GOD OR BEAST

Evolution
and Human Nature

Poor quality of ideas
Not worth Reading! Red Ryder

Books by Robert Claiborne

TIME

CLIMATE, MAN, AND HISTORY

ON EVERY SIDE THE SEA

THE FIRST AMERICANS

GOD OR BEAST

God or Beast

EVOLUTION AND HUMAN NATURE

Robert Claiborne

W·W· NORTON & COMPANY· INC.
New York

Library of Congress Cataloging in Publication Data

Claiborne, Robert.
  God or beast.

Bibliography: p.
1. Human behavior 2. Human evolution. 3. Aggressiveness
  (Psychology) 4. Civilization, Modern—1950–
I. Title.
GN273.C47   573.2   73–20454
ISBN 0–393–06399–2

This book was designed by Andrea Clark.
The type is Times Roman and Palatino,
and manufactured by Kingsport Press, Inc.

Contents

FOR SAM AND AMANDA

My first textbook in human nature and my
contribution to continued human evolution

Foreword

The cave man is in fashion. Certain unpleasant aspects of his life are being widely publicized and are used as a ready-made, pseudo-scientific explanation for our own misbehavior. Since we have inherited our genetic structure from him, it seems reasonable to assume that this heritage from the Stone Age accounts for our tendency to kill, even to kill our fellow men; for our pathological desire to control and spoil nature; for the crassness of our social relationships. Jean Jacques Rousseau believed that everything had been good in human nature before it was spoiled by civilization. The more popular view at present is that human nature was bad from the very beginning and that civilization has only made more evident man's fundamental bestiality.

It is obvious, of course, that in its tendency to kill, the human species does not differ biologically from animal species. But what is more remarkable and hardly ever pointed out—except by Robert Claiborne—is that a very large percentage of human beings find killing a painful experience; this is the reason why, despite the most subtle means of propaganda, it is difficult to make war appear desirable. In contrast, altruism is widespread and extends frequently to self-sacrifice. Altruism certainly has deep roots in our biological past, because it presents advantages for the survival of the group. However, the really human aspects of the problem are not the biological origins of altruism and its evolutionary advantages, but rather the fact that mankind has now made of it one of the absolute values by which it transcends its animality.

At the beginning of the Renaissance, Pico della Mirandola expressed the genius of humanism by affirming that man has it in his power to remain beast or to become angel: "With freedom of choice and with honor, as though the maker and molder of thyself, thou mayest fashion thyself in whatever shape thou shalt prefer. Thou shalt have in thy power to degenerate into the lower forms of life, which are brutish. Thou shalt have the power, out of thy soul's judgment, to be reborn into the higher forms, which are divine."

Robert Claiborne's book could be regarded as the modern scientific expression of Pico della Mirandola's statement of faith. There is no need to demonstrate once more that the organic structure and the behavior of mankind have their basis in animal nature. But what is needed and what Robert Claiborne provides is a better understanding of the fact that the human species has evolved socially into preoccupations and modes of behavior which transcend its animal origins. The progressive passage from instinctive reactions to willful actions based on reason has always involved difficult and painful choices and decisions. It is through these choices and decisions that humanity progressively emerged from animality.

RENÉ DUBOS

New York, New York
August 1973

Author's Preface

In the preface to an earlier book of mine, *Climate, Man, and History,* I happened to mention quite casually that one of my reasons for writing it was to make some money in an honest and interesting way. This offhand remark drew the attention of several reviewers, some of whom expressed surprise and pleasure at my "frankness," while one, a Canadian geology professor, cited it as evidence that the book was worthless. He, to be sure, managed to "edit" my remark into a declaration that money was my *only* reason for writing the book, which I would call a bit of scholarly misrepresentation.

Be that as it may, there seems to be some confusion here which ought to be cleared up. Writers—though a few may delude themselves otherwise—are not Pure Spirits, subsisting on air and writing for the sheer good of their souls or the elevation of mankind. They write for money, and for the same reasons that teachers teach for money, plumbers plumb for money, and geology professors do whatever it is they do for money: because they have a bias in favor of paying the rent or the mortgage and of eating regularly.

But of course I, like most writers, write for many other reasons as well. I—and they—enjoy the experience of exercising the writer's skill, of putting words together in a particular way. This is our version of the creative impulse, which—for reasons set forth at length in Chapter 11—I believe to be a well-nigh universal feature of human nature. I—and they—also write out of a desire to win the esteem and affection of friends and relations, a trait which is nearly universal not only among human beings, but also among our monkey and ape cousins.

Perhaps my chief reason for writing the present book, however, was none of the above, but rather a feeling that I had something to say that badly needed saying. Over the past ten or fifteen years, the American and European reading public has been regaled with a whole series of works which have said in essence that the long course of human evolution has made modern man into a first-class son of a bitch.* This view—as I hope to make clear in the body of this book—is a structure of nonsense, conceived in prejudice, founded on selective misrepresentation of the facts, and buttressed with fallacious reasoning. I have felt this ever since I began dipping into these books, and everything I have read in the course of writing this one has strengthened that feeling.

But the theory that man is fundamentally a son of a bitch is not just nonsense, it is dangerous nonsense, providing a perfect, built-in cop out for sons of bitches in both private and public life—of which, God knows, there are plenty. Like the evil duke in one of James Thurber's fables, who plaintively declared that "everybody has his faults; mine is being wicked," these gentlemen can offer the evolutionary excuse that their only fault is being human. (The same excuse—that man is basically violent and vicious—has been invoked by "auteurs" such as Stanley Kubrick and Sam Peckinpah who have become rich portraying violence on the screen.)

As a human being, and one who—like millions of others—not infrequently feels himself the victim of various prominent sons of bitches, I reject both the excuse and the slanderous picture of human evolution on which it is based. When I look around me at the several dozen people with whom I am personally acquainted, I observe that neither evolution nor anything else has made most of them sons of bitches—or bitches for that matter. Which implies one of two things: either the people whom I know well are mostly not part of the human race, not members of the evolutionary lineage that has begotten the world's sons of bitches, or the pop evolutionists have been peddling us a bill of goods.

I think these writers have indeed been conning us—albeit at times

* Modern woman has also gotten her lumps from these pop evolutionists, though in rather different ways.

unconsciously—and I think it is high time somebody wrote a book saying so, and saying why.

*   *   *

No writer, whatever the reasons he writes, operates in a vacuum; before, during, and after he works over his typewriter he depends on the help, counsel, and encouragement of others. Among those who have helped with this book are Professor Irwin Katz of the Graduate Center, City University of New York, who read the entire manuscript and made a number of valuable suggestions, as well as Professors Elwyn Simons, Ian Tattersall, and David Pilbeam of Yale and J. P. Robinson of the University of Wisconsin, who took time away from their own work to answer my questions about human prehistory and primate psychology. Eric Swenson, executive editor of W. W. Norton & Company, Inc., exercised exemplary patience in awaiting a manuscript that took considerably more time in the writing than either he or I had expected; Sherry Huber, his assistant, and Georgia Griggs, who copy-edited the text, both helped to clarify and tighten it. My greatest debt, however, is to my wife, whose perceptive, wry, and offbeat comments on human nature have done more to enlarge my understanding of it than any book I have read.

New York and Truro, 1973

*"He hangs between, in doubt to act or rest,
In doubt to deem himself a God or Beast."*

—ALEXANDER POPE,
Essay on Man

*"The essential predicament of man is that he is aware
of his situation as an animal but yet is potentially
divine."*

—GRAHAME CLARK,
The Stone Age Hunters

The monkeys, apes, ape-men, and primitive humans described herein are not intended to represent any
living individuals of our species. I cannot pretend, however, that any resemblance to such individuals is coincidental. All scientists named are, so far as I know,
quite real.

—R. C.

PART ONE

Animal among Animals

1

TO BEGIN WITH:
Looking Forward
by Looking Backward

"I don't know who my ancestors was, but we been descending for a long time."

— OLD SAYING

Almost everybody is interested in his ancestors. Whether they were or were not persons of general distinction, our own progenitors are distinguished to us because they are ours, part of us as we are part of them. If they do not usually define us (as ancestry defines such notables as the Roosevelts, Cabots, and Churchills) they at least help us define ourselves, to puzzle out who we are and what we might be.

In my own case, for example, both my grandfather and his grandfather were involved, albeit in no very prominent capacity, in attempts to overthrow the government by force and violence—one successful, the other not.* This fact, though it does not define me as a revolutionary, has certainly helped to solidify my conviction that any governmental or social structure is to some degree provisional, subject to radical change without notice if and when it becomes destructive of the proper ends of government—and that in such an event it would be my right, in fact my duty, to help bring about such change. (For the record and to avoid misunderstandings, I am not now engaged in any attempt to overthrow the government by force and violence, nor do I expect to be so engaged in the near future.)

Beyond this, and whether or not we can name our grandfather's grandfather, we are all descendants of some people or culture or

---

* My grandfather might be more accurately classed as an aider and abetter of subversive violence; as a surgeon with Lee's Army of Northern Virginia, he killed nobody—at least, not deliberately. His grandfather, however, fought the British as part of an "irregular" (nowadays we say "guerrilla") cavalry troop in southside Virginia.

nation. We are of the tribe of Cromwell, Shakespeare, and Elizabeth R., of Robbie Burns and Robert Bruce, of Wolfe Tone, Deirdre, and Cuchulain, of Rabelais, Abelard, and Heloise, Juarez and Moctezuma, Dante and Leonardo, Spinoza, Ruth and Jeremiah, Guatama and Gandhi, Kung Fu-tze and Sun Yat-sen, Nat Turner and Sojourner Truth and the unknown black kings who founded the lost empires of Songhay and Mali. And these tribal kin, no less than our blood kin, shape us and identify us—to others and to ourselves.

But beyond this again—beyond the ties of blood or speech, tribe or clan—all of us spring from deeper roots, from tribes no one can name and, deeper yet, from scattered bands of creatures that could not yet name themselves. Who we are, what we will be or might be, are in part the outcome of events and processes of inconceivable remoteness. If six or seven generations ago my great-great-grandfather was sniping at Redcoats from some swamp or pinewood, behind him (though he did not know it) lay five hundred thousand, a million, two million generations that had shaped the hand that held his musket, the eye that sighted it, and the brain and impulses that aimed and fired it.

Our interest in our more remote ancestors has burgeoned ever since Darwin suggested, to the mingled rage and fascination of the Victorians, that our species must be descended from an ape or something very like one. In the century or so since this theory was published, prehistorians have converted Darwin's hypothesis into a reality, fleshed out in sometimes startling detail. To the traditional evidence of the bones and stones—the skeletal fragments of primitive people and the objects they chipped or hammered out of rocks and pebbles— have been added clues from botany, zoology, climatology, and half a dozen more recondite specialities, to the point where we can tell not only what our ancestors looked like and what tools they made, but can plausibly conjecture how they made the tools and what they did with them, what they ate and how they got it, whether or not they clothed and sheltered themselves, and with what.

More recently, prehistorians and many others have tackled a far more difficult task: reconstructing the prehistory of human nature. They have tried to imagine not just what our ancestors did but why they did it—how they felt, how they thought (those of them who *could* think), and how they got along with their fellows. Some of the scientists who have been digging into our psychological prehistory have done so for the same reason they have tackled other prehistoric puzzles: curiosity about the past. But most of those—scientists and otherwise—who have concerned themselves with the problem are basically interested in the present rather than the past; in seeking to discover why primitive man did what he did, they hope to uncover clues to why modern man does what he does—and what he is likely to do next. If human anatomy—our upright posture, our dextrous hands, and our enlarged brains—is the outcome of a long evolutionary process, as it certainly is, then so, presumably, is what we call human nature: the preferences, predilections, and potentials that underlie all the myriad different human cultures, present and past.

The analogy is, I think, accurate—but also treacherous, for two reasons. First, it conceals the fact that reconstructing our physical evolution is a very different problem from reconstructing our psychological evolution, because in one case the final stage of the process is known, in the other it is not. Modern human anatomy has been weighed and measured to the last milligram and millimeter; the only question that confronts the evolutionist is how it got that way. Human psychological anatomy, however, is something else again; scientifically speaking, we know very little about it. Most of us, to be sure, feel confident that we know something about the nature of the people around us, and of course we do; this is not "human nature," however, but rather the nature of particular kinds and groups of humans. Without at this point getting into the intricate question of nature and nurture, it is obvious that what particular people do in particular circumstances, and why they do it, is enormously influenced by the group of which they happen to be a part; whatever human nature is, we can view it only darkly through the glass—or distorting lens—of human culture. To assess anatomy, we need only strip people of their clothes, whether bluejeans, sarongs, kilts, or loincloths, but we cannot divest them of the psychological garments they have acquired from their tribe, caste, or nation.

Moreover, while none of us has profound biases about human anatomy, all of us have at least some biases about human nature which can radically distort our perceptions of it. Many of us, to be sure, prefer white skins to black (or vice versa), brunettes to blondes, and so on, but never to the point of claiming that all skins are white or all women (or men) are brunettes. However, those of us who prefer submissive women are quite likely to claim that all women are by nature submissive; those with a taste for violence often allege that all men are naturally violent; those who have been notably successful in acquiring worldly goods may well insist that man is naturally acquisitive. "Human nature" all too easily becomes a Rohrschach ink blot in which we see not our fellow man but our own desires, hopes, and fears.

If this is true of people in general, it is no less true of most people who have written about human psychological evolution. With few exceptions, they have contaminated their inquiries into what man was with all sorts of preconceived notions about what he is. The result, to speak bluntly, has been an outpouring of nonsense. Of the half dozen best-sellers touching on human psychological evolution that have appeared during the past fifteen years, not one has put together a scientifically credible picture of the process, and every one of them has to some degree misread, misstated, or simply ignored much of the evidence on which any such picture must be based.

These are strong words; whether they are too strong is something the reader will have to decide after reading this book. In the meantime, let me emphasize that the question I propose to concentrate on is: what kinds of creatures, psychologically speaking, were our ancestors? The answers, insofar as we can arrive at them, will undoubtedly be relevant to what kind of creatures *we* are, and what we might be, and how we might better order our affairs. *But the answers must come first.* If the study of our past has any significance for our present and future—and I, for one, am convinced it does—we can discover that significance only by approaching the past, to the greatest possible extent, on its own terms, without biases drawn from the present. I do not expect, of course, to eliminate my personal biases altogether—no human being can do that—but I do hope to keep them under reasonably tight control. How well I succeed is something else the reader will have to decide for himself.

How does one go about reconstructing the prehistory of human nature, and on what kind of evidence?

The most fundamental bit of evidence is the fact that we are here talking about the evidence. Man has survived. His "evolutionary line" has persisted over tens of millions of years, while any number of other lines petered out into extinction. To be sure, the ancestral species that preceded him, such as the man-ape Australopithecus, are all "extinct" in the sense that they are no longer on this earth. But they are certainly not extinct in the sense that the dinosaurs are extinct; their genes, their physical and psychological traits, survive in us, though often in altered form.

The bare fact of human survival tells us that our line, like all the other evolutionary lines that have survived up to the present, had what it took. And what it took was, fundamentally, three things. First, our ancestors, in the various environments they inhabited at different times, were able to find things to eat, in sufficient quantity and variety to keep breath in their bodies. Second, they were able to avoid being eaten. And third, they successfully reproduced—meaning not merely the rather simple business of begetting and giving birth, but also seeing to it that the infants thus produced survived long enough to reproduce in their turn.

We are talking, of course, about our ancestors collectively, not individually. Unquestionably many of them, faced with temporary food shortages, died of starvation or the diseases that starvation fosters; others no doubt made meals for the local lions, leopards, wolves, or their contemporary equivalent. But from the evolutionary standpoint, it matters not a jot whether a given individual survives or not, or whether, or how prolifically, it reproduces—indeed, in most species the great majority of progeny do *not* survive. The female codfish, for instance, lays three million or more eggs a year, and the odds against any of them surviving long enough to reproduce is close to a million to one. But in cod or man, all that matters is that the evolutionary books shall balance—that the loss in population from disease, starvation, predation, or simple old age be compensated by the gain in population from reproduction. The alternative is evolutionary bankruptcy—extinction. And the fact that a species walks the earth or swims its oceans today is conclusive evidence that its books *do* balance and that those of its remotest ancestors did likewise.

The processes by which a species keeps its books balanced are, of course, what we call animal behavior; to eat, avoid being eaten, and reproduce obviously involve doing certain things and not doing certain others. And the characteristic things that an animal does and doesn't do are clearly part of what we call its nature, so that we say, for example, that a lion's nature is to eat meat, a cow's to eat grass, and so on. But there is more to an animal's nature than merely the characteristic things it does; there is also the matter of why it does them. Does the lion, for instance, kill and eat an antelope because the inherited structures of its nervous system are "programmed" to do these things, or is its behavior learned? And if learned, by what processes is it learned, and what motives or drives lead it to learn one thing and not another? It is questions of this sort that we must ask about our ancestors, hoping that the answers will tell us something about ourselves.

In seeking answers, however, we are handicapped by the total lack of direct evidence. Naturalists like George Schaller have learned much about the nature of lions by observing them in their natural African habitat, but Australopithecus and the rest of our ancestors are no longer here to be observed. Nor are the prehistorian's traditional bones and stones of much help. If I examine a plaster cast of an Australopithecine skull such as graces my living-room table, I can tell quickly enough that the creature looked much more like a chimpanzee than I do, and that its brain—and therefore, presumably, its intelligence—was a great deal smaller than mine. But the skull itself tells me nothing about how Australopithecus, limited intelligence and all, coped with his environment—which, on the fossil record, he did successfully for several million years. Again, if I survey, in a museum case, the clean, symmetrical lines of a "hand axe" some half million years old, they tell me that its maker was considerably more skilled at tool making than were earlier human models, and had even, perhaps, evolved a primitive esthetic sense, but they do not tell me whether the instrument itself was used to grub up roots or bash in the skull of a neighbor, or perhaps both these things, or neither.

Necessarily, then, we must fall back on analogies between human beings and other animals. Man's separation from the rest of the animal kingdom began no more than a few million years ago, with the emergence of the first ground-apes that can reasonably be called even halfway human; the final stages in the process may have occurred less than fifty thousand years ago—on the time-scale of evolution, only yesterday. What this means is that man was an animal long, long before he was a man, so that by studying what animals do and (so far as we can infer it) why they do it we should be able to deduce what our ancestors are likely to have have done, and why.

This assumption has been accepted by everyone who has been concerned with human psychological evolution. Where many have tripped up, however, is in deciding what animals to study, and how to study them. Some commentators, even some scientists, have taken testimony from a whole menagerie—geese, chickens, rats, leopards, deer, chaffinches, sticklebacks, baboons, tropical fish, and many more —apparently on the assumption that one animal is about as relevant to human prehistory as another. To disciples of B. F. Skinner, who (as we shall see in a later chapter) has constructed an entire theory of human nature from experiments with rats and pigeons, the assumption would doubtless make sense. But most of us, when we think about it, recognize that if we want to learn something about a man we have never seen we will do best to study his brothers and sisters, not his fourteenth cousins.

Evolutionarily speaking, our brothers and sisters, or at least our first cousins, are the primates, a group of mammals which has existed for at least sixty-five million years. Our family ties with such nonprimate mammals as the rat or leopard therefore date from some seventy million years ago, with the nonmammalian goose and chaffinch, more than thrice that long ago, while our links with such finny creatures as the stickleback must be dated in the hundreds of millions. By contrast, our ancestors were at least kissing cousins with the monkeys only thirty-five million years ago, and enjoyed intimate relations with some ancestral apes a mere fifteen million years back. If we are to learn anything about human nature from animal nature, it is the primates—and particularly their more advanced representatives, the monkeys and apes—that we must focus on, and the more similar the primate to man, the better. By that standard, the obvious candidate for close study is the chimpanzee, because by every known criterion— size, anatomy, the number and shape of its chromosomes, the chemistry of its blood, and the range of its intellectual and emotional capabilities—it is unquestionably our closest relative on earth, and even closer to our Australopithecine ancestors.

But evolution involves not merely anatomy but ecology. How an animal lives and what it does depend not merely on its physical and mental equipment but also on the environment it inhabits. By that standard, we ought to be able to learn a good deal from the baboons as well. In physique and brain power these monkeys are a lot less like human beings than is the chimp (though a lot more like them than a deer or a rat, let alone a chicken), but ecologically some baboons are more like humans. In contrast with chimps, which are essentially forest dwellers, many baboons live in open savanna and grassland, the types of country in which Australopithecus lived and in which the bulk of the human race has lived ever since. (Modern man often lives near forests, but seldom in them; he favors rather the artificial clearings and grasslands he has made with axe, saw, and bulldozer.) Thus the problems of survival which the baboons have solved are the same that Australopithecus and his descendants must also have solved.

Apart from the primates, we can safely ignore most other animals, since in anatomy, life-style, or both they are too remote from either us or our ancestors. Possible exceptions are the wolves and other wild dogs; these predators, like primitive man—but unlike either the chimp or the baboon—systematically hunt in groups. Genetically, to be sure, the dog family is no more closely allied to the human family than either of them is to a rat or a deer, so that any putative resemblances between canine behavior and human behavior are almost certainly the result not of genetic relationship but of what is called convergent evolution—similar life-styles begetting similar behavior. Still, it is just possible that the activities of these four-legged hunting bands may provide a few clues to those of primitive human hunting bands.

Having carefully chosen the most likely candidates for study among the animal kingdom, we must be no less selective about the conditions under which we study them. Nearly all the early scientific observations of primates were of captive populations in zoos or laboratories, which with hindsight makes about as much sense as studying people in jail or in crowded slums and calling the results human nature. Thoughtful laboratory experiments with monkeys and apes have taught us a great deal about how these animals behave, and why— even as thoughtless ones have generated a great deal of misinformation on the same subjects—but if we want to know what these animals are naturally prone to do, we must obviously study them under natural conditions. This is the more true in that, as has recently become apparent, the same animal may behave quite differently in one natural environment than in another.

There are two other kinds of evidence that we can make use of, though very cautiously. One of them is observations of infants and young children. In these little ones, where cultural influences have had only a limited time to operate, we may perhaps find traces of universal psychological traits characteristic of the human family. Unfortunately, there isn't much evidence of this sort. A newborn human infant is obviously not physically capable of much in the way of behavior, and by the time he is, cultural influences have been operating on him for months or years. However, a few observations have established some interesting and often unexpected facts about human nature, which will be cited in their proper place.

Finally, there are studies of existing human cultures—in particular, the simplest, most primitive of these. People with a simple technology who live in small groups and in an environment with only modest resources are probably living something like our ancestors of fifty thousand or even half a million years ago. If we can find among these peoples any more or less universal characteristics of patterns, it is a fair bet that similar patterns existed among our—and their—ancestors. Perhaps more important, if we do *not* find certain patterns present in these simple societies, we can be pretty certain that such patterns are *not* characteristic of the human animal, but merely of certain human cultures.

Before concluding this introductory chapter, I might as well say frankly that whatever answers emerge in subsequent chapters to the question of what human nature was (and is), I do not expect them to portray man categorically as either a god or a beast: the question of whether Homo sapiens is a Good Guy or a Bad Guy is, in my judgment, interesting only to those who view life and literature in these cardboard terms. But there still remains the very interesting question of what kind of a guy he is—and the no less interesting one of what kind he might be.

It is often said today that the world we live in, the societies we have so laboriously constructed, are in some sense destructive of basic human values. The statement is vague enough to make rational proof impossible, yet most of us, I think, feel intuitively that it is somehow true, even though we might be hard put to define what we mean by "basic human values"—and even harder put to agree on any definitions we arrived at. In this context, the study of the human past is "relevant" in the true sense of that rather weary word. If we believe that our human institutions are in some respects antihuman, as my great-great-grandfather and many of his contemporaries viewed British rule in America, then we obviously need to alter those institutions or to abolish them and construct something better. And surely an essential step toward contriving a more human, more humane society is to try and understand as best we can what it means to be human.

The study of the past—of a family, a tribe, a species—is fascinating in itself, but doubly fascinating because it is that past which has made the present and which will help make the future. Looking backward to what was is also a way of looking forward to what might be. Let us, then, look backward at our remoter ancestors, whose lives and deaths, successes and failures, adaptations and readaptations to the demands of nature are embodied in the play of our own muscles, the goading or calming secretions of our ductless glands, the electrical currents of our nervous systems that impel us toward love or murder.

2

INSTINCT, LEARNING, AND INCENTIVES: Why Animals Do What They Do

"The ability to learn, that is, to respond differently to a situation because of past response to the situation, is what distinguishes those living creatures which common sense endows with minds."

— EDWIN B. GUTHRIE

If we examine the infinitely varied behaviorial patterns which animals have evolved to cope with their environments, we quickly see that they fall into two broad categories: instinctive and learned. The categories overlap, as do virtually all categories in nature, but they are still distinct enough, and important enough, to be worth discussing at some length.

Instinctive behavior patterns are inherited. They are part of the animal's genetic makeup in precisely the same way as are the number and structure of its limbs and the color of its fur, fins, or feathers. A caterpillar's impulse to bite into a leaf is built into its nervous system in precisely the way a capacity to digest the leaf is built into its digestive system. Confronted by a leaf of the proper color, texture, and odor, the caterpillar chews on it for essentially the same reason a doorbell rings when you press the button: it's built that way.

An instinctive action, therefore, is automatic, species-wide, and stereotyped. It is automatic because the animal performs it in response to certain stimuli regardless of previous experience or training. It is species-wide because *all* members of the species perform it under the appropriate circumstances. And it is stereotyped because all members of the species perform it in the same way. A learned action, by

contrast, is none of these things. Whether or not an animal performs
it depends not just on the stimuli it receives but on its previous
experience in connection with those stimuli. Some members of the
species may never perform it at all, no matter what stimuli they are
subjected to. And those that do perform it may do so in different ways.

Some instinctive actions in man are coughing, sneezing, and giving
birth. A baby doesn't learn to cough; it does so automatically when
its respiratory tract is stimulated in certain ways. All babies cough
under these circumstances, and all cough in the same way—as, indeed, do all adults, though they may *learn* such refinements as covering the mouth while doing so.* No woman learns to give birth; when
her time comes, her body takes over and—unless something is seriously wrong—expels the baby automatically. As for learned actions
in humans, anybody can sit down and list dozens of them in a few
minutes, starting with a baby's first efforts to manipulate a rattle or
spoon and going on through reading, writing, and arithmetic to pilot-
ing a plane or operating a computer. No child is born with the ability
to write; millions of them never learn how, and those that do, write
in scores of different symbols, hundreds of different languages, and
millions of different handwritings.

There are several basic facts about instinct and learning that are
worth keeping in mind. First, the more similar an animal is to a
human being, the greater its learning capacity is likely to be. The
vertebrates as a group seem to have noticeably more learning ability
than such animals as the insects or molluscs; the mammals are
unquestionably the champion learners among the vertebrates, while
the primates are no less pre-eminent among the mammals, though
they get a certain amount of competition from the elephants and,
according to some authorities, the porpoises and dolphins.

This fact is generally recognized and accepted. Rather less widely
appreciated is a second fact: learning and instinct are two ends of a
seesaw. That is, to the extent an animal's behavior is governed by one,
it *cannot* be governed by the other. If an animal's feeding behavior
is automatic and stereotyped, as with the caterpillar on its leaf, then

* Many psychologists would call such actions as coughing and sneezing reflexive
rather than instinctive, reserving the latter term for more complex patterns of innate
behavior. For our purposes the difference is unimportant; simple or complex, the
actions we are talking about are in all cases automatic, species-wide, and stereotyped,
and thus, for simplicity, can be lumped together as "instincts."

by definition that behavior cannot be modified by experience. The caterpillar has no need to learn which leaves to eat, but it will starve to death in the absence of leaves to which its instincts are attuned, even though plenty of equally nutritious leaves of other types are available. Human beings, by contrast, do not know instinctively what to eat. Babies will notoriously put almost any substance into their mouths and, if it can be swallowed, swallow it; some thousands of them die every year from lack of the caterpillar's instinctive dietary conservatism. On the other hand, babies can eventually learn to eat anything edible that their environment provides, from caterpillars to their fellow man.*

As I have already intimated, some kinds of behavior in some animals appear to combine both instinct and learning. A male oriole, for instance, will instinctively sing at the appropriate time of the year even though it has never heard another oriole sing—but its song will bear little resemblance to those of other oriole males unless it *has* heard them sing; in effect, it sings by instinct, but precisely what it sings is determined by learning. (In many other birds, however, singing seems to be purely instinctive.) In humans, speech may be a somewhat similar blend of instinct and learning. All normal children make a wide variety of babbling sounds, comparable to the abortive song of the isolated male oriole, but if the child's babbling is to be transformed into speech, the child must hear others speak; if it does not (as with children born totally deaf) it learns to speak only with enormous difficulty, if at all.

Just how important a role instinct has played in our behavior and that of our ancestors is a subject we shall examine in more detail later on. Meanwhile, it is safe to conclude that its role is bound to be less in the human family than in other groups of animals. Evolutionarily speaking, the human line has "specialized" in learning, as the cats have specialized in hunting and the porpoises in swimming; as everyone known, Homo sapiens can learn far more, and more complicated, things than any other animal. And given this immense development of learning capacities at one end of the seesaw, we can safely assume that the weight of instinct is correspondingly light. If it were not, there would be no "room" for humans' elaborate learning ability to operate

---

* In practice, of course, their eating is generally limited to the relatively narrow range of comestibles sanctioned by their culture.

in, and it could not have evolved to its present state. For rather obvious reasons, animals do not evolve organs that do not contribute to their survival; if human behavior were specified by instinct to any considerable degree, our swollen brains, no less than the elaborate and sophisticated learning they make possible, would be evolutionary monstrosities.

However, to say that learning plays a preponderant role in the behavior of the human family does not mean that there is no un-learned, genetic component in human, or protohuman, behavior. Learning, in the human or any other species, does not depend *only* on the experience of the individual, shaped by the traditions of prac-tices of the group it belongs to. It is a psychological truism that we learn most easily those actions which we find pleasant or otherwise satisfying, or which are followed by pleasant or satisfying conse-quences, while painful or unpleasant activities are learned with dif-ficulty or not at all. Pleasantness or unpleasantness, to the extent they are innate, constitute a built-in incentive system, acquired during evolution, which insures that at least some kinds of actions will be learned easily and quickly, while others will be rejected just as quickly.

Not surprisingly, many of the most obvious examples of innate incentives bear directly on the key survival problems cited in the preceding chapter. In the matter of eating, for instance, we have first of all that sensation of emptiness, ranging from uncomfortable to actively painful, which reminds us that it is time for dinner. Psycho-logically, of course, it doesn't work quite that way. The concept of "time for dinner"—or breakfast, or lunch—is learned, as are the processes, many of them quite intricate, involved in procuring, pre-paring, and consuming food, from getting the job that yields the money that pays the grocer to washing the dishes. What the pangs of hunger give us are a powerful and frequently renewed motive for learning these things and, having learned them, doing them.

But eating, for animals no less than for humans, is obviously much more than simply filling the stomach with something or other; to stay healthy one must eat certain things and refrain from eating certain others. Evolution has therefore provided us with a whole set of innate incentives concerning what we "should" and "should not" put into our mouths. All of us have a built-in liking for sweets, doubtless evolved during our primate ancestors' long sojourn in the trees of tropical forests, where they lived as late as ten million years ago. In that habitat, sweet fruits provided a plentiful source of nourishment, so that a liking for sweets insured that these ancient primates would easily learn to consume fruits and to seek them out. Children still easily learn to seek out and consume sweets—many parents would say much too easily.

By contrast, we have a no less innate dislike of intensely bitter substances, which probably evolved during the same period as a protection against certain plant poisons, notably the group of compounds called alkaloids, including morphine, nicotine, and conine (the hemlock alkaloid that Socrates died of). While it is by no means true that all bitter plants are poisonous or that all poisonous plants are bitter (deadly mushrooms, for example, are usually quite tasty, according to those lucky enough to survive them), a sizable number of plants are both bitter and toxic. Our ancestors' innate dislike of bitter flavors ensured that they would spit out such plants if they happened to bite into them and shun the plant in future. Sweetness and bitterness are about as basic as one can get in the built-in incentive department. Indeed, they are so basic, so interwoven with our notions of pleasantness or unpleasantness, that we say that love or success or revenge is sweet, while poverty, rejection, or defeat is bitter.

A third innate taste preference probably evolved a good deal later: our dislike for strongly soapy tastes, an aversion taken advantage of by our grandparents when they washed their children's mouths out with soap to discourage bad language. While there are few soapy-tasting things in the tropical forest, by five million years ago our ancestors were living in the open, dry grasslands of eastern and southern Africa, where—unless they happened to be near a stream or river—they had to drink from springs, lakes, and water holes, some of which were undoubtedly impregnated with soapy-tasting alkaline salts, as they still are (Tanzania's Lake Natron takes its name from a word for washing soda). Our ancestors' innate dislike for soapy flavors helped insure that they would refrain from drinking water of this sort, which can produce consequences ranging from severe diarrhea to death.

Our fourth built-in taste preference is rather more ambiguous. We tend to like mildly salty things, a preference which encouraged our ancestors to consume enough salt in their diet to replace the salt lost in sweat and urine. Equally, however, we dislike intensely salty things (such as sea water) that could seriously derange our internal chemistry if we consumed them.

Just as eating nutrituous things and eschewing toxic things are crucial to the survival of the individual, so reproduction is crucial to the survival of the species. Not surprisingly, then, evolution has endowed us with another notable incentive plan in this area. Sexual pleasure insures that most of us will learn about sex (though perhaps not everything we always wanted to know about it) and will—like our forest ancestors with their nutritious fruits—devote considerable effort to seeking it out. Finally, of course, we possess a notable "negative incentive" in the shape of pain, which insures that we will rapidly learn to avoid many kinds of objects and situations that might otherwise injure us.

An important point about evolution's built-in incentives is that in humans—and probably most other mammals—they are relative, not absolute. That is, while they make it *more likely* that certain kinds of actions will be learned and repeated and others will not, they seldom if ever establish any certainty about such actions. Though the biases they establish are innate, the biases can nonetheless be negated and even reversed by experience. As we know, some people have learned to dislike sweets, while the numbers who drink their coffee black and sugarless are pretty cogent evidence that some of us can learn to like bitter substances (in this case, the alkaloid caffeine). Despite the notoriously powerful incentive supplied by sexual pleasure, some people forgo it throughout their lives, and a few find sex actively repellant. Evolutionary incentives, in short, do no more than establish certain presumptions about what people will do, "other things being equal"—but of course other things often aren't equal. If they were, understanding human nature would be a lot easier than it is.

A no less important point about nature's evolutionary incentives is that they can too easily become a rationale for a sort of instant morality: what is "natural" is automatically assumed to be right. This is nonsense, for several reasons. Perhaps the most important is that ethics—in my book, at least—applies to actions, not to the biases that are at the root of those actions. The fact that human beings naturally like sweets and sex is neither good nor bad, wrong nor right—it just is; one can no more apply standards of morality to these psychological processes than to the physiological processes of digestion. By the same token, I would say that any system of morality which claims that it is *wrong* for people to like sex—or sweets—is ridiculous on its face. Ethics become relevant to evolutionary incentives only at the point where these incentives lead the individual to do certain things—if, for example, an individual's liking for sweets leads him to steal candy from babies or a liking for sex induces him to engage in rape. When St. Paul—hardly an apostle of "permissiveness"—told the Philippians that "the love of money is the root of all evil" he did *not* say that it was in itself evil, but rather that it could lead to evil; the same could be said about a love of sweets, or sex, or almost anything else.

There is also a rather subtler fallacy sometimes attached to evolutionary incentives: the feeling that if men "naturally" like certain things, then those who dislike those things are "unnatural," perverted, and in fact immoral. Nobody, of course, would claim that a dislike of sweets is immoral, or even a dislike of sex—indeed, some would probably consider the latter morally desirable. On the other hand, people who dislike *heterosexual* sex but like homosexual sex —which, for reasons I shall give later, is no more or less unnatural than disliking sex in toto—are widely considered to be morally abhorrent. Whether homosexuality is moral, immoral, or both, or neither, can be argued, but the fact that it is "unnatural" has nothing whatever to do with the matter. A deeper understanding of human evolution and human nature can, as I shall argue in the final chapter of this book, help us to liberate ourselves and our fellows from some of the unnecessary and unnatural constraints with which our species has surrounded itself over the millennia—but not if we seek to turn "human nature" into some sort of straitjacket into which all human beings must fit on pain of legal or moral condemnation.

In all this discussion of evolutionary incentives, the reader may have noticed that I have said nothing about the human's inherited likes and dislikes as they concern the third essential of survival: avoiding being eaten. The reason is that our inherited reactions to danger are a much more complicated question and a much more controversial one, at least in the sense that more bunk has been written on the subject than on any other aspect of human nature; we shall therefore need an entire chapter to deal with the problem. Much of the remainder of this book, indeed, will be devoted to considering our inherited likes and dislikes—those built-in guide posts that so heavily influence what we learn and why we learn it. Before getting on with these matters, however, we need to explore *how* animals, including human beings, learn. Our exploration will necessarily be fairly lengthy, and also somewhat roundabout, since we must begin by retracing some of the lengthy blind alleys into which the scientific study of learning long ago wandered and in which it remained for far too many years.

3

HOW ANIMALS LEARN:
And Some
Psychologists Don't

"If the only tool you have is a hammer, you tend to treat everything as a nail."
— ABRAHAM MASLOW,
The Psychology of Science

"Ask a silly question and you get a silly answer."
— OLD SAYING

Few people, I think, would deny that our understanding of our own nature, as compared with our understanding of, say, geology or chemistry or astrophysics, is in a relatively primitive state. We talk a great deal about the nature of human nature, and some of us write books about it, but both the conversations and the books, whatever other virtues they may or may not possess, are uniformly distinguished by a dearth of hard, generally accepted scientific fact.

There are a lot of reasons for this conspicuous gap in the fabric of science, not the least of which is the complexity of the problem; it is a lot harder to figure out the nature of a man than that of a molecule. But a goodly share of the credit, I think, must be borne by the "school" of psychology that dominated psychological research in the United States (and, to a lesser extent, in several other countries) between 1920 and 1950, and in so doing—and despite some real scientific achievements—set back the science of human nature by thirty years.

This movement has gone by a number of names—behaviorism, stimulus-response psychology, and objective psychology (the last implying, in a neat bit of academic one-upmanship, that other schools of psychology were not "objective"—i.e., not scientific); for simplicity, I shall call it behaviorism. Like any important scientific or social movement, behaviorism was the work of many hands and minds, but its character can be illustrated pretty well in the lives and activities of its three leading figures, two of them dead, the third very much alive: John B. Watson, Clark L. Hull, and B. F. Skinner.

John Broadus Watson, born in 1878, grew up in the midst of America's Gilded Age, in a country becoming increasingly aware of, and intoxicated by, its own strength. It was a time of ferociously rugged individualists; robber barons like Andrew Carnegie, J. P. Morgan, and the elder Rockefeller were constructing the mammoth edifice of American (and their own) financial power, while their political counterparts sought outlets for American goods, capital, and self-assertiveness in imperial adventures. It was a time, too, of crusaders and tub thumpers, of Chautauqua lecturers bringing culture and enlightenment to the hinterland, of William Jennings Bryan inveighing against mankind's crucifixion upon a cross of gold, of Colonel Robert Ingersoll preaching agnosticism with the fervor of an old-time revivalist, of Carrie Nation wielding her hatchet against the Demon Rum. It was a time, finally, in which the "hard" sciences of physics and chemistry, with their technological offshoots, were pouring out a seemingly endless stream of wonders—steel and petroleum by the million tons, synthetic dyestuffs and drugs, electricity, the telephone, the horseless carriage. Science and scientific methods, it was perfectly clear, were about to usher mankind into a new utopia of permanent prosperity and (despite the regrettable resistance of some inferior races) peace.

In 1903, John B. Watson received the first Ph.D. degree granted by the new psychology department of the new University of Chicago. The psychology of that day—heavily influenced by Europeans—stressed experiment, but as a means of investigating the human mind and states of consciousness. Its goal, moreover, was Pure Knowledge; the notion that psychology could or should be useful for anything was unworthy of the dignity of science.

But Watson was an American—as brash, materialistic, and utilitarian as the steel, lumber, and meat-packing magnates whose millions had founded his alma mater. For him, a truly scientific psychology must rely on the objective, controlled experiments that had done so much for the older sciences of physics and chemistry —and, perhaps not incidentally, had brought their practitioners such impressive recognition as the prizes recently established by a Swedish millionaire, Alfred Nobel. The operative word was "objective." Mental activities, states of consciousness, existed only in the mind; they could only be known, inaccurately, at second hand. For the truly scientific psychologist, the only acceptable data was behavior—not what a man (or animal) felt or thought, but what he (or it) did. Any other approach was "mentalism," a word that Watson evidently equated with "supernaturalism," for he assailed it with all the verve of Bob Ingersoll exposing the mistakes of Moses. Among the young psychologists whom Watson attracted to his banner, such words as "consciousness," "sensation," "idea," and "pleasure" soon became as taboo as the word "orgasm" at a Georgia camp meeting.

The new, objective, scientific psychology, Watson was convinced, could do quite as much for human kind as the older sciences were already doing, a view that he summed up some years later in a famous passage: "Give me a dozen healthy infants . . . and my own specified world to bring them up in and I'll guarantee to take any one at random and train him to become any type of specialist I might select —doctor, lawyer, artist, merchant, chief, and, yes, even beggar-man and thief, regardless of his talents, penchants, tendencies, abilities, vocations, and race of his ancestors."

In the hands of behaviorist psychology, any American boy *could* become a millionaire, or even President; Watson disposed of the problem of human nature by declaring, in effect, that it did not exist. While in his early forties, in fact, he followed his own utilitarian logic by abandoning academic life for a career as an advertising counsultant, but he left behind him a set of dogmas that would warp psychology for another generation.

Dogma number one, the central one of the entire system, was that mentioned above: psychology, like chemistry and physics, must rely *only* on objective information obtained from controlled experiments. This, of course, completely begged the questions of whether psychology, as a science, is in fact "like" chemistry or physics, and whether the methods appropriate to the latter are, or can be, appropriate to the former.

Given this dogma, the implication for psychological research was clear: animal experiments, and lots of them. The amount of experimentation that can be done on human subjects is obviously very limited, and the amount of completely controlled experimentation virtually nil. For just as the chemist must obtain a pure sample of a new compound if he is to determine its properties, so the psychologist who studies learning must obtain a "naïve" animal—one that has not been previously exposed to uncontrolled learning experiences. No human being except a newborn baby could possibly meet this criterion; guinea pigs, rabbits, and especially rats, raised in captivity under controlled conditions, were the answer.

To apply the results of controlled experiments on laboratory rats to other animals, including humans, required several other dogmas. Chief among these was the "atomic" dogma: just as the myriads of chemical compounds are built up from a limited number of atoms, and atoms (as the physicists were then in the process of demonstrating) are composed of an even smaller number of fundamental particles, so the myriad patterns of learned animal behavior are actually built up from many small and simple bits—and if you understand how these bits are acquired, you understand learning. Moreover, no matter how many bits an animal adds to its repertoire, it will continue to learn in precisely the same way—bit by bit. This assumption, as Harry F. Harlow (a distinguished animal psychologist of a later and more sophisticated generation) was to remark, suggested that the psychologists who embraced it were quite as naïve as the animals they experimented with.

The atomic dogma led directly to two corollary dogmas. First, "all animals are equal"; the learning processes of a laboratory rat are the same as those of a human being. Obviously the human can learn more than the rat, and learn it faster, but the mechanisms in both involve the same bit-by-bit accumulation of small changes. Earlier generations of zoologists had too often anthropomorphized animals, crediting them with impossibly human motives; the behaviorists "theromorphized" man (*ther* being Greek for "beast"). The second corollary, closely akin to the first, was that animals under natural conditions will learn in the same manner as animals in the far simpler and more restrictive conditions of the laboratory. After all, the chemical properties of salt, say, are the same in the ocean as in the test tube.

None of these dogmas had been proved and some in fact were unprovable, yet for years they remained central to a major sector of psychological research. One reason was that they constituted a beautiful example of a self-validating system of beliefs, one which defines the problem in such a way that the search for solutions automatically confirms the definition. Thus, for example, a capitalist (communist) nation may adopt the assumption that the communists (capitalists) are determined to destroy it. If it then acts consistently on that assumption, the inevitable result will be an ingrained hostility on the part of the communists (capitalists), which will, of course, conclusively prove to the capitalists (communists) that They Are Out To Get Us. Just so, the behaviorists, having decided that animal learning is atomized, gave their naïve laboratory animals atomized tasks to learn; when the animals learned the tasks, this proved that learning mechanisms are indeed atomized. From the assumption that only certain kinds of data were significant, the behaviorists eventually began acting as if no other kinds of data existed.

The self-validating tendencies of behaviorist theories were strengthened by the self-perpetuating tendencies of the growing behaviorist establishment. Academic psychology in the United States expanded rapidly during the 1920s, and the behaviorists—partly because, as suggested above, they were in tune with the current American *zeitgeist* —were very much in on the ground floor. As a result, they rapidly came to dominate most university psychology departments, meaning that their definitions of what was, and wasn't, "scientific" psychology became official doctrine—and woe betide any graduate student brash enough to challenge it. When any doctrine becomes the vested interest of an elite (in this case, senior professors and department heads), truth suffers.

Clark L. Hull, the second great figure in behaviorism, though born only four years after Watson, was temperamentally poles apart—a scholarly theoretician rather than a rampaging utilitarian. Moreover, while Watson's views were formed in the years before World War I and reflected the ebullient self-assertiveness of that time, Hull's concepts crystallized far more slowly. His major work dates from the 1930s, a period when neither America nor most other nations were as sure of themselves as they had once been.

A major influence on his thinking was the great I. P. Pavlov, whose writings on conditioned reflexes were regarded by many behaviorists as the Old Testament of their authorized scriptures—the Gospel According to John (Watson) being the first book of the New. (Pavlov himself actually was very cautious about drawing broad conclusions from his highly specialized experiments.) Even more important, perhaps, was Hull's encounter with C. I. Lewis and some other philosophers during a summer's teaching at Harvard. Hull, who though modest in manner was by no means deficient in ego, asked them why philosophers had paid so little attention to some of his own early writings. Their precise answer is unfortunately not on record, but from Hull's subsequent course one can readily deduce it. Psychology, they must have said, was—well, interesting and no doubt important, but hardly rigorous enough in its thinking to satisfy a true philospher. If it were more precise, more *mathematical* . . .

Hull then bought and read Isaac Newton's *Principia* and the much more recent *Principia Mathematica* of Alfred North Whitehead and Bertrand Russell. The result is neatly summed up by the title of a subsequent book on which he was the senior collaborator: *Mathematico-Deductive Theory of Rote Learning.* Hull's subsequent writings on learning were in fact as systematically deductive as a theorem of Euclid, complete with equations such as $SER = f_b(N)$ and others even more recondite. If to Watson and many other behaviorists the best psychological experiment was the one most like an experiment in physics or chemistry, for Hull the best was the one most readily reducible to a mathematical expression. His equations, I am told, did indeed describe with reasonable accuracy the experiments on simple human learning tasks—nonsense syllables, word lists, and the like— from which they were derived. But neither Hull nor any of his disciples ever managed to demonstrate convincingly that they described anything else, in the laboratory or out of it.

A central feature of Hull's system, as it was of many other psychological systems of the time, was something called the drive-reduction theory. Any theory of learning must obviously explain why certain kinds or bits of behavior are learned while others are not; for Hull and most others, the answer was "drives." An animal, that is, is equipped by heredity with certain impulses which drive it toward the actions necessary for survival, meaning that if an action satisfies one or another of these impulses, it is learned; if not, not. Hunger is such a drive, so is sex, the avoidance of pain, and so on.

Thus far, we have a theory with which one could hardly quarrel, though, as we shall see, the reality is a lot more complicated. The trouble came when behaviorists tried to define what a drive actually consisted of. From the "objective" standpoint, to talk of "satisfying" a drive was hopelessly unscientific, while concepts such as pleasure, pain, and the like could hardly be mentioned in decent psychological society. Lifting some concepts from the theories of the great American physiologist Walter Cannon, behaviorism equated drive with various kinds of nervous impulses. Thus the hunger drive is the muscular impulses produced by contractions of the empty stomach, the sex drive is the pressure impulses produced by seminal fluid accumulating in the testicles (in males, of course; the behaviorists, very few of whom were women, never managed to explain why—or even whether— females possess a sex drive). Learning, then, occurs whenever one or another of the nerve impulses is weakened; drive reduction "reinforces" the connection between a particular stimulus (the sight of food, for example), and a particular response (eating the food).* In summary, an animal will learn to perform *whatever actions will minimize stimulation,* whether from within (e.g., hunger pangs) or without (e.g., the mild electric shock frequently used in learning experiments). Putting it in nonobjective terms (which no behaviorist would have done), the less stimulation, the more satisfaction—a notion which may come as something of a shock to any parent who has had to cope with the rainy-day complaints of a child: "Mommy, what can I *do*?"

B. F. Skinner was and is the logical successor to Watson and Hull as high priest of behaviorism, combining as he does the utilitarianism and dogmatism of the former and the mathematical bias of the latter. As such, he is still a major influence, both in the field of psychology and, especially, outside of it; indeed, he seems at times so omnipresent as to recall the last line of a famous limerick: "No, it was Skinner again, the bastard! "

Skinner, even more than Watson, has worked by elimination. Watson and his successors eliminated the "subjective" from psychology; Skinner has eliminated almost everything else. His theory of behavior, as he himself concedes, "leaves out of account habits, ideas, cognitive processes, needs, drives, traits, and so on." It also leaves out creativity, intuition, wit, and humor. The naïve reader, if not the naïve animal, may well wonder what on earth is left. What is left, for Skinner, is *the response,* plus various "contingencies" which reinforce it. Even the stimulus fades away like the Cheshire Cat, though—like the cat's smile—it retains a nebulous existence, not as something which *produces* a response (as in earlier versions of behaviorism) but merely

---

* Drive-reduction theories actually came in a number of varieties; the above explanation is therefore necessarily simplified.

as the thing which "sets the occasion upon which the response is more likely to occur."

Skinner has even managed to eliminate learning from psychology. It is, after all, difficult if not impossible to say "objectively" that an animal has or has not learned a particular action; all we can say is that it does or does not perform the action. Skinner's Law of Reinforcement, therefore, does not deal with learning but—again in line with developments in physics and chemistry—with probability. "Positive reinforcement" makes repetition of an action more probable; "negative reinforcement," less probable.

Now it is obvious that if an animal repeats an action, it must in some fashion have "learned" that action. *But the reverse is not true:* an animal's failure to repeat an action does *not* tell us that the action has not been learned, or that it has been unlearned. If, for example, a child learns to raid the cookie jar and thereupon receives negative reinforcement in the shape of a smack on the behind, it may perhaps leave the jar alone, at least for a while. But this is obviously not to say that it does not know, or has forgotten, how to get at the cookies. Indeed, as it grows older it may build on what it has already learned in this area, devising ways of securing cookies surreptitiously, thereby minimizing the probability of further negative reinforcement.

Skinner first achieved prominence in the 1930s when, after some ten years spent in studying the behavior of rats in the apparatus often called a "Skinner box"—a device for measuring reinforcement by counting how often the animal presses a bar under certain "contingencies"—he produced a work titled, with magnificent chutzpah, *The Behavior of Organisms*—the final word encompassing every animal from protozoa to humans. After another fifteen years of experiments, now including pigeons as well as rats, he produced his second magnum opus, titled—with even more remarkable chutzpah—*Science and Human Behavior*. This, of course, is the "all animals are equal" dogma with a vengeance. When taxed with drawing impossibly grandiose conclusions from specialized experiments, Skinner compares himself to Mendel, Pavlov, and other great pioneering figures in biology and physiology who, he says, also discovered fundamental truths by studying only one or two species. Subsequently, he has attempted to apply his animal findings to education, the origins of superstition, the construction of a fictional human utopia, and, most recently, a best-selling proposal for reforming society according to behaviorist principles.*

It would be unfair—and unscientific—to evaluate Skinner's work merely in terms of his own estimates; a man may not have achieved as much as he thinks and yet achieve a good deal. Thus his demonstration that animals tend to repeat actions that are followed by certain kinds of experiences obviously tells us something important about how and why animals learn. But the heart of the problem, surely, concerns the question of what *kinds* of experience—or "contingencies"—reinforce particular actions, and—perhaps even more important—how the actions originate in the first place.

Skinner has never faced up to the self-evident fact that many actions are learned, and repeated, for their own sake—that (in behaviorist terms) they are *self-reinforcing*. Thus people may engage in sexual intercourse for a variety of reasons: to express love, to conceive children, to relieve boredom, and so on. But most people who have actually engaged in it would, I think, testify that their primary reason is that the process itself, whatever its origins or results, is pleasant. Sexual intercourse, in other words, requires no "contingencies" to reinforce it; it is its own contingency.

Equally, Skinner has never really dealt with the possibility that patterns of behavior may not be built up bit by bit, but may be acquired "whole" *by imitating or observing other animals.* He notes that a rat, for instance, must press the lever of a Skinner box once "for other reasons" before it can learn to press it for food—but he has shown little interest in just what those "other reasons" might be. He has, indeed, conceded that imitation *may* be one source of an animal's behavior, but if one is to judge "objectively"—by his behavior—he still thinks in terms of what he calls "minimal units" of learning, which are, of course, the classic "atoms" of the behaviorist school. By reinforcing and combining such minimal units, he has trained animals to do remarkably complex things. A rat will pull a chain to get a marble from a rack, pick up the marble in its forepaws,

---

* To discuss Skinner as a social thinker would, unfortunately, take us far beyond the bounds of the present volume. I will say only that whatever the merit of his proposals, they are *not* based on any scientific knowledge of human nature—unless, of course, one believes with Skinner that man is merely a rat or pigeon writ large. I don't—for reasons that the balance of this chapter should make clear.

carry it to a tube projecting above the floor of its cage, and drop it in; pigeons can be reinforced into playing a simplified game of Ping-Pong. But such experiments, however effective they may be in a lecture-hall demonstration or television program, obviously prove nothing about how equally complex patterns are acquired by animals outside the laboratory.

There is, of course, no law that says a psychologist, or even a whole school of psychology, *must* investigate certain problems. What was unsettling about the behaviorists was their capacity to discourage even nonbehaviorists from asking the questions that they themselves ignored. Thus a standard textbook on learning theories published as late as 1956 contains exactly two sentences on imitation learning, though the author himself was not a behaviorist.*

Beginning about 1950, however, the seemingly impregnable edifice of behaviorism began to crumble, at least at the edges. One reason, perhaps, was that the "hard" sciences of physics and chemistry had turned out to be not quite so hard as had been thought. The physicist Werner Heisenberg, with his "uncertainty principle," had shown that in certain situations even the most "objective" knowledge was inherently unreliable; atoms, once deemed the indivisible constituents of matter, turned out to be catastrophically splittable. Advances in pharmaceutical chemistry revealed that the laboratory test tube was often a poor guide to living reality; chemists, physicians, and patients learned—sometimes the hard way—the difference between a drug's actions *in vitro* (in glass) and *in vivo* (in life). Equally, they learned that physiologically all species are by no means equal; morphine, for example, is a powerful sedative to a man, but a powerful stimulant to a cat; a cow is contented on a diet of grass that would starve a man.

These and similar developments probably had little impact on the behaviorists, since most of them had apparently forgotten the physical-science analogies on which their dogmas were based—if, indeed, they had ever known them. But changes in the hard sciences served at any rate to shake up the structure of science generally, suggesting to the newer generation of psychologists that there were perhaps more

* More recently, a number of behaviorists, though not Skinner himself, have accepted the reality of imitation learning and have done a considerable amount of experimental work on it. Better late than never, I suppose—but early rather than late would have been still better.

things in heaven and earth than were dreamed of in Watson's or Skinner's philosophy.

What really disintegrated the old dogmas, however, were new facts.

Soon after 1950, the Primate Laboratory of the University of Wisconsin set up a colony of captive macaque monkeys. Its purpose (in the words of Harry F. Harlow, its founder) was "to provide a steady supply of healthy newborn monkeys for the intensive study of learning and intellectual development." Baby monkeys were taken from their mothers shortly after birth and raised in individual cages where they could see and hear their fellows but not touch them. Fed a nutritious diet, first from bottles and then in solid form, they thrived; their death rate was lower and their weight gain more rapid than normal. Their physical drives (apart from sex, which they were too young to possess) were systematically and regularly "reduced," and by all the standards of behaviorist drive reduction they should have been—well, not *happy*, but at any rate well adjusted and well functioning.

The result was far different. As the young monkeys matured, they began displaying symptoms which in human beings would have indicated severe neurosis or downright psychosis. For hours they would sit motionless, staring into space; at other times they would rock back and forth in the manner of some human children suffering from the severe psychological disorder called autism. At the approach of a human being they might start biting themselves. Their sexual behavior, when the time came for it, was no less abnormal; though they showed clear signs of arousal in the presence of the opposite sex, they were quite incapable of doing anything about it, and would eventually attack their "partner" violently.

Drive reduction or no drive reduction, something was obviously wrong, and Harlow and his associates set about finding out what. The most obvious possibility was that the emotionally disturbed monkeys had missed out on mothering as infants, but Harlow and Company felt that this was too broad and vague a concept for experimental testing. Breaking it down, they concluded that "mothering"—considered in terms of the infant's experience—involved at least two important elements: reduction of the hunger drive, by being fed, and physical contact, by being held. Harlow thereupon contrived two surrogate mothers to test their effect on the infants: wooden-headed dummies with wire-mesh bodies. In one type, the wire was bare, in the other, it was covered with terry cloth and heated to body temperature by a small light bulb within; bottles of milk were attached sometimes to one type, sometimes to the other.

Almost instantly it became obvious that what was most important to the infants was not food but "contact comfort"—the softness and warmth of the terry-cloth dummies. If milk was available from both types, they would invariably ignore the wire mother; even when it was available only from the latter, they still spent nearly all their time, when not feeding, with the soft, cuddly surrogate. Scored in terms of hours per day with one or the other surrogate, it was Contact Comfort, 18; Drive Reduction, 1.

Evidently, then, the notion that reduction of stimulus is the only source of learning and other behavior is far from the truth; the corollary notion—the less stimulus the better—is even farther from it. More recent experiments have shown that human beings subjected to "sensory deprivation," with incoming stimuli of all sorts reduced to the lowest possible level, soon become temporarily psychotic. (In sensational fiction, the technique has been used for "brainwashing," though whether it would actually work is uncertain.) Indeed, experiments with rats and mice have shown that animals raised without adequate stimulation grow up not merely psychologically abnormal but physically abnormal as well; their nervous and endocrine systems do not mature properly, so that as adults they are more vulnerable to stress and disease.* Rats reared in isolation have noticeably smaller brains than those raised in an "enriched" environment—that is, one in which they associate with other rats and have a variety of objects to investigate; significantly, almost the entire difference is in the weight of the cerebral cortex, which as we know is the part of the brain most concerned with learning and intelligence.**

Another assault on drive reduction came from R. A. Butler, an associate of Harlow's, using a variant of the Skinner box in which reinforcement is measured and charted. In the standard Skinner box, a particular action such as pressing a bar or lever is reinforced by

* Oddly enough, the kind of stimulation does not seem to matter very much; a brief daily period of handling will do no better than periodic mild electric shocks. But stimulation of some sort there must be.

** The possible effect of similar environmental impoverishment on human brain development (such as in children raised in certain kinds of institutions or communities) is something worth pondering, though—since the variables are so numerous and controlled experiments are obviously out of the question—it would be hard if not impossible to determine in any scientific way.

presenting the animal with a pellet of food; in Butler's version (which his friends soon called the "Butler box"), a rhesus monkey was "reinforced" by the opening of a window, through which it could reach an object that it could manipulate or look at something interesting, an electric train running around a small track, for example, or another monkey. The sight of a monkey was the most potent reinforcer of all—and all three were more potent, at least part of the time, than drive-reducing food.

The final drive-reductio ad absurdum has been provided by a recent experiment in which rats were first trained to eat "free" food from a dish and then to "earn" food by pressing a lever. Although their hunger drive was equally reduced in either case, they uniformly *preferred* to press the lever so long as it yielded a reward—but only if they had to press it once or twice; if they had to press it ten times before they received food, they quit pressing and fed from the free dish. Evidently rats, like men, do not live by drive reduction alone; even in the absence of the much-maligned Puritan ethic, "work," for a rat, is somehow desirable in itself. And, clearly, free food does not ruin the animal's character—though if forced to work too hard for too little, even the most industrious rat will prefer to go on welfare.*

Findings like these, it hardly needs saying, put the cat among the laboratory pigeons. Skinner and his disciples were not much troubled; if you are dealing not with drives but with "contingencies," then one contingency is as good as another. Nonetheless, they were forced to reword their theories somewhat. If "positive reinforcement," that is, could not be objectively described as drive reduction, like the hunger reduction produced by the food pellet in a Skinner box, it must be, objectively, something else. Skinner thereupon defined it as *any* contingency which makes an action more likely to be repeated—thereby, unwittingly, turning his much-touted Law of Reinforcement into a literally meaningless tautology: an action is more likely to be repeated if followed by any contingency that makes it more likely to be repeated; a rose is a rose is a rose.

---

* Some months after writing the above, I read—with no surprise—that a study of human beings had yielded similar results. Over a three-year period, the Institute for Research on Poverty at the University of Wisconsin gave "income supplements" to some hundreds of poor families, such that they would continue to receive part or all their accustomed income whether they worked or not. Virtually nobody stopped working, not even those people who wouldn't have lost a nickel if they had.

Other drive-reductionists evolved even more tortuous explanations. For example, Neil Miller of Yale found himself arguing that Butler's monkeys, penned in their boxes, underwent a rise in tension simply from the *lack* of stimulation, which tension could be reduced by any change in the environment, so that the monkeys had really undergone drive reduction after all. In plain English he was saying that the monkeys were tense because they were bored, and therefore welcomed anything new. Which may well have been true—though not, as we shall see, the whole truth. But this amounted to saying that under certain circumstances an *increase* in stimulation (e.g., a new toy) could amount to the same thing as a *decrease* in stimulation (e.g., a reduction in hunger pangs)—now you see the drive-reduction pea, and now you don't.

Salvage operations of this sort, however, could not conceal the fact that drive reduction had been fatally undermined, though its complete collapse took a long time. Even today, indeed, the ruins of its temples survive here and there, like the lost cities of Yucatan, to astonish travelers in the psychological jungles. And many experimental psychologists still retain traces of superstitions reverence for the old religion, eschewing such taboo words as "pleasure" or "pain."

Before exploring some of the other widening cracks in the edifice of behaviorism, let us sum up some of what Harlow and Butler's experiments accomplished. In addition to beginning the dismantlement of drive reduction, they considerably expanded the scientifically acceptable list of monkey (and, there can be little doubt, human) motives. They established, in fact, that monkeys like the sight of other monkeys; that monkeys like to manipulate things; that monkeys are strongly motivated by curiosity; and that baby monkeys like to be cuddled.

On the face of it, demonstrating that babies like cuddling and monkeys are curious seems like a pretty silly way for two grown men to have spent several years of their professional lives. It *was* silly—but only if you ignore the abysmal silliness they were contending with. If the Wisconsin primatologists spent much time and trouble in proving the obvious, it was because so many of their behaviorist predecessors had spent even more time and trouble in denying the obvious.

Even before Harlow and his associates set off their first blast beneath the foundations of drive reduction, they had begun chiseling away at another behaviorist dogma: atomism. As early as 1949, Harlow had reported a series of experiments dealing with what he called the formation of learning sets. The basic experiment involved a classic situation in animal psychology: teaching an animal (in this case, a monkey) to distinguish between two objects (for example, a black cube and a red ball), one of which is rewarded and the other not. Discrimination problems of this sort are well within the capacity of a monkey, or even a rat (indeed, as we shall see in a moment, simple versions can be solved by fish).

Harlow ran his monkeys through three hundred and forty-four different pairs of objects. Invariably, the monkey learned to consistently pick the rewarded object sooner or later; what was interesting, however, was that the more problems the animal learned, the quicker it learned new problems. At the beginning, the monkey's success in picking the right object of a given pair climbed only fractionally with each trial, but as the experiment continued the solutions came more rapidly. By the time the animal had done three hundred problems or so, it usually required only a single "preliminary" trial to determine which object was in fact rewarded, after which it would almost unerringly choose the right one. The monkey had not simply learned; it had *learned to learn*. It had acquired not merely three hundred solutions to three hundred different problems—in behaviorist terms, three hundred new stimulus-response connections—but a *generalized* solution applicable to any problem of that type.

To Harlow, the implications for human beings were clear: a man's emotional, personal, and intellectual characteristics are not produced by the mere piling up of innumerable atoms of behavior; for human beings, as for other primates, the piling up of enough atoms of a given kind will itself create a new pattern *that determines the impact and arrangement of subsequent atoms.* It is this "learning how to learn efficiently in the situations that the animal frequently encounters," he declared, that "transforms the organism from a creature that adapts to a changing environment by [simple] trial and error to one that adapts by seeming hypothesis and insight." Having thus paid his respects to what he called the "rat psychologists"—a term, I think, chosen with a certain malicious deliberation—he closed with the hope that his approach to learning would be extended "by those brave souls who study *real* men and *real* women."

Harlow's work on learning sets not only initiated the demolition of the atomistic dogma but also, and by no means incidentally, pointed up the basic fallacy of the "stick to naïve animals" experiments on which the behaviorists had so heavily relied. For Harlow's monkeys, as they became less and less naïve, *learned in a different way—and one that could not have been predicted from their naïve behavior.* Ask a naïve question, in fact, and you get a naïve answer.

But Harlow had done something more: he had opened a crack in another behaviorist dogma—the "all species are equal" dictum. If learning is purely atomic, then the only possible species differences will be how many atoms a given species can pile up, and how fast; if, however, "emergent," nonatomic mechanisms play a role in the learning of some species, it is at least possible that they play no role in others. And this has in fact turned out to be the case.

Perhaps the clearest set of experiments on this point has been conducted by M. R. Bitterman at Bryn Mawr College. Many of them deal with what is called reversal learning, which involves a simplified variant of the object-discrimination experiments just discussed. The animal is first taught to choose the rewarded one of two objects; then the reward is "reversed" and the animal must learn to choose the other object.

Bitterman tested five kinds of animals in this manner: monkeys, rats, pigeons, turtles, and fish. For the monkeys and rats, the results were precisely what one would expect in the light of Harlow's earlier experiments: not only did they learn reversal more rapidly than the other species but their performance also improved with each reversal. A rat, after a dozen reversals or so, would begin picking the new rewarded alternative almost as soon as the former one ceased being rewarded; in Harlow's terms, it had acquired a learning set. The fish, however, completely lacked this ability. Not only did they learn reversal much more slowly than the rats (which anyone could have predicted), but their performance improved not at all. Putting it loosely, one could say that the rat had learned to "expect" reversal, while the fish could not do so.

Interestingly, though not surprisingly, the other species proved to be intermediate between rats and fish. The turtles could acquire a learning set on some kinds of problems but not others; the pigeons could do so, albeit with difficulty, on all the reversal problems, but in certain other experiments proved to be "fishlike" rather than "ratlike." (The experiments were evidently too simple to distinguish between the learning characteristics of rats and of monkeys.)

What we have here is clear evidence of a new learning mechanism —learning-set formation—which has emerged in the course of vertebrate evolution. Fish do not have it at all, being presumably dependent on instinct and pure trial-and-error learning; turtles have it in some situations but not others, pigeons in most situations, while rats and monkeys (and, presumably, most or all other mammals) show it all the time. Obviously, then, all vertebrates are equal only in the sense that all of them can learn; when it comes to *how* they learn, some are a great deal more equal than others.*

Another emergent form of learning—though present information is still too sparse to support conclusions on just when (in evolution) it emerged—is learning through imitation, or, as psychologists now usually (and more accurately) call it, observation learning. Like all forms of emergent, nonatomic learning, this was long rejected by behaviorists, and on evidence at least some of which seems, in retrospect, unbelievably fragile, not to say unscientific.

One such experiment was carried out as early as 1914 by John B. Watson himself. He used only four monkeys—a baboon, a cebus, and two rhesus macaques. For the first two, Watson himself served as the "demonstrator," performing certain tasks to see whether the animals would imitate him. Neither one did, nor did the two rhesus that were set to imitate one another. Watson himself ruled the baboon results out of consideration, declaring that the animal was too stupid to make its performance meaningful—though just where the stupidity lay in this experiment is a matter on which one might reserve judgment. On this extraordinarily slender evidence, he then concluded that imitation did not exist; a later commentator has noted that "the whole situation was so unnatural as to preclude the likelihood of any imitation occurring."

Imitation did, in fact, remain difficult to demonstrate rigorously in the laboratory, even for the occasional psychologists who cared to hunt for it. Animals do not always behave to order; they can, for example, be distracted by the presence of the experimenter (as in Watson's experiments) and also by one another. Experiments on imi-

* Not at all surprisingly, the capacity to form learning sets parallels the anatomic importance of the cerebral cortex, the portion of the brain most concerned with learning. Rats have more cortex than turtles, which have more than fish. And when Bitterman surgically removed part of the cortex from rats and then tested them, he found that their performance dropped to the turtle level.

tation have doubtless contributed to the formulation of what some psychologists call the Harvard Law of Animal Behavior: "Under carefully controlled experimental conditions, animals do as they damn well please."

Nonetheless, experiments continued to be done, and eventually to yield results highly displeasing to the behaviorists; ironically, part of the credit goes to the increasingly sophisticated experimental techniques which the behaviorists themselves had developed. A key experiment was reported in 1959 by C. L. Darby and A. J. Riopelle, of Emory University in Atlanta. They used the same basic approach with which Harlow had earlier demonstrated the formation of learning sets—setting an animal a long series of discrimination problems of the same type and measuring his improvement in performance. The difference was that two monkeys were involved: a "demonstrator" which tried to solve the problem and an "observer" which watched the demonstrator—and then tried in its turn.*

The "demonstrator" was given one opportunity to pick the rewarded one of two objects; its chances of doing so were of course precisely 50 per cent. When the observer was given its chance, it at first did no better than this. Gradually, however, its performance improved; by the time it had been exposed to five hundred problems, it could pick the rewarded object three times out of four *simply from having watched the demonstrator succeed or fail.* Significantly, too, its performance was not mere "imitation," since half the time a "correct" solution involved doing the opposite of what the demonstrator had done—that is, if the demonstrator had picked the unrewarded object, the observer must then pick the rewarded one. In fact, the observer seemed to learn somewhat more rapidly from the demonstrator's "mistakes" than from its successes. There is no way I can think of to describe this performance except to say that the observer, having seen the demonstrator pick either a rewarded or an unrewarded object, learned to draw certain conclusions about which object was in fact rewarded—and act on them.**

---

* This account is of necessity rather simplified.

** It has gradually become apparent that the term "observation learning" actually encompasses two more or less independent phenomena. The one that Darby and Riopelle observed is now often called "empathetic learning": the capacity to learn from observing the reinforcement (or nonreinforcement) of another animal's actions. "Imitation learning" in the literal sense, by contrast, involves rather a tendency to perform a particular action (or series of actions) simply from having seen another animal perform it.

Once again, experimental psychology—thanks to the retarding effects of behaviorism—had taken fifty years to catch up to popular observation: monkey see, monkey do. And not, as it turned out, just monkeys. In 1968, a group at New York Medical College headed by E. Roy John reported even more remarkable results with cats.

John and Company were not initially very interested in learning mechanisms as such; their concern was rather with the effect of learning upon the electrical patterns (brain waves) of the cortex. To study this, they would surgically implant tiny electrodes in the animals' brains (a largely painless procedure; brain tissue has no pain-sensitive nerves) and then record the changing wave patterns as the animal learned various conditioned actions. Hitches developed, however, when the cats—despite being exposed to the best Skinnerian reinforcement techniques—learned either slowly or not at all, to the point where experimental schedules were sometimes disrupted. The experimenters thereupon began hunting for quicker and more reliable ways of training, in the course of which they explored the possibilities of observation learning.

In the first experiment, the animals were trained to jump over a hurdle at the sound of a buzzer, the "incentive" being a mild electric shock to the feet. They were divided into three groups: "observers," "students," and "teachers." The students were trained in the normal Skinnerian way; the observers, after being given an initial shock to establish "empathy" with the students, merely watched them being trained. After each day's observation session, the observers would then see a teacher—which had been previously trained—actually perform the jump.

When the students had learned the hard way to jump consistently, the observers were put into training. They learned far more rapidly than the conventionally trained students—in several cases, requiring only one or two training sessions where the students had required up to twenty. A second experiment, on a simpler task (lever pressing), showed that the teacher alone could do the job; one observer, after having observed the teacher press the lever three times, learned to do likewise during its first training session.

John himself makes two points about these experiments. First, he notes that his observers, like Darby and Riopelle's monkey observers, were not engaging in simple imitation; while the teachers had been trained to press the lever only with the paw, the observers learned to press it with paw, elbow, or nose. What they had learned was not a specific physical action but a generalized *kind* of action. His second point—and to me the clinching one—has to do with the brain-wave changes that were the initial object of the entire exercise. Student cats' waves showed specific kinds of changes as they learned their tasks —and the observer cats showed much the same kinds of changes *while they were observing*. If, then, the changes in the students reflected the fact that they were learning by doing (and it is hard to see what else they could have reflected), then clearly the same changes in the observers must have reflected learning by watching.

John's own summary of his results is worth recounting, not merely because of what it says but also how it says it—a beautiful example of the "objective," dead-pan scientific put-down.

Undoubtedly, he says—his tongue well into his cheek—behaviorist conditioning techniques "have been of great utility in the quantitative study of learning." Against this, however, we have "the impressive speed and efficiency of observational learning, contrasted with the potentially catastrophic slowness and need for repetition which often characterize conventional conditioning." What he is saying is that in a natural situation, where failure to learn may well mean not the laboratory electric shock but being snapped up by a predator, an animal forced to rely on slow trial-and-error learning would often be dead before it had learned very much. Thus, says John, conventional conditioning "may well be a phenomenon of limited relevance, utilizing relatively unnatural mechanisms." In particular, "observational learning may be the primary method of acquiring language, ideas, and social habits in man. . . . The behavioral and physiological study of more natural learning situations may be essential for adequate understanding of learning mechanisms."

Even more interesting is something that John failed to point out: his experiments, taken together with earlier experiments on observation learning, knocked the props out from under Skinner's famous Law of Reinforcement. The observer animals had clearly learned something from watching the teacher; in Skinnerian terms, their observations had made it more probable that they themselves would perform the action. Yet they themselves *had not been reinforced*—because they had performed no action that *could* be reinforced.

What John had to say about Skinnerian conditioning is simply a more genteel version of what I have been saying in this chapter: behaviorism, with its interminable naïve and atomized experiments, at best explored only a tiny corner of animal (and human) behavior. For all its "objective," scientific pretensions, it has in fact told us very little about why animals and people do what they do; it has labored mountainously—and brought forth a laboratory rat.*

Having observed the crumbling of various subsidiary behaviorist dogmas, we might as well conclude this chapter by a backward look at its central dogma: that a scientific psychology (or a scientific anything else) must rely only on objective data from controlled experiments. So far as the experimental end of this dogma is concerned, the statement is pure moonshine. Geophysics—the science of how the earth is constructed and how it changes—does not rely primarily on experiments of any kind, and never will. The processes by which mountains are built, or by which (as we are now learning) the continents and sea bottoms slide back and forth upon the semiliquid rock beneath them, are far too spacious to be encompassed by the walls of any laboratory, as their time span far exceeds the life span of any scientist. Astrophysics—the science of how stars originate and change—is, if anything, even less experimental; like geophysics, it became a science less in the laboratory than by observing the natural world, formulating hypotheses to explain the observations, and confirming (or disproving) the hypotheses by further observation. Scientific psychologists please copy!

As for the behaviorists' obligatory "objectivity," the best one can say is that it is a cop-out. Admittedly, it would be much more convenient if psychological phenomena *were* totally objective. The behavior of a rat in a Skinner box is simple, and easy to describe—and the descriptions are reliable; the experience of being human is seldom simple and often almost impossible to describe, nor can we place any

---

* Space prevents me from tackling the fascinating question of how Skinner—dogma, tautology, and all—has managed to retain enormous prestige among his own scientific colleagues, so that as late as 1971 the American Psychological Association could hail him in the most fulsome terms as "a pioneer in psychological research, leader in theory, master in technology, who has revolutionized the study of behavior. . . . A superlative scholar, teacher, and writer." The mechanisms may be somewhat similar to those by which generals who have fouled up in command are given medals and promotions; I commend the problem to historians of science. Likewise, I cannot let myself be sidetracked into a discussion of behaviorism's impact on American culture generally—though I hope some cultural historian will one day tackle the question. As just one example, the notorious "Look, look, look! See Spot run!" approach to early-grade reading, which has stultified two generations of American kids, can fairly be described as at least the bastard offspring of behaviorist atomism.

automatic reliance on the accounts of it that we get from our fellows, since as we well know they may be lying, to us or to themselves. If it has taken more than a century of observations merely to begin to understand the formation and evolution of a star, it may well take another century before we can comprehend the far more complex and elusive processes that shape and change a man.

Science, if it is about anything, is about the real world; to the extent that it turns its back on that world, or on part of it, it ceases to be science and becomes theological disputation about how many conditioned responses can dance on the head of a pin. Subjective phenomena—pleasure, pain, hopes, dreams, the contrivance of a new invention, the writing of a poem—are part of reality; to deny them, to whittle man down to rat size (or less) for the convenience of publish-or-perish professors, is to deny human nature and humanity.

4

THE FAMILY OF MAN:
Meet the Primates

"The key to [the primates'] success has been their adaptability, their own 'specialization' being that they have remained unspecialized."

—L. B. HALSTEAD

"The wild infant monkey or ape does not survive except in the group."

—K. R. L. HALL

Before considering how the principles of animal behavior, so long obscured and obfuscated by the dogmas of behaviorism, apply to our ancestors, let us take a quick look at the place of those ancestors in the animal kingdom.

Man is, to begin with, a vertebrate, possessed of the tough internal skeleton and efficient circulatory system that have characterized vertebrates since their appearance on earth some half billion years ago. As such, therefore, he is a member of that group of animals which almost from the first has dominated life on earth in terms of size, mobility, and—eventually—intelligence. The internal skeleton, and especially the circulatory system, which pumps oxygen- and nutrient-laden blood through a closed system of vessels to all parts of the body, enabled the vertebrates to produce the largest land animals (in the shape of the now extinct dinosaurs), the largest marine animals (in the shape of the almost extinct great whales), and the largest flying animals (the birds). (The latter, though for aerodynamic reasons they are pretty small stuff compared to a whale or even a dinosaur, are enormous in comparison with their nonvertebrate competitors, the insects, who never managed to evolve a circulatory system adequate for a body weighing more than an ounce or so.)

Largely because of their size, the vertebrates can also travel farther and faster than any other group of animals. And size and mobility taken together have given them an enormous advantage in nature's perpetual eat-or-be-eaten sweepstakes: many vertebrates eat invertebrates, from the early robin catching the worm to the majestic blue whale guzzling shrimplike krill by the truckload, but the reverse seldom happens—at least not so long as the vertebrate is alive and well. Mobility, which implies exposure to varied and rapidly changing environments, also gave the vertebrates a powerful evolutionary incentive to develop high-grade instruments for getting information from their surroundings; in fact, they can see better than any invertebrate and hear better than all but a few. Not very surprisingly, their equipment to process that information—their brains and nervous systems—is also, by and large, the best in the world, though of course it varies enormously in quality from fish to man.

Humans are also members of the class of vertebrates called mammals: animals with a high metabolic rate which, aided by hair or fur insulation where necessary (in humans, of course, artificial insulation), can maintain a relatively constant body temperature under conditions of cold or heat that would render other animals torpid or lifeless. Perhaps more important, mammals possess the superefficient lungs and circulatory system which seem to be absolutely necessary for supplying oxygen in the quantities required by a large and complex brain. Accordingly, while a fish's information-processing capability (as the computer men would call it) is not much above the invertebrate level, even the stupidest mammal is smarter than the smartest representative of any other animal group.

Mammals, of course, are conventionally defined by a quite different criterion: the possession, by the females, of mammary glands for nourishing their young.* In and of itself, this reproductive refinement was probably of only minor evolutionary significance; certainly millions of other species have survived and thrived despite a disinterest in their offspring for which "child neglect" would be the feeblest of euphemisms. But mammary glands provided a foundation for other, and considerably more important, developments, since they imply a close and relatively prolonged association between adult and young.

---

* Those women's liberationists who see male conspiracy in terminological trivia, demanding that "history" be converted to "herstory," might reflect on the fact that the most successful and intelligent class of vertebrates has been defined—by male scientists—in terms of its females, not its males.

This was clearly an essential precondition for the later evolution of observation learning, so superior to the simple step-by-step conditioning found among fish and behaviorists, as well as the development (in humans) of communication, language, and social cooperation. Of course suckling the young did not of itself produce these behavioral refinements, but without the close association between mother and child that it involved they could hardly have developed at all.

Thus we mammals are not only the sole group physiologically capable of maintaining a high-grade learning apparatus but also the only group *socially* equipped to make use of such an apparatus. And evolutionarily speaking, we owe it all to our mothers!*

Moving higher up (or farther out) on our family tree, we classify our species as a member of the order of mammals called primates. It is a difficult group to define, including as it does animals ranging from man down to the tree-shrews, small squirrel-like animals of Southeast Asia with anatomies so unspecialized that zoologists still cannot agree on whether to classify them with the primates or with the even more unspecialized insectivores (the shrews, moles, and hedgehogs) or to duck the issue by assigning them an order of their own. The distinguished anatomist LeGros Clark has suggested that primates can be most usefully defined in terms not of specific anatomic characteristics (of which they have none that distinguish them as a group from other mammals) but of their long-term evolutionary trends. From this standpoint, then, a primate is a relatively primitive mammal that has become more or less adapted to living in trees, the adaptations centering on the limbs, eyes, and brain.

Primates, except for the tree-shrews, possess hands (in most cases, feet also) adapted for grasping tree branches, either between fingers and palm or between fingers and thumb.** The eyes are improved in several respects. First, they can form especially sharp images with the aid of the fovea, an area in the retina unusually rich in light-sensitive cells. The fovea—which is present even in the tree-shrews,

* Here, as in the matter of size, birds are a special case. Like mammals, they are warm-blooded, well insulated, and well oxygenated; like mammals, they nourish their young, though without the aid of special organs. Yet despite these advantages they are not intelligent in anything approaching the mammalian sense; their small size has doomed them to remain—well, bird-brains.

** The tree-shrews do their climbing with the aid of claws, but this method is unsafe for most larger animals, since with increasing weight the claw is increasingly likely to tear loose from the tree's bark.

albeit in rudimentary form—is the reason you can read this book. If you shift your eyes to the edge of the page, so that the image of the words no longer falls on your foveas, you will be able to see the type, but not to tell one word from another. Second, all primates, including the tree-shrews, can see in color. Third, all primates except the tree-shrew possess at least a degree of binocular vision. That is, their eyes, instead of being located on the sides of the head, as is the case with most other mammals, have moved around to the front of the head, allowing the animal to fuse the images from the two eyes into a single, three-dimensional picture.

The primates' improved eyes are clearly a consequence of treetop life. An airborne or partially airborne existence forces an animal to rely more on vision and less on smell, that other prime resource for learning about the environment, since scent does not "lie" well off the ground. We note, for example, that birds, which are even more airborne than the primates, have retinas that are "all fovea" and can also see in color, but have virtually *no* sense of smell. The primate olfactory sense, though it still exists, is far less acute than that of, say, a dog: the part of its brain that handles signals from the nose is proportionately rather small, while its visual centers are, as one would expect, enlarged.

Binocular vision, and the 3-D perception it makes possible, has an even more specific evolutionary rationale in terms of mobility in the trees. To move through treetops at any speed inevitably involves a certain amount of leaping from branch to branch—and a branch leaper unable to judge accurately the distance to the next branch stands an excellent chance of breaking a leg, or its neck.* And 3-D vision brings with it other important consequences. Since its possessor no longer sees the world as a flat picture, objects literally stand out from their surroundings (even more, in many cases, if they are seen in color), so that the animal can become aware of them as separate entities. Try the experiment, for instance, of covering one eye and looking at a tree or bush; you will probably see it as a relatively homogeneous mass. Seen with two eyes, however, it becomes not just a green-and-brown lump but something composed of individual

---

* Unless it is a lightweight like the tree-shrew or the squirrel, in which case the relatively high air resistance of its body—in particular, its bushy tail—will slow its descent sufficiently to prevent damage.

branches, twigs, and leaves. As both hunters and nature watchers know, most wild animals, with monocular (and usually black-and-white) vision, respond far more readily to *moving* objects than to objects as such; if one remains still or moves very slowly, one can get on surprisingly intimate terms with many shy creatures.

It is almost certainly the interaction of the grasping limb with acute vision that first nudged the primates toward their third evolutionary trend: the enlarged brain. A hand that can grasp a branch can also grasp a fruit or an insect—manipulate it, pull it apart, turn in around to be examined from different angles. The object can be brought up to the nose to tickle the dulled smelling nerves, while the fingertips, which do not support the body and therefore are not covered by hoofs or tough calluses, can perceive the object's shape and texture. But if all this information is to be of any use to the animal, it must possess an apparatus for coordinating and classifying it—an improved brain, in fact.

The primates' trend toward braininess was doubtless accelerated by a peculiarity of tree life. As the writer John Pfeiffer has pointed out, the treetop environment is full of discontinuities. A bird flies in a medium—air—that is relatively homogeneous, and therefore predictable; the same goes for a ground-based animal on terra firma, or an aquatic one in the water. But an animal moving rapidly about in the treetops must constantly cope with sudden and often unexpected irregularities and changes: gaps that may require a short leap or a long one, or that may be too broad to leap at all, requiring either a change of direction or a detour on the ground; branches that may or may not be thick enough to support its weight—and that even when apparently thick enough may yet break from rottenness, requiring a quick grab at an alternative support. For the primates, life in the trees meant "decisions, decisions," with the penalty for wrong decisions ranging from injury to death. Small wonder, then, that their decision-making apparatus expanded. And when we say "decisions," we are of course talking about learned responses, not instinctive ones. To the extent an animal's behavior is governed by instinct, it *cannot* make decisions, any more than a man who has just inhaled pepper can decide whether or not to sneeze.

Having defined the primates as well as we can in evolutionary terms, let us now consider just what kinds of animals are included in the definition. Conventionally they are divided into two major groups. First is the prosimians, which includes the tree-shrews,* the lemuroids—now found mainly in Madagascar, but worldwide fifty million years ago—and the tarsioids, another formerly widespread group which today is even more obscure than the lemuroids. The second great tribe of primates, the anthropoids, is made up of the cercopithecoids or Old World monkeys, the ceboids or New World monkeys, and the hominoids, which, as their name ("manlike") suggests, include humans and their close relatives, the apes.**

Just how do our ancestors fit into this scheme of classification? To begin with, we can be certain that our forebears of perhaps sixty-five million years ago must have been pretty similar to today's tree-shrews, at least in anatomy; their behavior can only be guessed at. By perhaps fifty million years ago they must have evolved into lemuroids of some sort—probably not very similar to any of today's lemurs, but close enough to the generalized lemur design that underlies all these modern species.

Thus far we have necessarily gone on inference; though tree-shrew-like and lemuroid fossils have survived, all of them possess enough specialized anatomic features to make it unlikely that they are part of man's lineage. Our actual ancestors of perhaps thirty-five million years ago, however, seem to have left their remains in the shape of a creature called Aegyptopithecus ("Egyptian ape"), dug up a few years ago near Cairo by Elwyn Simons of Yale. Simons himself calls it the first ape, but his own description of it casts some doubt on that classification. It had, he says, "the teeth of an ape in the head of a monkey," probably possessed a tail (as no ape does), and also retained certain primitive skeletal features which even modern monkeys (as well as apes) have lost. On the whole, then, I am inclined to label it a cercopithecoid monkey, though one with certain anatomical aspirations toward apehood.

Aegyptopithecus, like his ancestors, lived in a tropical forest; his bones lie amid fossil treetrunks, some nearly a hundred feet long. As to what a tropical forest was doing near the future site of Cairo, today one of the driest spots on earth, we need only note briefly that thirty-five million years ago the earth was a good deal warmer overall and

---

* If, that is, one considers them to be primates, as I do.
** I have pretty much ignored the ceboids in this book, since they are quite remote from our own family tree.

in many places much moister than it now is.* As a tree-dwelling monkey, it is very likely that Aegyptopithecus lived primarily on fruits, shoots, and other juicy and tender vegetation, as most modern forest monkeys and apes still do. Though we do not have enough of his limb bones to be certain, it also seems very probable that he moved about his treetop home as today's Old World monkeys still do: by leaping and landing on all four feet, rather than by swinging from arm to arm ("brachiating"). He was, in short, still essentially a quadruped.

By twenty million years ago, our ancestors were to be found among the genus Dryopithecus ("tree ape" or "oak ape"), a wide-ranging group of extinct apes whose remains have been found in Europe, Asia, and Africa. Which of the known fossil Dryopithecines was our ancestor, if any of them was, is uncertain. What is certain is that they were as a group considerably larger than Aegyptopithecus—one was almost the size of a gorilla—and, partly for this reason, had acquired some anatomic characteristics of the true ape. Their arms, in particular, possessed considerable sidewise mobility, enabling them to distribute their weight among two or three branches. By the same token, they could reach out to grab fruits and such in almost any direction, and if they could do that, it is not unlikely that on occasion they stood on their hind legs to reach things, as all modern apes do. Dryopithecus, that is, was probably on the road to becoming a part-time biped—an obviously necessary stop toward becoming the full-time biped that man is.

By fifteen million years ago, some Dryopithecine or other had evolved into Ramapithecus ("Rama's ape"), whose fossils have turned up in both India and Kenya. These are, unfortunately, very fragmentary—we do not have even a complete skull—but the fragments are enough to place Ramapithecus either on or very close to our family tree. His teeth were arranged in his jaws, not in the straight-sided U found among all other apes, but in a continuous curve rather like the geometer's parabola, as ours are. Moreover, the arrangement of these teeth and certain other features about them indicate, in the opinion of Simons and some other paleontologists, that he fed in part on grass seeds, which would mean that he spent a certain amount of time on the ground. Certainly his habitat was consistent with that possibility.

* The interested reader can find out more about prehistoric climates and why they changed in my book *Climate, Man, and History.*

Like his ancestors, he lived in forest country, but it was a rather more open forest, interspersed with grassy glades offering a useful dietary supplement to any primate with the adaptability to exploit it.*

It seems not unlikely, then, that Ramapithecus lived much as do today's chimpanzees—he was about as big as the smallest of them— spending a fair amount of time on the ground but also taking to the trees for food as well as for safety. There is also some rather tenuous evidence that he may have used natural objects as tools, as chimps quite frequently do, though we cannot be sure of this and probably never will be. He may have killed and eaten small animals, as chimps sometimes do. It would be fascinating to know just how far he had adapted toward a bipedal gait, but we will not know this until the fossil-hunters have dug up many more Ramapithecine bones.

Between the time that Ramapithecus bows out of the fossil record, perhaps ten million years ago, and the appearance on stage of our next ancestor, there is a gap of some five million years. The main thing we know about this period is that world climates grew drier. The tropical rain forests where Aegyptopithecus and Dryopithecus had lived did not disappear completely, but more and more of them were opening up into the moist savannas that Ramapithecus had favored. And these, in turn, were opening up further into dry savannas—grassland interspersed with trees instead of trees interspersed with grassland—while the dry savannas were transformed into open, grassy steppes, and some of the latter, into outright deserts.**

This long trend toward drying climates—it had been going on for at least twenty million years—naturally begot numbers of new animal species adapted to live in the open savannas and grasslands that were covering an increasing proportion of the earth's surface. Notable for their expansion, in both number and variety, were the ungulates—the grassland grazers and the forest-edge and savanna browsers, including the horse, cow, deer, sheep-goat, elephant, and antelope families.

---

* It is worth noting that grass seeds—in the shape of wheat, corn, rice, oats, rye, and millet—contribute more to the diet of modern man than any other category of plant or animal product.

** Whether, and to what extent, deserts had existed earlier is an old argument among specialists in ancient climates. Both sides of the dispute, however, agree that deserts and other dry or semidry habitats had become a great deal more prevalent by five million years ago than they had been previously.

Along with them came predators endowed with the necessary teeth, claws, cunning, and fleetness of foot to feed on the ungulates.

And along with these came representatives of the primates, moving out of the trees in which they had lived for tens of millions of years. The generalized traits and capacities they had acquired from treetop life—the grasping hand, sharp eye, and active brain—turned out to be quite as useful for life on the ground, as we can see from the fact that not one but several primate groups begot down-to-earth representatives. The Old World monkeys produced the baboon-macaque family, all of whom spend much of their time on the ground, though not all of them live in open country; the lemuroids, holed up in the island of Madagascar where higher primates had never penetrated, produced the extraordinary giant lemur, as big as a two-year-old calf, which was at least a part-time ground dweller. And no fewer than three branches of the hominoids made the transition from treetop to ground. One was the ancestral gorillas—which, however, were probably forest and wet-savanna dwellers, as their descendants remain; a second was a supergorilla, Gigantopithecus, whose massive bones have been found in deposits indicating that he lived in grasslands, perhaps feeding primarily on grass seeds. And the third, of course, was Australopithecus ("southern ape"), one variety of which was pretty certainly our ancestor.*

In contrast with the other new arrivals on the ground, Australopithecus was a true biped; his feet had lost the power to grasp and were instead adapted to supporting and transporting his body on the ground. His size was about that of a modern chimp, while his brain was perhaps a fraction bigger. Certainly his activities were rather more complex and sophisticated than those observed in chimps; he

---

* The scientific classification of this group of ground-living hominoids (technically called homin*id*s) is at present in a very confused and controversial state. Some experts (notably Elwyn Simons) lump them all together as members of the genus Australopithecus, embracing several species differing considerably in both anatomy and probable life-style; others (notably the late Louis Leakey and his son Richard) have shifted some species into our own genus, Homo. Mainly in the interests of simplicity, I have chosen the former course. Hereafter, then, "Australopithecus" can be taken as referring to the hominids between about five million and one million years ago and, more precisely (unless otherwise indicated), to those species within the group whose anatomy and life-style indentifies them as probable ancestors of man. Later members of the human family will be called "Homo."

made crude tools of stone, as chimps do not, and doubtless of other, more perishable materials, as chimps occasionally do. In addition, there can be little doubt that along with these natural objects which he had modified to make them more useful, he also used a variety of unmodified objects for various purposes, as chimps frequently do; according to one theory, he employed the leg bones of ungulates as clubs and their horns as stabbing daggers.

Ecologically speaking, Australopithecus must have lived much as do today's savanna baboons, eating just about anything edible—the traditional primate menu of fruits, buds, and shoots in season, grass seeds, roots, and succulent underground runners out of season, as well as the eggs of ground-nesting birds. In addition, he undoubtedly ate meat—at least in some cases, for certain varieties of Australopithecus are suspected of having been vegetarians. Both baboons and chimps occasionally catch and devour young mammals of several species, including young monkeys.* The chimps, moreover, sometimes catch their prey by acting in semiorganized groups; there can be little doubt that Australopithecus was at least as sophisticated.

There can be no doubt whatever that Australopithecus, whatever and however he hunted, was also hunted himself; the savanna-grass-land predators, though they lived primarily on ungulates, had no prejudices against primate on the menu. How Australopithecus avoided being eaten is a subject for a later chapter, but we can note at this point that tool use and tool making very probably played a key role. The ground-living gorilla was (and is) protected by its size, as was, *a fortiori,* Gigantopithecus, who weighed in at a quarter of a ton or more; the ground-living baboons were (and are) protected by the tusklike canine teeth of their males. Australopithecus, not much bigger than a big baboon, but without the latter's tusks, had only his two hands—and whatever weapons they could wield.

At this point the human line, having produced a full-time biped dependent on tool use and tool making for survival, has clearly separated from the rest of the primates. Whether Australopithecus can be classified as a "man" or as something less than a man is arguable, but he was, despite his name, unquestionably something more than

---

* It is suspected that chimps also occasionally make off with a human baby—which, unpleasant though the thought may be, is only turnabout, since a number of African tribes relish roast chimp.

an ape. The story of his descendants, over the last million or two years, is therefore a rather different kind of story than the one we have been recounting up to this point, for though these creatures still faced the same basic survival problems of eating, avoiding being eaten, and reproducing that they had confronted first in the forest and then in the grassland, they increasingly tended to solve them in uniquely human ways, rather than by generalized primate survival techniques. This human phase of human evolution will be discussed in Part II.

Meanwhile, having introduced the primates and placed our ancestors among them, is there anything we can say about primates generally that may throw some light on human nature? As it happens, there is. Before saying it, however, I should emphasize that any statement about the behavior of primates as a group needs at least a pinch of salt. Since most primate species live in trees, they are difficult to observe under natural conditions, and in fact only a minority of them have been studied in this manner, while many have never been studied even in captivity.* Just how misleading the latter type of investigation can be may be noted from some early studies of caged tree-shrews, which because of their small size are peculiarly difficult to observe in the wild. The animals were catagorized as "gluttonous, wrathful, and libidinous"—traits in which the anthropologist Carlton S. Coon (rather a fast man with a conclusion) professes to see "a caricature of uninhibited human nature." More careful studies, in much larger cages where some effort was made to simulate the animals' natural environment, established that they could at least as accurately be described as sociable, affectionate, and playful.

For what the various primate studies are worth, it appears that the latter characterization of tree-shrews also applies to primates generally. They are, above all, sociable animals: nearly all of them live in groups (the only exceptions, significantly, are found among the lower primates). The size of the group varies greatly, from the "nuclear family"—male, female, and young—of some gibbons to the hundred-plus individuals of some baboon bands; moreover, in some species group members may at times go off on their own. Nonetheless, all

---

* Happily, chimps and baboons, the two primates cited in Chapter 1 as most relevant to man's psychological past and present, *have* been studied extensively in the wild, the former by such investigators as Irven DeVore, Thelma Rowell, and the late K. R. L. Hall, the latter by Vernon and Frances Reynolds and, above all, in the magnificent studies of Jane Van Lawick-Goodall and her associates.

members of nearly all primate species spend most or all their time in company with their fellows—and, so far as we can judge, like doing so.

To talk of the likes or dislikes of a tree-shrew, or even a monkey, may, indeed, seem like the most arrant guess work—and is certainly, from the behaviorist viewpoint, the most heinous heresy. To those psychologists who eschew the very notion of animal likes and dislikes, on the grounds that an animal after all cannot tell us about its feelings, I would say the following. First, some animals can "tell us" very clearly about their feelings, as anyone knows who has ever stepped on a cat's tail, or who has stroked the animal and listened to its vocal response. And pussy's outraged squall and contented purr are "behavior" quite as real as pressing the lever in a Skinner box—and a great deal more natural. Beyond this, animals define their likes and dislikes by what they do and don't do. If a monkey in the wild systematically seeks out and consumes fruits, it seems to me perfectly reasonable to conclude that it likes fruits—as we ourselves do. By the same token, if a cow brushes away biting flies with its tail, it hardly seems over-imaginative to conclude that it dislikes being bitten—as, again, we ourselves do.

Thus when we observe that virtually all primates in the wild voluntarily spend their time with other members of their species, when we note that Butler's experiments with monkeys showed that they may find the mere sight of another monkey a more potent "reinforcement" than food, and, finally, when we find in Harlow's experiments that young primates separated from their fellows showed clear signs of alarm or distress, surely the only rational conclusion is that something in the primate psyche finds group life appealing and prolonged solitude unappealing—as we ourselves find solitary confinement.*

But ingrained likes and dislikes, as I have pointed out earlier, don't just happen; they have evolved as ways of implanting types of behavior useful to the survival of the species. If, then, primates consistently favor life in groups, that life-style must help them survive in one or more ways. There can be little doubt as to what some of those ways are. To begin with, the group serves as an early warning system. A

---

* In recent years, even most behaviorists have come to accept the existence in many animals of what they call an "affiliative drive"—a built-in impulse to seek the company of other members of the same species, both because it is intrinsically gratifying and because, in frightening situations, it seems to be intrinsically reassuring.

group of animals can obviously spot the approach of a predator far more certainly than can a single animal—assuming, of course, that the "spotter" can communicate his observations to the rest of the group. Primates, from the tree-shrews on up, do communicate, making various noises whose significance is "understood" by other group members. The number and variety of these noises varies enormously, of course, from the two or three types of squeak employed by some tree-shrews to the thousands of words found in human vocabularies. But virtually universal among primates is an "alarm" noise that alerts the group to a possible external threat.

For primates living in or near trees, the standard reaction to danger is, as one might expect, flight into a tree, or from one tree to another more removed from the danger. For those living in open country, where flight into trees is less feasible, responses to danger can be grouped under two general headings: scatter and hide (as with the patas monkey) or bunch up and threaten (as with the grassland baboons). Here, of course, we have another group function: mutual defense. This, however, is what we might call an optional function; even baboons do not threaten on all occasions, and in a forest or near-forest environment are much more likely to run away. We can say, in fact, that primates generally prefer running to fighting (the ultimate stage of threatening), and for a fairly obvious evolutionary reason. Unless an animal is big enough (as is an elephant) or formidable enough (as is a lion) to make the outcome of a fight a foregone conclusion, escape—assuming that there is somewhere to escape to—is a much more reliable survival technique than confrontation. In anything approaching an even contest there is always the possibility of either losing outright or of winning at the cost of serious injury—which, in terms of the "winner's" future survival, may well be equivalent to losing. Although a degree of aggressiveness is characteristic of some primates, a sizable measure of caution is characteristic of all of them.

But if the primate group is important in detecting and sometimes coping with emergencies, it is even more central to the day-to-day business of living: the group is where primates learn to be primates. The capacity to learn quickly and efficiently by observation learning is obviously worthless in itself; there must also be somebody around to observe. The primate group insures that there *will* be somebody, that the young primate will constantly have around him (or her) "role models" from whom he can learn the skills and behavioral patterns he needs to survive.

We do not, actually, know much about the relative importance of observation learning in different primate groups, or even if it exists in all of them. Since this type of learning was until fairly recently an almost unmentionable subject among experimental psychologists, we do not yet have comparative studies (like Bitterman's experiments on learning-set formation). In principle, of course, observation learning might occur in any mammal or bird, in the sense that in both groups the young associate with their elders for fairly prolonged periods—but "might" is the operative word. In fact, it seems to play only a very minor role in birds, and I would guess that the same is very likely the case with the more primitive mammals, such as the opossum and other marsupials, the insectivores, and, perhaps, even the tree-shrews. On the other hand, it clearly exists in both apes and monkeys as well as in cats, dogs, and perhaps rats; it is not, in other words, a primate specialty. It seems likely, as a general rule, that the more varied and complicated actions an animal engages in, the more heavily dependent it will be on observation learning, since such actions, outside a behaviorist laboratory, will be learned with difficulty or not at all by sheer trial and error; the animal won't live long enough.

The group as a focus for observation learning is important for the adults as well as for the maturing young, since it insures that useful skills picked up by one or another group member will spread fairly rapidly to the others. This process has actually been observed in an experimental colony of Japanese macaques, which for years has lived under semiwild conditions on an island in Japan's Inland Sea. The animals are regularly fed (the island's natural food resources are modest), mainly on sweet potatoes, which are dropped off at feeding stations still dirty as they come from the earth. Some years ago, a bright young female learned—no one knows how—to remove the dirt by washing the tubers in a stream; within a few years, all the macaques in her group were doing it. Later still, the same female (she must have been something of a macaque genius) also learned a trick for making more palatable the grain the animals were sometimes given. Heaped on the ground, it became mixed with sand, but the female discovered that by careful manipulation in water she could wash away the sand, leaving the grain cleaned and ready to eat. And this skill, too, was gradually taken up by the rest of the group.

This process of "group learning" in effect multiplies the learning capacity of the individual animal, enabling him to learn not only from his own experiences but from those of his fellows. It also insures that the group's knowledge will be passed on from generation to generation. Irven DeVore cites the case of a troop of baboons, one of whose members was shot dead from a car. Thereafter, the group consistently made off whenever they spied a car—and were still doing so years later, though by that time most or all of the original group which had actually seen the death had themselves died. The dead baboon, as DeVore suggests, had not died altogether in vain.

What all this adds up to is that the continuity and integrity of the group is central to the survival of all higher primates and nearly all lower ones—and has been since before the days of our ancestor Aegyptopithecus. Clearly, then, evolution must have favored those tendencies and those patterns of behavior—whether inherited or learned—that made for group survival, and weeded out those that threatened group disruption. Thus, for example, an ancestral primate with a hyperaggressive temperament that led him to constantly attack other group members would have been driven out sooner or later; living in isolation he would not have survived long, nor would he have had much chance to pass on his "aggressive" genes—assuming his temperament was in fact hereditary—to the next generation.

On the positive side, there is a whole complex of behavioral traits whose "purpose," at least in part, seems to be the maintenance of group solidarity. A notable one is what is called grooming—picking over the fur and skin of another animal to remove dirt and parasites. Grooming seems to be pretty much of a primate universal, from the tree-shrews on up, and all the evidence indicates that primates enjoy grooming and being groomed, even as many human beings enjoy being massaged.* Grooming has its "practical" side, of course; removing dirt from a wound helps it to heal, and wild primates seem to be generally freer of external parasites, such as ticks, than other wild animals, since their fellows can remove the unwelcome visitors from otherwise unreachable places. But a great deal of grooming seems to be purely sociable—the primate equivalent, perhaps, of human small-talk.

Somewhat akin to grooming, perhaps, but more active, is play. All or nearly all mammals play in early life, of course, their "games" serving to train them in physical coordination and often in the skills

---

* I mean real, as opposed to "massage parlor," massage.

they will need as adults; a kitten pursuing a crumpled-up cigarette wrapper is obviously learning something about the pursuit of other small, fast-moving objects, such as mice. Many if not all primates, however, also play as adults, which few other mammals do (dolphins and porpoises are a notable exception). Tree-shrews play "follow the leader," with as many as four animals taking turns chasing one another, and also will "steal" a piece of cloth or other object from a fellow, who then steals it back; other "games" have been observed among other species, though who plays with whom, and how often, varies greatly. There seems no doubt, certainly, that all primates spend a certain amount of time in vigorous social activities that have no discernible connection with such "practical" pursuits as food, safety, and sex. How and why these activities originated is unclear; I myself am inclined to view them as more or less incidental consequences of being a primate. That is, any animal which is notably active in body and mind (as most primates certainly are) will, when its activity is not focused on the functional tasks of survival, tend to seek an outlet for its vitality in nonfunctional activities—play, in fact. (Certainly there seems no other very plausible explanation for the variety of games that our own species has designed to occupy its leisure.) Be that as it may, the liking for play also provides primates with a further incentive for living in groups.

Quite another approach to maintaining group integrity is seen in the type of behavior called dominance, which is found among primates from tree-shrews on up. Dominance amounts to saying, in human terms, that certain individuals in the group defer to certain others, a deference that is enforced by threatening noises, grimaces, or postures and occasionally by fighting. Some sort of dominance hierarchy seems to exist in most if not all primate groups, though as we shall see later, its importance varies enormously from species to species and, within species, from environment to environment. As we shall also see later, it varies with sex; to the extent it exists, it is mainly (though not exclusively) a male concern. Dominance promotes group cohesion in a number of ways. The dominant male or males often determine when and where the group will move, thereby helping to insure that it stays together.* They also, where circumstances require

---

* Thelma Rowell, however, has found that leadership in some primate groups can be rather more complicated. Among the baboons she observed, a series of males would,

it, constitute the group's "defense establishment" which drives off predators that threaten the group and in particular its females and young. The dominant males also tend to play a preponderant rule in disciplining the young when their play becomes too boisterous, and in breaking up fights between adults; they are the prototype of law and order. Finally, the very existence of a dominance hierarchy provides a built-in, efficient, and usually peaceful means of settling disputes, so that if two males reach for a ripe fruit—or ripe female—at the same time, the higher-ranking one gets it—or her—without squabbling and, so far as we can tell, without grudges.

Looking back for a moment at the tree-shrews, we note that dominance hierarchies, for reasons poorly understood, are very noticeable among some species, which was perhaps what led to their characterization as "wrathful." Most tree-shrews, however, are not very status-conscious, or "wrathful" in any other way. As regards their being "gluttonous" and "libidinous," these are slanders. They undoubtedly like eating, as do most or all mammals—and, in proportion to their weight, eat a good deal, since, like all small mammals, they have extra-active metabolisms that burn up energy quickly. But they do not overeat, nor indeed could they; an animal whose life-style involves active movement in the trees can hardly afford to develop a weight problem. They also doubtless enjoy sex—again like other mammals— but it would take a remarkably blue-nosed Puritan to see this as censurable. Indeed, of all the primates only man indulges in orgies either of eating or of copulation; whatever significance these phenomena may have for man's nature they certainly have nothing to do with any heritage from his primate ancestors. As we shall have occasion to observe many times in subsequent chapters, jumping to conclusions about human nature on the basis of a few studies of a few primates is quite as risky as jumping from branch to branch without binocular vision.

---

as it were, "suggest" that the group move in one or another direction, by moving that way themselves. It was the females, however, who ultimately decided which way the group would go, by following one or another of the males. As somebody once remarked, man proposes—but woman disposes.

5

MOTHER AND CHILD:
And Father (Sometimes) Makes Three

"The mother-newborn-infant relationship is the strongest and most intense bond in the life of a langur monkey."
— PHYLLIS JAY

"A child, like a caterpillar, is an organism in his own right, adapted to his own ecological niche."
— MICHAEL T. GHISELIN

"A boy's best friend is his mother."
— OLD SAYING

In seeking to delineate what we may call the basic primate personality—the pattern of likes, dislikes, preferences, and propensities that form the foundation for human personality—the most logical place to begin is at the beginning, the point at which a new primate is born. And a good primate to begin with is the Indian langur monkey.* In their mental capacities, langurs probably do not differ much from our ancestors of perhaps twenty million years ago. Moreover, though they are basically arboreal animals, as were those ancestors, they spend a considerable proportion of their time on the ground, as those ancestors may already have begun doing (they were almost certainly doing so a few million years later).

Langurs have apparently learned over the centuries to coexist quite comfortably with humans in densely populated regions—an adaptation probably related to the fact that they are sacred animals to Hindus, so that while they may be chased if their toll on crops

* Hereafter, "primate" will refer *only* to higher primates—the monkeys, apes, and man—unless otherwise indicated.

becomes onerous, they are seldom hurt or killed. Even forest langurs, though initially much more skittish in human company, get over this if tactfully handled. This relative unflappability makes them fairly easy to observe, as does their tendency to frequent the ground—up to 50 per cent of the time in forest country, as much as 80 per cent in settled regions—though they never move far away from trees, which are their refuge in times of danger and their dormitories at night.

In the years around 1960, Phyllis Jay, now at the University of California at Davis, spent more than a thousand hours observing langurs in various habitats. She became sufficiently accepted by them that adults would sometimes cuddle up against her and infants would try to get her to play with them. Her observations of langur infants have revealed resemblances to human infants which primatologist Irven DeVore and writer Sarel Eimerl describe as "quite extraordinary," since, as they stress, "human infants are not monkey infants." This is obviously true—yet, thinking about it, I am not so sure that the resemblances are particularly extraordinary. Our ancestors, after all, were monkeys long before they were men, and for a much longer span of time. In viewing the life of a langur infant and its parents, we are probably seeing something reasonably close to what the pro-verbial man from Mars would have seen had he conducted scientific observations of our ancestors some twenty or thirty million years ago.

The strong and intense bond between a newborn langur and its mother cited by Jay in the quotation heading this chapter flows from the fact that a langur baby, though not as helpless as a human baby, is at birth totally "dependent on its mother for food and transport." A langur band may cover more than a mile in a day's foraging—far beyond the capacities of an infant. The baby must therefore cling to the mother unaided very shortly after birth, "so tightly," says Jay, "that she [the mother] can run on the ground or make long jumps through the air without dislodging it." And in evolution, "must do" means "can do"—the ones who can't, die.

But why does an infant monkey, with no conception of either evolutionary necessity or the law of gravity, cling to its mother? Obviously, as we saw in Harlow's experimental monkeys, because it finds the experience of clinging pleasant and reassuring. This is not anthropomorphic speculation; Harlow actually demonstrated the reassurance experimentally. When he confronted an infant monkey with a strange and menacing object—a mechanical toy, for instance —or merely moved it from its cage to a large room, it immediately showed signs of anxiety, and ran to the terry-cloth "mother" to cuddle against it. Then, its anxieties relieved, it would cautiously proceed to explore the room or examine the toy, though with frequent trips back to "mother" for reassurance.

If you have ever watched a young child and its mother when it encounters a similar "tense" situation, the relevance of these monkey observations to our own species will seem pretty clear. How does any human mother soothe a frightened or hurt baby? By picking it up and cuddling it. We may also note as not without interest the fact that a newborn human baby, feeble though it is in almost every respect, has a surprisingly powerful hand grip, and within a week or so can support its own weight, sometimes even with one hand. It has long been known, moreover, that one of the few sensations that is intrinsically frightening to a human infant is that of falling. I commend these facts to those who question whether observations of other primates are relevant to understanding man. To be sure, the fact that human babies are reassured by Harlow's "contact comfort" hardly needs rationalization from the distant past; on the ground, as in the trees, the safest place for an infant confronted by a strange (and therefore potentially dangerous) situation is close to mother. But it has been well over five million years since our ancestors were swinging through the trees like the langur mother with her baby, more than five million years since the infant's grip on its mother's fur was crucial to its survival—yet the capacity to grip is still there, part of our primate inheritance.

Thus there seems to me every reason to believe that bodily contact, holding and being held, is for monkey or for man the first, and most ingrained, source of comfort, reassurance, and safety. It is the first physical, sensory basis of that complex of emotions we call love, the shelter we intuitively, almost automatically, seek out in times of deep distress. I remember, years ago, seeing a photo of two young soldiers who had been drafted into one of America's periodic crusades to make the Orient safe from Orientals. The cameraman had caught them at the end of that terrible winter retreat from the Yalu River—hungry, exhausted, with the look of boys who had seen too much horror too soon. They sat slumped on the ground, one of them holding his friend cradled in his arms; in posture and in expression, they were hardly distinguishable from the frightened monkey babies of Harlow's experiments.

So much, for the moment, for the primate infant. But what of the primate mother? So far as I know, mother love has not been investigated experimentally, but we can surely assume that its development is a rather more complex business than the development of infant love, as mothering is a more complex job than being mothered. Judging from Jay's observations, a major factor is that the mother finds physical contact with her infant intrinsically pleasurable. As Jay describes it, she "inspects, licks, grooms, and manipulates the infant from the hour of its birth." Even when it is quietly resting—i.e., making no overt demands on her—"she grooms and strokes it softly without disturbing or waking it."

And not just the mother is affected. *All* langur females, says Jay, from juveniles on up, "are intensely interested in newborn infants." As soon as the troop's females notice the arrival of a newborn baby, all of them "immediately cluster closely around its mother. She is surrounded by a group of from four to ten females, all reaching out gently and trying to touch, lick, and smell" the newcomer. Within a few hours after the birth, the mother begins allowing other females to handle it. "One of these females takes the infant from the mother's arms and holds it. . . . She inspects it minutely, gently manipulating, licking, and smelling the infant. At the first sign of discomfort . . . it is taken by another of the waiting females, although if the mother is sitting nearby she often reaches out and intercepts the infant. . . . As many as eight females may hold the infant during the first day of life."

Have you ever attended an old-fashioned christening party and observed the female relatives with the new baby? Or watched a group of mothers in a city park when a neighbor wheels in her new arrival for its first outing?

Jay's observations seem to me to imply three main conclusions:

1. Female langurs find physical contact with infants intrinsically pleasant.

2. Female langurs find infants intrinsically interesting.

3. Female langurs possess some built-in need or propensity to respond to the needs of infants ("at the first sign of discomfort . . .").

Precisely *how* the female responds to the infant's needs, how she goes about soothing an uncomfortable or fractious baby, are evidently learned. There is, says Jay, "considerable variation among mothers in caring for their infants and among females in holding infants of other females"—and the reader will recall that variation is one of the hallmarks of learned as against innate behavior. "Not all females can keep an infant quiet and content," says Jay, "and a few are awkward and clumsy. . . . Competent females are casual but firm." Significantly, she notes that "older females that have given birth to many infants appeared, in general, more efficient mothers than very young females. These older and more experienced mothers are usually more confident and expend little effort keeping a newborn calm and quiet." In mothering, as in any other kind of learned behavior, practice makes perfect. But what clearly is *not* learned is the female's interest in and desire to handle infants, which provide the built-in motivation to learn about mothering both by watching and by practice. This learning process works well enough, indeed, so that by Jay's reckoning only a fraction of 1 per cent of langur females can be classed as really "inept" with babies. And necessarily so; were the learning less efficient—that is, less highly motivated—the langurs would long ago have become extinct. As would any other primate.

I have devoted considerable space to Jay's description of langur mothers and infants because—among other reasons—it is notably clear and vivid. We should be aware, however, that not everything she describes is universal among primates. In particular, there is a great deal of variation in how soon, and how much, a new mother will allow other females to touch or hold her baby: among chimpanzees, and some macaques, not at all; among some baboons, almost as much as among Jay's langurs. What do seem to be universal are the infant's *attraction* for the older members of the group—sometimes the males, but invariably the females—and the satisfaction the mother (and sometimes other females) derives from touching and otherwise caring for it. Evolutionarily speaking, the attraction insures that, whether or not a young female has ever had the chance to "practice" with someone else's baby, as does the young langur female, by the time she becomes a mother herself, she will at any rate have spent much time in *watching* babies—and their mothers. Evidently in some species the females can learn as much as they need to know about child care simply by observation learning coupled with the built-in satisfaction derived from caring for an infant; the refinements emerge from trial and error. Certainly not a few mothers in our own species appear to become tolerably adept at mothering simply by looking—at least if one includes looking into Dr. Spock's *Baby and Child Care.**

Another primate universal in what might be called the child-care department is what Jane Goodall calls the "amazing tolerance" adult primates show for infants of their own species.** She was speaking of her chimps, of course, but the observation is true of all primates that have been studied in the wild. The most bad-tempered elderly male—and some of them can be pretty crotchety—will put up with annoyance and even harassment from an infant that, from an adolescent or adult, would bring an immediate threat, or worse. Male chimps, Goodall reports, will even allow one or more infants to climb on and interfere with them while they are engaged in sexual intercourse—which is rather more than most human males would put up with. Again, there are powerful evolutionary reasons why this tolerance must exist. Young primates, like all young animals, are much smaller and weaker than adults. They are also—unlike the young of some other animals—much less mobile than adults, so that they cannot easily escape from a threat, whether from their own species or another. Finally, because they mature relatively slowly and because so much of their behavior is learned, it takes time for them to grasp what they "should" and "should not" do—in objective terms, what will and will not annoy their elders. (This fact will come as no surprise to anyone who has had any contact with young human children.)

Since a young primate has a high capacity to annoy its elders, and since the latter, were they to respond "normally" to the annoyance, could easily injure or even kill the young one, there evidently must be some intrinsic quality about the infant which, even as it stimulates the friendly interest of adults, also short-circuits their aggressive impulses toward it. In many primates the quality probably has to do with the infant's color. In the langur, for instance, the infant is a dark, almost blackish-brown as against the adult's light, grayish-tan coat; in the chimp, the infant's naked facial skin is—in human racial terms—not "black" but "white"; moreover, it has a conspicuous

---

* Not only Dr. Spock but most other pediatricians and child psychologists would probably agree that the "casual but firm" attitude which Jay noted among her most experienced langur mothers is also a good capsule description of a capable human mother.

** As already noted, some primates eat infants of *other* primate species.

white tuft of hair where its tail would be if it had one. and as the infant loses its distinctive coloration, the adults' special interest in, and tolerance of, it diminish or disappear.* By that time, however, the infant has learned enough do's and don't's to reduce, if not eliminate, his "irritation capability." Human infants, of course, show no such sharp color contrast with adults, and exactly what about them acts to disarm adult aggression remains to be determined. Their small size is one possibility, and from my own observation, a baby's smile also has an extraordinarily disarming effect. But some comparable "disarming factor" there surely must be—otherwise infanticide would be a lot more common than it is.**

As I have already implied, the attitude of male primates to the infants of the group shows rather more variation than that of females. While they are uniformly tolerant of infants, their degree of active interest in them varies widely, from the almost total disinterest of the langur male to the active involvement of the male baboon or chimp, who from DeVore's and Goodall's accounts evidently enjoy tickling and romping with the young members of the group.

The reasons for these variations are not altogether clear. Part of the answer seems to be differences in habitat. As DeVore points out, langurs, which never stray far from trees, can escape into them at the first sign of danger, while baboons, most of which live in much more open country, must be prepared to defend themselves—a job which falls almost entirely on the adult males, the females being too often encumbered with infants. Largely for this reason, a mature male baboon weighs twice as much as a female, and his biting muscles, which supply power to his tusklike canine teeth, weigh nearly five times as much as the female's. As the defender of the group's young, therefore, the male baboon must presumably be motivated by a concern with and interest in them; as DeVore notes, "an animal is hardly likely to risk its life to save an infant for whom it feels no emotion."

---

* My wife has suggested another evolutionary function for the primate infant's distinctive color. At the beach years ago, she recalls, she and her friends used to dress their kids in dayglo bathing suits to keep track of them amid the hordes of other little ones. The similar arrangements among other primates might help the mothers single out the most helpless infants, who would require immediate assistance in case of an emergency flight into the trees.

** Infanticide is even less common among nonhuman primates—though not unknown.

By contrast, the male langur, which need not and does not defend the infants of its group, shows a correspondingly feeble interest in them.

But though the habitat argument is persuasive in comparing langurs and baboons, it breaks down when applied to the chimp. Like langurs, chimps seldom if ever stray far from trees, and can escape into them if need be. Like langur males, chimp males do not act as group defenders, yet they show quite as much interest in, and enjoyment of, infants as do baboon males.

For whatever the habitat argument is worth, however, it certainly applies to our own Australopithecine ancestors of five million years ago, who like the baboons were savanna and grassland dwellers. Moreover, as we shall see in a subsequent chapter, there are even more persuasive reasons why these and, especially, later males of the human line must have possessed some sort of built-in concern and involvement with infants and children. Certainly common observation tells us that human males, by and large, derive a certain pleasure from playing with infants and young children—if not always other people's children, at least their own. Some human males, to be sure, do find the prospect of fatherhood daunting, but more often, I suspect, because of the financial responsibilities involved than from any actual dislike of their prospective progeny.

If observation learning in the primate group is the means by which primate females learn to be mothers, it is no less the means by which primate infants learn to be adults. To the newborn infant, of course, the "group" means primarily its mother. If only because of its physical helplessness, it spends most of its time with her, and as it becomes able to move about it still returns to her frequently—for food and for the reassurance that Harlow demonstrated in the laboratory. It also learns about life by watching her. When a langur infant is old enough to begin taking solid food, for instance, it follows its mother about while she is foraging, sampling the plants she eats. Many other examples of such observation learning have been reported among other primate species.

Interestingly, some recent experiments indicate that at least some infant mammals learn more rapidly by observing their mothers than by watching other adults. The work was done by Phyllis Chesler, an associate of E. Roy John in the "observation learning" experiments cited in the last chapter.* Chesler found that kittens who watched their mothers pressing a lever for a reward (food) learned to do likewise far more quickly than kittens who watched strangers. Some never managed to learn, even though the strangers were "friendly" (as shown, for example, by their licking the kittens) and the kittens showed no signs of being afraid of them. Chesler suggests that the difference may be due to the existence of an "affective or social bond" between mother and kitten, which comes into existence only slowly, if at all, with strangers. This suggestion—which amounts to saying that learning may be greatly aided, or hindered, by the learner's emotional relationship to its "model" or teacher—is certainly consistent with many of our intuitive judgments about education: notably, that children learn badly from teachers they don't like, or who they feel don't like them. It also suggests one reason why children, despite being exposed to many adults, tend to pick up primarily their parents' individual mannerisms; like father (mother), like son (daughter).

As the infant primate grows older (in the langur, as early as two months) it begins to develop an interest in its peers. At first, this is expressed in physical exploration—touching, sniffing, and licking—but before long the babies are playing together much like human children, though usually a good deal more vigorously. In part, the play serves simply to develop muscles and coordination, but it also serves a very vital function in the development of personality. The exact nature of this function is hard to define, but its importance is shown by more of Harry Harlow's experiments. In further work with infants raised with cloth "mothers," Harlow found that their severe emotional disturbance, including an inability to develop normal sexual behavior as they matured, could largely be prevented if they were allowed to play together, even for as little as twenty minutes a day. By contrast, lack of such contact with the "peer group" engendered abnormality *even in infants raised by a natural mother.* Infants with neither maternal nor peer-group contact were, as one would expect, the worst off of all; their behavior, says Harlow, "is a pitiful combination of apathy and terror." Those who had spent their first twelve months in isolation could not subsequently relate to normal juvenile monkeys, and indeed had to be removed from the communal cage in fairly short order lest they be seriously injured or even killed. Later

* Subsequently, she became better known as the author of *Women and Madness.*

on, they swung to the other extreme, attacking the normal monkeys viciously, including even "suicidal attacks upon large, adult males."

These observations, clearly, have considerable relevance to the sources of "aggression" in primates, including humans. A full discussion of the problem will have to wait until a later chapter, but even at this point it seems fairly evident that one prime source of aggression is fear. A man or monkey confronted with a frightening situation is pretty much limited to two reactions: attacking or running. And if he (or it) is sufficiently terrified, his choice between the two may have little appropriateness to the actual reality he confronts.*

Exactly why these isolated monkeys should find other monkeys so terrifying—apart, of course, from the fact that they are disturbed monkeys to begin with—is not clear. My own guess is that they are frightened in part because they have suddenly been confronted with an unfamiliar and complex situation in which they have *no clue how to behave.* They may, in fact, be suffering from something like the monkey equivalent of "culture shock," a phenomenon not uncommon among humans (such as Peace Corps members) suddenly transferred from, say, an American college campus to a back-country village in Kenya. Suddenly, almost none of the behavior patterns they have unconsciously picked up over the years "work"; people's actions, words, and expressions do not mean what they "ought" to mean—nor do the victim's own words and actions convey what he intends them to convey.** Significantly, we are told that symptoms of culture shock include both anxiety (fear) and apathy.

Be that as it may, there can be no doubt that normal primates, in playing with their peer group, are not just learning new and useful patterns of physical action; they are also learning patterns of social behavior—how to get along with other primates. Among langurs, says Jay (and her observations are paralleled in many other species), "most basic patterns of social behavior, including dominance and sex, first appear in play groups. As a context for learning to get along with

* The isolated monkeys' suicidal attacks against large adult males—the monkey "power structure"—may tell us something about the psychological roots of suicidal "revolutionary" terrorism indulged in at one time by a few way-out radical grouplets.

** An almost classic case of cross-cultural failure to communicate is that of the anthropologist who tried to tell the story of *Hamlet* to elders of a West African tribe she was studying. When she recounted how the prince of Denmark was incensed because his uncle had married his widowed mother, they insisted she must have got the story wrong. That, they said, was what any decent uncle would have done.

other monkeys, the play group provides [a] social environment in which experimentation and mistakes go without punishment or the threat of danger from other monkeys."* It seems clear, then, that though primates, for all the reasons we have been discussing, need to live in groups, and by innate preference *like* to live in groups, the actual techniques of group living are learned, not innate. Obviously, any primate group can continue to exist only by grace of the fact that its members do certain things and refrain from doing certain others, and it seems clear that in practice they learn these things primarily in childhood, both by contact with their elders and especially through play with their peers.

Although the play of young primates may be exceedingly vigorous and even rough, the juveniles somehow sense where to stop before anybody gets hurt. Thus though they may at times nip one another, the skin is never broken. The adults seldom intervene in these squabbles—except in two situations. One is when, because of the small size of the group, there are few youngsters of the same age, so that the play group includes members of quite different sizes and strengths, with the resulting chance that someone may get hurt by accident. The other is when, in any group, the play becomes too noisy. When young langurs engage in "sharp or loud outcries or continuous squealing," says Jay, adult females may "break up the play group by slapping the ground or mildly threatening the playing animals." ("If you kids don't quit that racket I'm going to come in there and . . .") In fact, the young langurs rapidly learn to be seen but not too loudly heard.

Given the large importance of the play group for young primates, there obviously must exist some mechanism to insure that these groups are formed. Just as baby primates are—must be—intrinsically interesting and attractive to female primates, so they must be equally interesting and attractive to one another. And of course they are. Harlow says flatly that "affection of age mates for one another is universal within the entire primate kingdom." That this is true of human infants has been shown by studies extending back for decades, and it can, as Harlow says, "be confirmed informally by anyone who

---

* The fact that juvenile primates normally engage in a certain amount of sex play may perhaps help assuage the anxiety of parents who discover their kids playing "Doctor" or similar games. Whatever its moral aspects, which are pretty much a matter of personal taste and conviction, this sort of thing has evidently been going on for a long, long time, with no evident ill effects on the primate psyche.

looks in on a pediatrician's waiting room." The children "strain toward one another, and if close together, they reach out to one another. They smile at each other, and they laugh together." Sometimes, indeed, the young primate's play extends beyond the bounds of his own species. Goodall's young chimps not infrequently played with young baboons which happened to be in the neighborhood, and in at least one case chimp and baboon formed a relatively long-lasting friendship. Young humans, too, play with other species—cats and dogs, for instance.

While the infant is playing with, and familiarizing himself with, his fellows, he is also, of course, familiarizing himself with other features of his environment. Earlier I mentioned Butler's experiments demonstrating that monkeys are, in fact, full of curiosity, and the existence of curiosity—an animal's drive to explore and familiarize itself with its environment—has since been repeatedly demonstrated in species from rats to man. In human infants, indeed, this exploratory drive often reaches the point where it threatens to destroy the environment—or the infant.

The existence and importance of curiosity-exploration in mammals generally and primates in particular has now become so obvious that we need not belabor the matter further. One series of experiments, however, is worth mentioning, both because of its intrinsic ingenuity and because it has demonstrated the existence of curiosity in human infants as early as the first week of life. The experiments are the work of T. G. R. Bower of Edinburgh and J. M. Broughton and M. K. Moore at Harvard.

The three psychologists knew before they started that infants appear to reach out for objects and, when they can, touch and sometimes grasp them. However, some psychologists (including so well known a figure as Jerome Bruner of Harvard) had dismissed this as mere random thrashing about. As a first step, then, the researchers filmed a number of infants from six to eleven days old in the presence of a bright orange ball. The ball was moved to various positions, and analysis of the films showed that invariably the infants reached in the direction of the ball—though of course their aim at that age was a good deal less than perfect. Whatever the nature of the reaching, it clearly wasn't random.

But the investigators wanted to go further—to prove that the infants were not reaching merely as an automatic response to a conspicuous object but with the intention of investigating it. On the face of it, this might seem an impossible dream—how on earth does one determine the "intentions" of a week-old baby? The method they adopted was not only ingenious but also demonstrated that experimental psychologists, if they have the wit to ask the right questions, can often come up with persuasive "objective" evidence for distinctly "nonobjective" phenomena. One group of babies was exposed to various objects and, as expected, reached out for them and touched them. Another group, by means of a complicated arrangement of lamps and polaroid filters, was exposed to *images* of the same objects. They too reached out—and when they found they couldn't touch the "object," began to cry, though the other group had remained perfectly happy. Evidently, even in the first weeks of life infants actively desire to reach out and investigate—and if their desire is frustrated, they get upset.

Experiments with a number of species have established not merely that the curiosity drive is a reality, but that it has been shaped by evolution in specific ways related to survival. Thus animals find unfamiliar objects or events more interesting than familiar ones, meaning that their information-gathering equipment is geared to extract the maximum amount of information from the environment, ignoring things about which they already possess information in favor of those concerning which they have none. Again, moving objects are more interesting than motionless ones—which pretty clearly ties in with the fact that a moving object is more likely to be dangerous than a fixed one. If an animal is confronted by two predators, one lying down and the other actively hunting, there isn't much doubt as to which of the two is most likely to require immediate defensive or evasive action.

If we define intelligence as an animal's capacity for varying its responses to a varying environment, it seems fairly obvious that without curiosity, intelligence could function only at the most primitive levels. The mere capacity to alter behavior in response to environmental change is worthless unless the alterations are *appropriate* to the change, which means in the first place that the animal must possess information about the environment. And since many changes in the environment are quite sudden, the animal's responses must be equally sudden, meaning that it will have no time to take in more than the most obvious features of the situation. Thus unless its response is going to be based simply on this very modest amount of "instant information," meaning that the response will often be inappropriate (sometimes fatally so), it must *already* have absorbed and stored up as much information as its nervous system can absorb. Which is to say that simply as a matter of survival it must be equipped with a drive to investigate its surroundings, including some intrinsic pleasure or satisfaction attached to absorbing new information. Curiosity may have killed a few cats—and primates—but it helped a lot more of them survive.

So far as man is concerned, indeed, a certain minimum flow of information seems absolutely essential for normal psychologic functioning: as noted earlier, individuals experimentally subjected to "sensory deprivation," in which incoming stimuli of all sorts are cut to the minimum, rapidly develop severe, though temporary, psychoses. A need for information is evidently a fundamental property of our nervous systems, so that long before our ancestors were able to formulate in words the common inquiry, "What's new?" they were acting it out in deeds.

I know of no studies that compare the relative strength of the "curiosity drive" in different species—or even if such studies are possible. Assuming they could be carried out, however, one would expect them to show that a species' strength of curiosity is related to its intelligence: the greater the capacity to make use of information, the greater the drive to acquire information. I don't think it is coincidence that folklore has endowed primates, whose intelligence is well above that of such familiar animals as dogs, cats, and horses, with an especially powerful sense of curiosity, or that humans, the most intelligent of the primates, can also be fairly described as by far the most inquisitive. Indeed there exists a whole class of humans who spend a large proportion of their waking hours systematically satisfying their curiosity about the world around them. To be sure, scientists engage in their investigations for diverse reasons—not least, to make a living.* But nearly all scientists, I think, would freely admit if asked that the pursuit of knowledge is satisfying in itself, quite apart from any financial or honorific rewards attached to it.

And if young (and often not so young) primates derive an intrinsic satisfaction from acquiring new information, equally, I suspect, do they derive satisfaction from acquiring new skills. Again, I don't know

* Though some scientists seem to find this motive rather disreputable—see the preface to this book.

whether this has been (or can be) demonstrated experimentally, but it seems reasonable enough so that some experimental psychologist should have a try at it. We know, indeed, that the acquisition of some skills has an immediate payoff attached, perhaps the outstanding example being the skills involved in copulation. But there are other skills involved in primate survival which by their very nature require considerable practice to learn—as copulation does not—yet which cannot yield any obvious payoff *until* they are learned.

Jane Goodall, for example, has described how infant chimps over a period of months will practice building the nests that they sleep in as juveniles and adults. The ultimate payoff attached to the nest is perhaps that it provides a comfortable and secure place to sleep in a tree—but this payoff comes only when the youngster has actually learned to build a nest that will hold together. And this takes considerable time. Goodall describes one infant who at ten months "bent a small twig and sat on it on the ground in the approved manner"—that is, presumably as he had seen adults do. Later on, she saw him "trying to make nests as he dangled in midair, bending down twigs and attempting to hold them under him with his feet as he reached for more." Over the next few months he became increasingly proficient; "he often made a nest while he was playing by himself in a tree. Sometimes he just bounced around in it, frequently breaking it apart, and then after a few minutes making another. *This constant practicing means that when a youngster is four or five years old and ready to sleep on his own he is skilled in nest-making techniques*" (my emphasis).

Yet this constant practice obviously does not occur because the infant chimp in any way foresees the time when he is ready to sleep on his own; the only reasonable explanation is that he derives some inherent satisfaction from his growing skill at nest building. If ones watches a human infant learning to walk—a skill even more central to human survival than nest building is to chimp survival—it is hard to avoid the impression that it gets a kick out of learning. And certainly a good deal of play among human infants—particularly what the psychologists call solitary play—seems to be of much the same nature as play nest building among young chimps: the acquisition of new skills which, though they may well turn out to be useful later on, are at the beginning acquired "in play"—for their own sake.

Here, then, we have our archetypical young primate: initially dependent on and emotionally involved with its mother—and she with her infant; increasingly involved with its playmates, with whom it jumps, tussles, swings from the branches—and acquires the basic techniques of social living; tolerated by its elders in infancy, disciplined by them in childhood; watching its mother, and increasingly its fellows, for clues on what to do and how to do it; inquisitive and experimental, delighting in the exploration of its environment and in the acquisition of new physical skills to deal with that environment.

This is, of course, a thumbnail sketch, in which many details have necessarily been suppressed, or deferred for later examination, yet there seems to me every reason to believe that so far as it goes it is an accurate sketch of the young Australopithecines of five million years ago. For that matter, my own observations of and readings about young children give me little reason to think that they have changed much since that time.

6

THE PRIMATE MYSTIQUE: Male and Female

"Of all the animals, the boy is the most unmanageable."
— ARISTOTLE

"Oh men, respect women who have borne you!"
— THE KORAN

"Vive la différence!"
—OLD SAYING

Generalizing about human nature is a bit risky at any time. Nowadays, however, generalizing about masculinity and femininity is downright dangerous. If the Male Chauvinist Pigs don't get you, the Castrating Radical Feminists must.

My own view of the masculinity-femininity question can be summed up in four questions and answers:

Q. Do innate differences in behavior and temperament between the two sexes exist in the animal kingdom?

A. Unquestionably.

Q. Do primates (other than man) show such differences?

A. Consistently.

Q. Are there evolutionary reasons for thinking these differences have persisted in our own species?

A. Undoubtedly.

Q. Does this mean men are superior to women—or women to men?

A. Don't be silly.

Before trying to document these statements, however, it might be well to enumerate my own "credentials" in the field. Like just about everybody else writing on sex differences, I start with certain biases, and it seems only fair to the reader to give him (or her) some notion of what they are.

To begin with, then, I am fortunate in that the women to whom I have been closest during my lifetime have all of them been bright, intellectually curious, and independent-minded. My mother was involved in the women's rights movement before World War I, and until her retirement worked at administrative jobs; at this writing she is, at eighty-six, still actively interested in people, ideas, and public affairs. My sister is a college teacher and author (as well as the successful mother of four). My first wife was (and is) a highly paid advertising copywriter and, more recently, also a teacher; my second is a short-story writer and an activist in the peace movement (both are also mothers). And I am happy to say that my daughter, now seventeen, gives every evidence of following the family tradition.

Given this sort of background, it will probably not surprise the reader much to learn that for most of my life I have generally preferred the company of women—interesting ones—to that of men. Not just some of my best friends but nearly all of them have been women. Evolution and genetics aside, then, I obviously find women distinctly different from men—and so far as I am concerned, *vive la différence!*

Professionally, as a writer and editor, I have worked with women and had them work for me over many years, and have found no noticeable professional differences between them and the men I have worked with: in both cases, some were more competent than others. (For what it's worth, the only employee I ever fired for incompetence was a man.) I also, for a year, had a woman as my immediate boss. She was one of the most capable people I have ever worked for, and one of the most pleasant—far more so than the overbearing, hysterical male who was *her* immediate boss and later (when she got pregnant and I took over her job) mine.

Both personally and professionally I have also, of course, known women of the type sometimes called "typically feminine"—deferential to men, feather-headed, and possessing few ideas of their own (or reluctant to express them). I can't, however, say that I have known any such women really well—principally because I find them boring.

Having gotten these matters on the record, let us now look at what evolution can tell us about the probable nature of human sexual differences. To begin with, we find behavioral differences between the sexes widespread among the vertebrates.* The female stickleback lays

---

* And in not a few invertebrates. A notable example is the mosquito, the female of which bites while the male doesn't.

eggs; the male tends them in the nest he has built. Male deer fight with one another during the rutting season; the females are fought over. Lionesses do most of the hunting, but their mates take the lion's share of the meat. Among hyenas, by contrast, both sexes hunt, and share the kill more or less equally, but in other respects the females are the dominant sex.*

Sex differences are if anything even more consistent among the primates than among other vertebrates. We saw in the last chapter how the female langur has an active and evidently innate interest in and concern with infants, while the male finds them uninteresting at best and a nuisance at worst. We noted that male baboons may band together to defend their females and young against predators; the females, by contrast, remain with the young (whether or not they happen to have infants of their own at the moment), encouraging them to remove themselves from the source of danger. In addition, the female chimp may retain an emotional bond to her offspring for years, even after they have grown up, while the male, though clearly interested in and attracted by the infants of his group, shows no special interest in any of them once they move out of infancy into childhood.

In the latter case, to be sure, there is no hard-and-fast evidence that we are dealing with an innate sex difference; it may be that mature male chimps fail to form emotional relationships with young ones not because they lack the capacity but simply because they lack the opportunity. The female and her infant maintain a relatively prolonged association, the infant depending on its mother for food, transportation, and reassurance-by-contact for as long as three years after birth; by the same token, the mother clearly "knows" which infant is hers. Given the relatively secure habitat of the chimp, there appears to be no comparably important function for the mature male vis-à-vis the infant; given the chimp's sexual promiscuity, there is equally no way in which the male can tell his own infant from another. (Indeed, even human scientists cannot determine the father of a given chimp with any certainty, though they occasionally guess on the basis of physical resemblance.) Certainly mere maleness does not appear to present any

* Hyenas, long considered carrion eaters, turn out on closer study to be hunters as well, though they also do scavenging—and on occasion have been seen to forcibly take over the fresh kill of some other predator. Which method of food-getting predominates in a given hyena pack seems to depend on the environment.

barrier to the formation of prolonged emotional bonds; male and female offspring of the same mother, provided they are not too far apart in age, are likely to establish a special emotional relationship —as shown, for example, by their playing with one another more than with other youngsters. (It is not yet known, however, how long these brother-sister bonds persist into adult life.) It would appear, then, that emotional bonds among chimps are the product of relatively long association (as, indeed, they usually are in humans), whether between mother and child or between two children of the same mother; since there is no occasion for such association between male and child, the bond does not form.

On the other hand, male chimps do seem to have a less active interest in youngsters than do females; for example, they show little or no concern if a young chimp shows signs of alarm or fright, whereas the youngster's mother will take out after it to see what's the matter. Goodall also notes that though male chimps naturally show great interest in sexually receptive females, at other times they may spend much of their time in all-male groups. It may be, therefore, that in the chimp, as more certainly in the baboon and langur, we are dealing with innate differences in temperament and interest between the two sexes.

The case for such differences in primates is strengthened by the fact that other sex differences manifest themselves at quite an early age— well before sexual maturity or (in the female) child bearing, could exert any influence on personality. Among langurs, says Phyllis Jay, "the active running and wrestling of male infants brings them into contact with adults more than the quieter play of female infants. As a result, adults threaten and chase male infants more than twice as often as they do female infants." The young male langur's high "Irritation Quotient" in respect to his elders reaches a peak during the years from two to four, when he will be in trouble with the adults more than three times as often as his female contemporary. In a human boy, this period would roughly correspond to age seven to twelve.

Similar observations have been made on other species of monkey. Harry Harlow, indeed, finds sex differences universal among these animals. They begin to appear, he says, "by the third or fourth month and increase steadily until the animal is mature. Male monkeys become increasingly forceful, while the females become progressively more passive." In play, males are the pursuers, females the pursued. As they grow older, moreover, the sexes tend to segregate, with the young males playing together and associating with male adults, while the young females become part of the overall female group, sharing its interest in babies and similar subjects. Among chimps, on the other hand, sex differences in childhood seem less marked than among monkeys. Goodall notes, however, that young males show more independence than young females, tending to leave their mothers at an earlier age, and for longer periods.

Finally, we should note another kind of sex difference—this one among adults—which appears to be universal among primates.* This concerns dominance. Now the nature and significance of primate dominance is a large and complex subject, and one on which I shall have much more to say in the next chapter. In particular, as we shall see, its importance varies greatly from species to species and, within species, from environment to environment. Nonetheless, dominance in *any* species and environment, to whatever extent it exists, is primarily a male concern. In langurs, for example, Jay describes the female dominance hierarchy as "relatively unstable and poorly defined. . . . Dominance is often a matter of degree, and an adult female that is dominant in one situation may not be in another." Among males, by contrast, "the status of each individual is well defined and constant for long periods of time." Much the same can be said of other species. Often a female's status seems to depend at least in part on her relationship to the dominant male or males of the group. If she is sexually receptive, her status may be high because of the males' interest; in the case of some baboons, a female with an infant is protected by the dominant males, and therefore ranks higher—temporarily—than females without infants. Among langurs, the new mother simply drops out of the status hierarchy, such as it is; she shows no interest in dominating other females, nor they her.

The other universal thing about dominance in primates is that males dominate females. Again, the degree of dominance varies greatly from species to species and from habitat to habitat, but insofar as there is a dominant sex, the males are it. The close connection between sex roles and dominance is seen by the fact that the gesture called "presenting" is a well-nigh universal gesture of appeasement

* Here, as earlier, we are talking about the higher primates—monkeys and apes.

from inferior to superior primate. That is, if a dominant animal threatens another, the latter may turn and "present" his or her rump, in very much the way a female in heat will present *her* rump to a male. The dominant animal, in turn, will often "mount" the presenting animal, as he would mount a receptive female. There is little true sexual content to these gestures; the mounting animal may at times show signs of sexual excitement, but never carries matters to the point of actual or attempted intercourse. Rather, presenting and mounting seem to be a sort of dialogue without words in which the presenting animal is saying, "I am (at least temporarily) a female—I am no threat to you," to which the mounting animal replies, "I accept you as a female—I don't feel threatened." (Female baboons sometimes present to other females as a "friendly" gesture, though in a somewhat different manner than they do to males. Significantly, however, the other female never mounts.)

Before considering the evolutionary origins of these sex differences, and what relationship (if any) they have to human sex differences, we should first satisfy ourselves thoroughly that they *are* the product of evolution—that is, that they are in fact innate rather than learned.

So far as sex differences among juvenile apes and monkeys are concerned, there seems no plausible way in which they *could* be learned. A young female langur certainly does not interest herself in baby langurs—as a young male never does—because any Feminine Mystique has told her she "should"; only humans have mystiques, feminine or otherwise. Nor does a young male langur play more actively and noisily than his female contemporary because his group allows him (but not her) to get away with it. On the contrary, as we saw earlier, he receives far more negative reinforcement, in the shape of threats or chasing, than does the female—but continues to "misbehave" anyway. Boys, it appears, will be boys. Or as my sister put it, after some months of comparing her baby son with his two older sisters, "Little boys are just the same as little girls—but much, much more so!"

Some feminist writers, to be sure, seek to argue—or at least to suggest—that primate sex differences, whether in youth or in adult life, are not innate but are in some sense the learned product of the primate social group. Thus Naomi Weisstein of Loyola University, for example, argues that "since primates are at present too stupid to change their own social conditions" we cannot know whether sex differences are either innate or fixed "until we change the social organization of these groups."* Now the first thing that can be said about this statement is that it makes very little sense even on its own terms. It is not inconceivable, indeed, that human experimenters could "change the social organization" of a primate group so that the sex roles were in some sense reversed, the females becoming dominant over the males. But assuming this could be done, it would in no way show that there was no innate component in (normal) primate sex roles—merely that these roles could be modified by experience. This would be an interesting fact but—in the light of what we have noted earlier about the ways in which powerful human drives, including the sex drive, can be modified by experience—by no means a surprising fact.

The true weakness of Weisstein's argument, however, emerges when we consider what actual learning processes might be implied by her rather vague term "social structure." The fundamental facts we must deal with, remember, are that sex differences are universal in primates (leaving humans aside for the moment) and that they are, moreover, the same general *kinds* of differences in any primate we choose to name: the males more concerned with dominance, aggression, and defense, the females more concerned with, and involved with, the young. There seem to be three general ways of accounting for this situation (not all of them mutually exclusive).

1. Female and male primates are born with the same psychological tendencies, but something in the primate social structure emphasizes certain tendencies in the female and certain others in the male. There are a lot of objections to this. First, primate social structures vary enormously, from the tightly organized and disciplined band of grassland baboons to the very loose and "permissive" society of forest chimps (in addition to other structures too numerous and varied to mention)—yet the sex differences are nothing like so varied. Moreover, even assuming that one could discover some consistent, "sexist" bias underlying all this diversity, one would still have to explain where *it* came from. From some basic similarity in living conditions or environment? Primates, as we saw earlier, live in just about every

---

* Curiously, the underlying premise of this as well as other much more dogmatic, feminist statements on the subject appears to be that if women *are* innately different from men, they must be inferior to men. Needless to say, I violently disagree with this notion.

environment to be found in a warm or reasonably warm climate, excepting only outright desert, from the treeless, rocky cliffs of the Ethiopian mountains to the towering vegetation of the Congo forest. The only alternative would be some *innate* sexist bias—which brings us back to heredity and evolution.

2. Female and male primates are born with the same psychological tendencies, but learn their sex roles by watching their elders. There is undoubtedly a certain amount of truth in this (remember the female langur learning how to be a mother), but it cannot be the whole truth, since it fails to account for the fact that females always learn female roles, and males, male roles. To explain this, we would have to assume that females have some sort of inherent predisposition to model themselves on older females, and males, on males—which brings us back to heredity and evolution again. The "role model" theory, moreover, does not account for how the roles originated in the first place—see the preceding paragraph.

3. Female and male primates are *not* born with the same psychological tendencies: something built into their nervous systems makes them find different features of their world attractive and different kinds of activity satisfying—not, indeed, in any absolute sense, but merely in such a way that the female will tend to focus her attention, or more of it, on certain things—babies, for instance—and the male on certain others—status rivals, for instance. Given this difference in attention and interest, intensified by differences in temperament, the females will inevitably, or almost inevitably, learn certain kinds of behavior and the males certain other kinds.

This is not to say, as some commentators have put it, that male and female primates are somehow "preprogrammed" or "wired" to perform their distinctive actions. There is no reason to think that the roots of primate sex-role behavior are any different from those of primate behavior generally; in both cases, the prime mover is the built-in incentive plan which encourages the animal to learn certain things and not others—plus, I would say, a psychological-physiological "temperament" which makes certain kinds of actions "come easier" than others.* What seems clear, however, is that female pri-

* Just what "temperament" is cannot be defined at all concisely, if it can be accurately defined at all. One element, certainly, is the "excitability" of the nervous system, either in general or in relation to specific types of stimuli (food, sex, or what have you). Differences in excitability have been observed in human infants during the first few days of life—and they persist into childhood and adult life.

mates are born with somewhat different incentive plans and temperaments than males.

The biological roots of these differences are, at this writing, anything but clear. One important factor, certainly, is the sex hormones.
These—as even the most far-out feminists are constrained to admit—
differ considerably between males and females, and experiments with
several species have established that the differences can produce differences in behavior.

Not surprisingly, some of the most conspicuous of these differences
concern sexual behavior. The female rat, for example, when sexually
receptive gives the "lordosis response" to a male; this rather resembles
presenting in primates (if you have ever seen a female cat in heat with
a tom, you will know exactly what it looks like). The male, of course,
mounts her and, if all goes well, copulates with her. A female injected
with the male hormone testosterone, however, will often show a degree of male behavior, mounting a female and occasionally making
copulatory movements.

Interestingly, however, it is not simply a matter of testosterone
being present at the moment; an important factor is whether it was
present immediately after birth. Thus a female rat who received a
testosterone injection at this critical time will show much more
marked and consistent "male" responses to testosterone as an adult.
By the same token, a male rat injected with female hormones as an
adult will show little or no "female" sexual response (presenting)—
unless he was castrated (that is, deprived of testosterone) immediately
after birth. As David Levine of Stanford has put it, testosterone does
not merely influence sexual behavior in adult rats, it also, when given
during the critical period, "produces a profound and permanent
change in the sensitivity of the brain to sex hormones." The same
observations also apply to other, nonsexual behavior in rats: normal
females, placed in a large cage, tend to explore more actively than
males, and defecate less, but testosterone injections in the critical
period make them behave like males under these conditions.

Rats, of course, are not primates, and we cannot automatically
transfer findings on them to other species—not even other rodents,
in fact. Among golden hamsters, for instance, both sexes are relatively
aggressive, but the females dominate the males. Only if the males
receive "extra" testosterone in the critical period can they be induced
to attack females, apparently because these early injections make their

brains more sensitive to testosterone later on. Thus sex-role behavior is not simply a matter of hormones, but also of how the brain of a particular species responds to hormones.

Experiments with primates in this area have been much less comprehensive than those with rats, because, among other reasons, their "critical period" seems to occur before birth, not after, meaning that manipulating the hormones is a lot harder. It has been established, however, that in adult monkeys of several species testosterone injections can produce more aggressive behavior in both males and females; whether, or to what extent, their nervous systems are "sensitized" to testosterone in prenatal life is not yet know. It has also been shown that among male monkeys aggressive and/or dominant males tend to have higher testosterone levels in the blood than other males. To be sure, the relationship between testosterone and aggression (or dominance) is a very complicated business, as we shall see in the next chapter. Nonetheless, to the extent male primates are of a more aggressive temperament than females—as they consistently are—testosterone would seem to be an important part of the reason. Similar interaction between sex hormones and the brain could explain the other innate primate sex differences we have noted, as they evidently explain the female rat's greater tendency to explore under certain conditions.

Having established that innate sex differences in behavior exist among primates, and having noted some of the mechanisms that may be responsible for them, let us now consider the evolutionary function of these differences as a way of determining what functions they might have served in primitive humans.

As regards the "child-orientation" of the primate female—her interest in babies, her capacity to enjoy contact with them and caring for them, and to form emotional bonds with them—the function is obvious. Young primates are helpless at birth and for a considerable time after it; moreover, the larger and more intelligent the primate, the longer it is dependent to some degree on adults—in the first place, its mother, the adult closest to it. As one indication, we note that langurs become physically mature from about three and a half years (females) to about six and a half (males), chimps from ten (females) to twelve (males), while humans, as we know, do not attain full growth until their middle or late teens.

Thus the necessities of infant and child survival which engendered the evolution of "child-orientation" in the primate female must certainly have continued to operate in the protohuman and human female—if anything, with even greater force, considering the human child's longer period of dependence. For this reason I find it inconceivable that this female primate universal, without which no young primate would have any hope of reaching maturity, does not also exist in human females. I do not, in other words, believe that little girls play with dolls—as they do in most human cultures—simply because "society" has told them they ought to; rather, their play reflects a basic female impulse without which our ancestors would not have survived long enough to produce either little girls or dolls.

But to say that these impulses exist in human females is not to say that they exist to the same extent in all human females. Unless they are quite different from all other human traits—intelligence, size, strength, aggressiveness, and so on—they must vary considerably from one woman to another, simply as a matter of birthright. And for the same reason, they must vary even more as the result of experience. If individual experience can suppress, or even reverse, the sex impulse, it can certainly do the same for the mothering impulse, which is evolutionarily much more recent than the sex impulse* and very probably not as powerful.

Even less am I suggesting that because women are likely to possess this mothering impulse (or impulses), to one degree or another, that therefore all women *ought* to possess it. In evolution there are no "oughts"—merely traits and characteristics which, more or less probably, exist. To say that little girls are likely to find dolls and babies interesting does not in any sense imply that any given little girl should be compelled to play with dolls—or discouraged from playing with a bat and ball if she cares to. My moral judgment in this area is limited to saying that every little girl ought to have the *opportunity* of enjoying dolls—and, eventually, of enjoying babies. In my view, a woman who has been deprived, whether through circumstances or her own choice, of the chance to mother an infant has been deprived of an important part of the female experience, which is to say of her own humanity. But this certainly doesn't make her "wrong," merely—at worst—unfortunate.

---

* Copulation evolved in vertebrates long before mothering.

What about human males and children? As we saw earlier, primate males are remarkably tolerant toward young primates, though this tolerance diminishes as the youngsters approach adolescence. And baboon and chimp males are not merely tolerant but actively interested in and "involved" with infants, though seemingly less so than the females. The evolution of the tolerance is obvious; without it, a young primate's chances of surviving an encounter with an irritated or angry male would be slim. The evolution of the more active concern is less clear; though it has clear protective functions in baboons (at least those living in open country) it does not seem to in chimps, for whom the best and most available defense is flight. But perhaps we don't need to resolve this problem; whether we take the chimp as a model (because of its physical and mental resemblance to our ancestors) or the grassland baboon as a model (because of its ecological resemblance to them), the concern with infants is still there.

Thus it seems to me very probable that human males possess a built-in tolerance for infants and young children, as well as a built-in interest in them and capacity to become emotionally involved with them—a conclusion which seems wholly consistent with what we know about human societies. I would also suspect that, like both baboon and chimp males, the human male has a less powerful tendency to become involved with the young than does the female. I can't prove this, and indeed am not certain that it can ever be either proved or disproved. Nonetheless, it seems to me at least arguable that the emotional rewards of fatherhood are somewhat less than those of motherhood. Be that as it may, however, the rewards exist and I, for one, would hate to have forgone them.

Of course, the reservations already cited concerning the mothering impulse apply equally to the "fathering impulse." It undoubtedly varies from man to man, both by birthright and by experience, and it can be weakened or even totally suppressed by experience or circumstance. Men have murdered children, even mass-murdered them, as we know from the history of Nazi Germany and (though it gives me no pleasure to say so) from that of our own Vietnam War. Nonetheless, I find it significant that, judging from reports of the Mylai massacre, the overriding of the basic male impulse to tolerate and protect infants was a shocking emotional experience for most of the participants, as well as for those who only read about it—shocking enough, indeed, that a sizable number of American seem to have persuaded themselves that it didn't really happen, or that if it did, it wasn't a massacre.*

When we turn to the other notable sex difference between male and female primates, centering on dominance and aggression, the evolutionary reasons behind it seem no less clear. To the extent that the dominant males in any primate group have a distinctive social function, it is as the keepers of order within the group and, especially, as the group's defenders against outside enemies. Such activities have been observed repeatedly among both baboons and their Asian cousins, the rhesus monkeys. The dominant male or males are the spearhead of resistance against attack, and have also been seen to "escort" females with young who for one reason or another had become separated from the group or were lagging behind it.

David Pilbeam of Yale, who has eloquently and convincingly denounced "the fashionable view of man as a naked ape," has, indeed, claimed that these observations are based on baboons which "are almost certainly abnormal. They live in game parks—open country where predators, especially human ones, are present in abundance —and are under a great deal of tension." Though I share Pilbeam's views on many subjects, this is one on which we part company. I know of no evidence that the grassland is any less "normal" a habitat for baboons than the forest in which some of them live and in which they have, as we shall see later, evolved a quite different life-style. Be that as it may, however, the grassland has been the normal habitat of *our* ancestors, or most of them, for more than five million years. It was a habitat in which there were unquestionably predators, and in which the primate's preferred method of dealing with predators—climbing a tree—must have often been unfeasible because there were no trees nearby.

Even modern man (to say nothing of modern woman or child) occasionally falls victim to a lion, tiger, or leopard, rare as these predators now are. And the ancestral men we are talking about were for most of the five million years in question smaller than modern man (the male Australopithecines weighed eighty to one hundred pounds) and armed with only the crudest weapons. Doubtless as human weap-

* We also find the same sort of denial among not a few Germans who lived through the Nazi period.

onry improved the menace of animal predators became less, though this may have been somewhat offset by the rise of human predators. Much more certainly, however, any lessened importance of defense was balanced by the increasing importance of hunting, an activity that appears to involve some of the same temperamental qualities as group defense, and therefore seems more congenial to the male than to the female temperament. Chimpanzees hunt only occasionally, but when they do it is the *males* that hunt; in human societies, hunting is without exception predominantly or entirely a male occupation.

It seems to me highly improbable, therefore, that those qualities of the male temperament which evolved in response to the need for group order and defense in open country, and lent themselves to the later need to hunt for food, have disappeared in modern man. It seems to me even less probable in light of the fact that men still possess special *physical* characteristics which make them more effective fighters—or hunters—than women. They are, in the first place, bigger than women, outweighing them by 15 to 25 per cent. The greater length of their legs, and the anatomy of their pelvises and hip joints, enable them to move faster than women, while their longer arms and broader shoulders mean that, simply in terms of mechanical leverage, they can wield a club or throw a rock more powerfully. Given these physical differences relevant to fighting and hunting, it would be surprising if the equally relevant temperamental differences we observe in other primates were not also present in man.

Thus it seems to me clear that men, on the average, possess a higher potential for aggression than do women. This is not to say that men are "more aggressive" than women—merely that they learn aggressive behavior more easily, whether because their nervous systems are intrinsically more excitable or because they find vigorous, exciting physical activities more pleasurable, or both. But how aggressive a given man, or group of men, is, and under what circumstances, and toward what or whom, are matters not of evolution and heredity but of environment (as they are in the primates)—in particular the culture of which the man or group is a part.

If there are strong evolutionary reasons why men have retained the primate male's capacity for aggressive behavior, there are no less pressing ones why women have retained the primate female's disinterest in, or even distaste for, such activities. For all of human prehistory (and, indeed, for most of human history) the human female was deeply involved in the production and care of children, to the point that during the fertile period of her life she would for most of the time be carrying a child within her or carrying an infant about with her. In either case she could not afford to get involved in any aggressive dominance or status games that her male relatives and neighbors might be engaged in; the risk to the infant would be too great. A secondary reason may well have been the fact that a *less* excitable nervous system, a *less* aggressive temperament, should be something of an advantage in dealing with young children, as most parents today will attest. Even given the general primate tolerance for infants, there are limits to what the most tolerant primate can take, and a tendency to explode violently at a child who passed those limits could have seriously menaced the survival of the species—meaning that any such tendency would likely have been bred out of those members of the species (women) who were most involved with children.

Since more aggressive individuals tend to dominate less aggressive ones, it seems clear that men, to the extent they are actually (rather than merely potentially) more aggressive than women, will tend to dominate them, other things being equal. But in human cultures other things seldom are equal, so that it would be going far beyond the facts to say that men "naturally" dominate women—and even farther to suggest that such domination, to the extent it exists, is good for either men or women. The most I would be willing to say is that in man as in the other primates, where we find that one sex in fact dominates the other we would expect it to be the male sex, as it almost invariably is. More tentatively, in view of the fact that in all primates male dominance is most marked where enemies are most dangerous (notably, for instance, among the grassland baboons), we might also expect to find machismo particularly marked in frontier and militarized societies, which again seems to be the case.*

It would be going even further beyond the facts to declare, on the basis of what we have just said, that women are naturally "submissive" or "passive"—a misreading of the evidence in which both feminists and antifeminists sometimes indulge. There is nothing in our observations of male-female dominance among primates that cannot

---

* In many such societies, the "enemy" is, of course, begotten by the society's (in particular, its males') own actions—as in the case, for example, of American frontier society and its enemy the Indian. But psychologically speaking, a self-created enemy (or even an imaginary one) is still an enemy.

be explained simply on the assumption that the female temperament is less prone to aggressiveness than the male.* There is no reason to invoke any "innately submissive" temperament in women, still less to intimate that women *enjoy* being dominated by men or that they are, as Sigmund Freud and other psychologists have claimed, "natural masochists." From my own personal observations, even in our own culture, with its centuries-long history of male domination, not all women enjoy being dominated, though some undoubtedly do; in fact, a few men evidently enjoy being dominated by women.

Indeed, if we look at the primates, we see that the extent to which females defer to males depends considerably on circumstances. If an adolescent male chimp is attacked by an older male, Goodall tells us, its mother may gang up with her son to drive off the persecutor. And even if the attacker is a dominant male (that is, one with which the mother has learned to avoid confrontation), the mother will still remain in the vicinity, making threatening noises. As for "passivity," just try interfering with a female chimp's or baboon's baby and you'll discover, quickly and painfully, just how "passive" she is!

We should not leave the subject of sex differences without taking a quick look at some of the more notable bits of nonsense that have been written on the subject. Perhaps the most prominent offender in this regard is Freud. However, since his fantasies on the subject have been dissected at length by such writers as Kate Millett and Richard Gilman, there seems little point in my rewriting the same arguments. There is, however, one central point about Freud that is not often mentioned, and that seems to me relevant to understanding his errors (on sex differences and other things): the man was not a scientist. He was a great philosopher, even a great poet, of the human psyche, and very likely a genius, but a scientist he was not. His theories of human nature were erected on the most tenuous factual foundation (his theory of paranoia, for example, was based on exactly one case—which he himself had not observed), and having formulated them he then proceeded to "verify" them with evidence of the most ambiguous sort—dreams and "free associations" which all too often could be interpreted to mean anything he pleased. Like all great poets, Freud

---

* It is also quite likely that females find the pursuit and achievement of dominance less interesting and/or rewarding than do males, as males appear to find babies less interesting, and their care less rewarding, than do females.

had profound insights into human nature—and equally profound blind spots, feminine psychology being one of the blindest.

More recent contributors to the mythology of male-female differences are the anthropologists Lionel Tiger and Robin Fox, who are as casual in dealing with evidence as was Freud, but without his genius as an excuse. For example, they state in their book *The Imperial Animal* that "the aim of the primate male is to get to the top of the male hierarchy and so control the females for purposes of sexual satisfaction." This is, at best, a quarter truth. It is true that *one* aim of *some* primate males, in *some* environments, is to get to the top of the hierarchy. It is not true at all that this is done "for purposes of sexual satisfaction." There is no evidence that primate males pursue dominance—when they do—for any other reason but that they enjoy pursuing it; to suppose that a male baboon is intellectually capable of grasping the connection between a scuffle for dominance today and intercourse with a female next month, or even next week, is to strain credulity. Moreover, there is no very convincing evidence that dominant males achieve significantly more sexual satisfaction than nondominant males; as the authors themselves say elsewhere, "everyone copulates; only dominants propagate" (the second statement, by the way, is also false). In the case of our closest primate cousins, the chimps, in fact, dominance has absolutely no connection with sexual satisfaction; when a female is in heat, all the males, dominant or otherwise, take turns with her quite peaceably.

Even more outrageous is the Tiger-Fox description of primate male dominance in relation to meat eating, where, they allege, the dominant male "either keeps [the meat] for himself or at best allows his nearest male bond-mates to take a little. But the females are given nothing." So far as baboons are concerned, the statement is less than half true; as regards chimps, *it is false from beginning to end.* A dominant male chimp *never* keeps all the meat for himself, even assuming he caught the animal in the first place; moreover, if a nondominant male catches an animal, the dominant male will not attempt to take it away from him. And males, dominant or otherwise, *do* give meat to females who "beg" for it.

Most outrageous of all is the fact that this false statement is refuted by one of the works that Tiger and Fox cite in "support" of it—Jane Goodall's *My Friends the Wild Chimpanzees.* The only possible conclusions are that the authors (a) didn't read the book they cited or

(b) "forgot" what it said because it conflicted with their own oversimplified theories or (c) lied. Either way, their readers would be well advised to take any "facts" they cite about human nature with a peck or two of salt. In the subsequent chapters, we shall further examine the Tiger-Fox approach to human evolution and human nature, including the facts—and "facts"—on which it is based.

7

EVOLUTION AND EVIL:
Aggression
and Its Mythology

"Arguments for the spontaneity of aggression do not bear examination."

—R. A. HINDE

"The ruthless fighter who 'knows no fear' does not get very far."

—NIKO TINBERGEN

Man has been pondering the origin of evil at least since the days of the Sumerians some five thousand years ago, and probably a lot longer than that. Medicine men and high priests have ascribed it to witches and demons, theologians to original sin or the devil. More recently, psychoanalysts have linked man's inhumanity to man with the unresolved Oedipus complex, psychologists with the wrong kind of reinforcement, neurologists with imbalances in the humors that bathe our brain cells. Historians have chalked it up to history, sociologists to society.

There has, God knows, been plenty of recent evil to ponder: Guernica, Lidice, and Auschwitz, Vorkuta and Budapest, Hiroshima and Mylai, Biafra and Bangladesh; like Macbeth, we of the mid-twentieth century have supped full with horrors. The scale, no less than the number, of these and other manifestations of human brutality is probably one major reason for the rise of yet another theology, which sees evil not as an aberration engendered by external intervention, whether societal or satanic, or as an individual malfunction, whether physical or psychological, but as something bred in the bone of the human animal. Biotheology, as I have christened it, personified by such exponents as Robert Ardrey and the team of Tiger and Fox, whom we met in the preceding chapter, sees evil—man's tendency to oppress, injure, and kill his fellows—as the inevitable, or at least expectable, outcome of human evolution.

In providing a supposedly scientific foundation for the belief that man is basically a brute, biotheology does more than "explain" evil; it also supplies a prefabricated excuse to those who, for their own reasons, choose to celebrate (and thereby encourage) brutality. Thus Stanley Kubrick, taxed by critics with dwelling overlovingly on the old ultraviolence in his immensely profitable film, *A Clockwork Orange,* retorts that "man isn't a noble savage, he's an ignoble savage. . . . I'm interested in the brutal and violent nature of man because it's a true picture of him." And a picture, moreover, whose accuracy has ostensibly been certified by science.

The truth is that biotheology is anything but scientific; like all theologies, it is founded on faith, not reason. Its linking of evolution and evil has been accomplished only by ignoring many key facts about both, as well as by citing numerous facts that are not evidence and much evidence that is not fact.

In discussing the role of evolution in human evil, and the biotheological myths that have obscured and obfuscated that role, pride of place must surely go to Robert Ardrey, whose pioneering view of evolutionary human evil, as summed up in his *African Genesis,* is that "man is a predator whose natural instinct is to kill with a weapon."* Before examining this fundamentalist version of biotheology, I must confess that I find the necessity for doing so somewhat embarrassing. Ardrey has written very warmly about an earlier book of mine, and to repay him by attacking his own writings seems like rank ingratitude. Still, facts are facts, and must be faced; the reader can at any rate be assured that my attack on Ardrey is not motivated by personal animus. I should add that if I consider Ardrey a very sloppy thinker, as I do, I also deem him a superb writer.

The kind of "evidence" Ardrey relies on is typified by his repeated insistence that prehistorians are in some sort of conspiracy to conceal man's predatory nature—among other ways, by using the word

---

* I should note, in justice to Ardrey, that his latest book, *The Social Contract,* is much less dogmatic on the subject of instincts. He is still, I think, wrong about many things, but not so categorically wrong as he was in *African Genesis.* Unfortunately, it was the original, crude version of his theory that caught the public fancy, and is still parroted by the Kubricks of this world.

"tools" when what they really mean is "weapons." Now this is simply not so. When prehistorians talk about tools, which they constantly do, they mean exactly what you or I mean by the word: *any* objects, natural or man-made, used to manipulate the natural world. The cottage where I sit writing this contains dozens of objects that any anthropologist would class as tools, including a saw, a hammer, an egg beater, a couple of corkscrews and bottle openers, forks, spoons, and knives. Not one of them is used as a weapon. To be sure, most of them in a pinch *could* be used as tools for assault, with or without intent to kill—but so, indeed, could my copy of *African Genesis*. This fact does not lead me to class Ardrey and his publisher as members of the military-industrial complex.

To move back to our ancestor Australopithecus, whose alleged homicidal instincts Ardrey discusses at length, we note that his sparse tool kit included rounded hammer-stones, presumably used (among other things) for smashing animal bones to get at the marrow, as well as crudely chipped pebbles. These were perhaps employed as weapons—though to use them on any sizable animal would have involved operating at uncomfortably close quarters to the creature's sharp horns or hoofs—but more probably served to cut up game or chop tough roots. And if the practices of modern primitives are any indication, it is likely that Australopithecus also used sticks to unearth the roots, though these digging tools would of course have rotted away long since.

To this not notably homicidal tool assembly Ardrey has added the lower jaws of antelopes, whose jagged teeth, he alleges, were used to cut and slash—the prototypes, he claims, of the switchblade knives in *West Side Story*. Now I must confess that I have no evidence that these objects were not so used, but neither does Ardrey have any evidence that they were, or even that they were used as tools at all. It so happens, however, that shortly after reading his account of the antelope jaws, I had occasion to visit the American Museum of Natural History. There, in an exhibit on the Cherokee Indians, my eye fell on an object made from the lower jaw of a deer—larger than Ardrey's proto-switchblade, but otherwise virtually identical. According to the label, it had been used for the murderous purpose of scraping dried corn kernels off the cob. Evidently a weapon, like beauty, is often in the eye of the beholder.

Yet another bit of Ardreyan evidence is an Australopithecine lower jaw, broken across the middle, which supposedly proves that its owner was clubbed to death by a neighbor. On this I have consulted my old and valued friend, William Ober, M.D., who as Chief of Pathology at a large New York hospital is not unacquainted with injuries produced by violence. He tells me that it is virtually impossible to determine—particularly after a lapse of a million years—whether such a fracture was produced immediately before death or after it, and altogether impossible to say whether, if indeed it occurred before death, the cause was a blow or a fall. But one need not have a consulting pathologist on tap, merely a little imagination. If you are clubbing a man—try the experiment with a friend, using a rolled-up newspaper—you can quite easily hit him on the arm, the shoulder, the cheek, the side or top of the head, and perhaps the nose; the one place you will find virtually impossible to hit is the point of the jaw. Which pretty much eliminates the point of Ardrey's Australopithecine jaw.

To clarify the point at issue here, I should emphasize that Australopithecus and his descendants were unquestionably "predators" —a scare word meaning merely that they killed animals for food. Dogs are also predators and, in evolutionary terms, have been so for a much longer time than man, since their ancestors were killing for a living when ours were still subsisting on fruits, shoots, and roots. This fact does not inhibit dog owners from encouraging their children to play with man's best friend.* As predators lacking claws or powerful teeth, Australopithecus and his successors undoubtedly employed weapons, whether natural or manufactured, to kill game—and, quite as important, to avoid becoming game themselves for other predators. It is not unlikely that they occasionally used the same weapons to kill their fellows, as men still do. The question is whether "instinct" played any role in such activities.

In Chapter 2 we noted that instinctive behavior is typically species-wide, automatic (occurring invariably in response to certain stimuli), and stereotyped. On none of these grounds can homicide be classed as instinctive. It is not species-wide; only a minority of men ever kill, and if we exclude those who do so under compulsion—such as the soldier whose alternative to killing is being killed himself, or at least being court-martialed—the minority shrinks almost to the vanishing

* The same also applies, of course, to the predatory domestic cat.

point. In our own culture—not widely known for its abhorrence of violence—I would estimate the proportion of adult men who have deliberately killed another human being as perhaps one in ten, even including soldiers, policemen, and the like; if one excludes these killers-by-necessity, the proportion, judging from our national incidence of homicide, drops to something like one in a hundred.* How many murderers do *you* know? To the question so often, and so disingenuously, posed by the biotheologians—"Why do we kill one another?"—the only possible answer is that most of us don't; attempts to answer it in any other way inevitably beget mere variations on the theme of "ask a silly question . . ."

Nor is there anything automatic or stereotyped about human homicide. The Eskimo, the Zulu, and the American all instinctively cough in precisely the same way and under the same circumstances; their wives all give birth in the same way. But if they kill—and most of them never do—there is almost endless variation in whom they kill, and under what circumstances, and by what methods. Man is often described as notoriously ingenious in devising new techniques for eliminating his fellows, but the very diversity of these methods—plus the rarity with which he uses them—proves conclusively that they are learned, not instinctive.

Remarkably enough, killing appears to be learned even by some animals in which it is, by necessity, species-wide. The lion, for example, must kill to live; neither by physique nor by physiology is he equipped to subsist on plants. Yet Elsa, the famous lioness of *Born Free,* raised by human beings, simply didn't know how to kill; before she could be released into the wild she had, in the words of the old song, "to be carefully taught," or she would have starved.**

However, proving that man is not an instinctive killer obviously does not prove that there is no unlearned, genetic component in human violence. In previous chapters we have noted the innate psychological payoffs attached to certain primate activities, such as eating sweets or engaging in sexual intercourse, which encourage primates to learn about these things. If there is indeed some evolutionary

* Since it is generally conceded that killing, instinctive or not, is overwhelmingly a male activity, I have deliberately excluded women from these figures; their inclusion would of course lower the proportion of killers among us even further.

** Even more remarkably, Ardrey himself cites the case of Elsa in *African Genesis,* apparently unaware that it undermines his whole argument about instinctive killing.

impulse to evil, some built-in propensity to violence or oppression in the human animal, it must be of this type: not an instinctive command to kill but rather some innate pleasure or satisfaction in murderous, or at least violent, encounters with other human beings. This is presumably what Tiger and Fox are talking about in *The Imperial Animal* when they claim that we are "turned on" by violence—as most of us are certainly turned on by sex. It is also what Ardrey is talking about in *The Social Contract* when he declares that "we enjoy the violent." Interestingly, these authors couch their generalizations in terms of the rhetorical device that I have elsewhere called the Evasive We. Neither Tiger nor Fox is willing to admit that *he* is turned on by violence, and even Ardrey, while intimating that he would enjoy violence if he weren't a timid soul, concedes that in fact he has "no great taste" for it. But let that pass.

If evolution has in fact endowed us—or at least the male half of "us"—with some innate delight in violence, then that incentive plan must have originated as an evolutionary necessity—that is, as an incentive to learning some sort of behavior needed for survival of the species. An obvious candidate for the behavior in question, as we saw in the previous chapter, is dominance. As we shall see, the dominance of one (male) primate over another depends on a number of things, but its ultimate basis—there is no use in denying it—is force or, much more often, the threat of force. As the biotheologians have correctly grasped, an understanding of dominance—what it depends on, and to what extent a liking for it, comparable to a liking for sweets or sex, is built into primate genes—is obviously central to understanding the origins of evil. In fact, as we shall see, the importance of dominance varies widely from one primate species to another and, significantly, *within* some species, depending on the environmental conditions.

Consider first the chimp, which—it cannot be too often emphasized—is by every physical and mental criterion we can think of our closest relative on earth, and even closer to our Australopithecine forebears, at least in its anatomy; a chimp could be converted into a very passable imitation of an Australopithecine simply by "remodeling" its feet, legs, and pelvis so that it could comfortably walk upright. So far as the chimp is concerned, dominance plays a very small role in its life. Vernon and Frances Reynolds, who observed several groups of forest-dwelling chimps, note that although "there was some evidence of differences in status between individuals, dominance interac-

tions formed *a minute fraction* of the observed chimpanzee behavior"
(my emphasis). Jane Goodall's chimps seemed somewhat more concerned with dominance, but even so, she says, "aggressive and submissive interactions between individuals are infrequent." And a considerable proportion of these interactions, she believes, was unwittingly
produced by the human observers: by feeding the animals regularly
at a particular location, they drew together large numbers of chimps
around an especially desirable food (bananas), with a resulting increase in tension and squabbling. When the feeding was cut down,
so was the squabbling. If we are to judge an animal's liking for
particular activities in terms of the time it spends doing them—and
it is hard to think of any other basis for judgment—then these close
cousins of ours find dominance and aggression far less pleasurable or
interesting than such pacific occupations as feeding, fornication,
mutual back scratching, and playing with their young. And to the
extent that we, or our ancestors, resemble them, we would expect a
similar hierarchy of "innate values," with violence well down on the
list.

But resemblances, as we have had occasion to note earlier, involve
ecology as well as anatomy. From this standpoint, we should expect
to find clues to man's alleged propensity for violence among the
grassland baboons, whose habitat is so similar to that of Australopithecus and many or most of his descendants. Like Australopithecus,
these baboons live in the open, meaning that the trees in which primates typically seek refuge from danger are often inaccessible. Their
alternative, as we have seen, is self-defense—notably, by the large,
vigorous dominant males who lead the baboon band. Similar tactics,
it seems virtually certain, must have been employed by Australopithecus. If man indeed possesses some innate drive for dominance,
some built-in liking for violence and aggression, then here, clearly,
is where it must have begun: among the aggressive, dominant Australopithecine males who, like baboon males, needed to be ready to
fight if their band was to survive.

Well, then, what about the baboon male? How does he get to be
dominant, and how much do inherited drives and traits enter into the
process? At one time, baboon dominance was thought to be almost
entirely a matter of inheritance: of innate size, strength, and aggressiveness. These qualities, it was held, were passed on by dominant
males to their sons by a process of sexual selection. The dominant
male, or males, that is, were thought to mate with the band's females

—and to prevent their subordinates from doing so—at the point in the female sexual cycle when conception was most likely, thereby transmitting his, or their, "dominance genes" (not to be confused with "dominant genes," a purely genetic concept) to a large proportion of the group's offspring.

More recently, it has become evident that matters are not all that simple. For example, Robert Wingfield and the late K. L. R. Hall observed one group of South African baboons continuously for nine days, during which three females were in heat; the dominant male mated with only one of the three. Moreover, the other two males in the group mated with this same female, though less often than their superior—and *only* they mated with the other two females. If we assume that all three females conceived, the result would have been at best one infant with "dominance genes" and two with "submissive genes"—which is to say, the same proportion as already existed among the group's males. Not much sexual selection here.

In addition, however, it must be obvious that if any such process of sexual selection does or did play a role in baboon or human evolution, it must have operated within very narrow limits. If genes making for dominance and aggression were continually being transmitted to more and more of the group's offspring, while those making for submissiveness were being weeded out, it would not have taken many generations before *all* the males in the band were innately aggressive, or even ultra-aggressive. The result would have been catastrophic: a band with all chiefs and no Indians, group disruption, and, inevitably, extinction. As I have repeatedly pointed out, the integrity of the primate group is utterly essential to the survival of the group, and whatever the role of inherited dominance and aggression in primate evolution, it must always have played a distant second fiddle to this fundamental fact.

More sophisticated studies, in fact, show that dominance in baboons depends on many things, some inherited and some almost certainly not. Size, strength, and, very probably, intelligence are obviously important, and these are undoubtedly inherited to a large degree.* But so, significantly, is a capacity for attracting allies and

---

* Intelligence seems to be clearly significant in dominance interactions among chimps. Goodall gives an amusing account of how Mike, one of the males in the group she was studying, made himself number one by sheer ingenuity: he discovered that by rattling empty kerosene tins he could produce a racket so appalling that even the dominant males were overawed.

cooperating with them. Among many baboon bands, leadership is exercised not by an individual but by a syndicate, which by acting in concert can face down a competing male who, considering merely his own size, strength, and aggressiveness, could be expected to dominate any individual member of the band's power structure. Evidently domination of others and cooperation with others are by no means the polar opposites they are often portrayed as; the one often depends on the other. We do not, indeed, know whether "cooperativeness" is in any sense a matter of heredity—apart, that is, from the general primate trait of sociability toward one's own kind. The most we can say is that a male baboon conspicuously deficient in this trait, whether by heredity or by upbringing, would have a rather meager chance of becoming part of his band's power structure.

No less important in achieving dominance in the baboon group are such hard-to-define qualities as self-assurance and what can only be called the will to power. And whether these are in any sense inherited is, to say the least, doubtful. Irven DeVore, who has probably spent as much time watching wild baboons as anyone in the world, suspects that self-assurance is largely or entirely learned. Male infants born to subordinate females, he believes, "will take on the attitude of subjection they perceive in their mothers," while the offspring of a dominant female "is likely to acquire the same sense of self-assurance." Like mother, like son, in fact. Among humans, as we know very well, sons of rich and powerful families—even adopted sons with few or no "upper-class" genes—easily learn to expect, even demand, the deference and privileges their parents enjoy. The will to power, too, seems more likely to be acquired rather than innate; at any rate, DeVore cites cases of dominant males who voluntarily "dropped out" of the power structure and the group, preferring, one might say, to get out of the rat race—or baboon race—and live as loners. (Adult baboon males, unlike females, are evidently big enough and tough enough to survive outside the group).

Yet another factor in baboon (or, for that matter, human) dominance is individual aggressiveness; a dominant baboon achieves and maintains his position in part through his willingness to carry out, or threaten, aggression against competitors. But here too there is considerable doubt whether this trait is inherited to any marked degree. For example, DeVore cites two cases in which male baboons changed groups, which seldom happened among those he observed.* Both animals were well down in the hierarchy of their original groups, yet *both quickly became top baboon in their new groups.* If their original status reflected some sort of hereditary nonaggressiveness, what did their new status reflect?

But, the reader may well protest, surely you are contradicting yourself! Only a few pages back you were arguing that the greater aggressiveness, or potential for aggressiveness, among primate (and human) males in contrast with females was the result of the males' much greater supplies of the hormone testosterone—and this is certainly a matter of genetics, not learning. This is, of course, quite correct. I *do* believe that male primates are more "aggression-prone" than females, that testosterone is one important reason why, and that—obviously—males produce testosterone in quantity because they are genetically males. What I do not believe is that there is anything like so clear-cut a relationship between differences in aggressive potential *among* males and inherited differences in testosterone production. My reasons are somewhat complicated, but I think convincing.

To begin with, there is any amount of evidence pointing to a connection between aggression, dominance, and testosterone production. Studies of captive monkey groups have shown that high testosterone levels tend to correlate with high aggression and/or high rank, and moreover that injections of testosterone can turn a nonaggressive individual into an aggressive one.** But the relationship is anything but simple. Thus a group of researchers from Walter Reed Army Institute of Research and the Yerkes Primate Center in Georgia, in a study of rhesus monkeys, found that "the most aggressive animals are not always the most dominant, nor are the least aggressive necessarily lowest in dominance." Out of thirty-four males in the group, the dominant male ranked only twelfth in frequency of aggressive behavior, while the most aggressive animal ranked number ten in dominance—yet had over a third *more* testosterone than did number one.

Further studies, this time by Irving S. Bernstein of Yerkes and

---

* In other regions, such changes are almost routine, though the reasons for the difference are not well understood.

** For that matter, the technique of turning the aggressive, dangerous bull into the tractable ox by castration—i.e., by removing its source of testosterone—has been known for at least five thousand years.

Robert M. Rose of Boston University, strongly suggest that much of the time it is not the high testosterone levels that lead to aggressiveness and/or dominance, but the aggressiveness and dominance that produce the high testosterone levels. When they placed a single rhesus male in a group of females, he quickly dominated them (as rhesus males normally do)—and his testosterone levels rose sharply, though whether because he dominated them or because their presence stimulated him sexually is not clear. When the same male was then placed in a group of strange males, they quickly ganged up on him and forced him to the bottom of the totem pole (which is also normal in such situations)—and his testosterone levels fell precipitously. In the final experiment, a dominant male in another rhesus group was converted into a "lower class" male by removing the male allies who had helped make him dominant—and *his* testosterone levels also plummeted. To make matters even more complicated, it has also been determined that high testosterone levels can make primate males feel sexy.*

This bewildering situation, in which sex, aggression, and testosterone play ring-around-the-rosy, with no one able to say which is cause and which is effect, is largely explained by recent discoveries about the incredibly complex system of interlocking controls that govern the release of hormones, including sex hormones. Twenty or thirty years ago, it was generally agreed that the release of hormones by the endocrine glands was governed by the pituitary, a tiny organ buried deep in the brain, which was then known as the body's master gland. More recently it has become apparent that the pituitary itself has a master—a portion of the brain known as the hypothalamus, which can turn on or turn off various pituitary functions just as the pituitary turns on or turns off hormonal release by other endocrines.

Nor is the hypothalamus a free agent. *Its* activity, which governs the pituitary and, through it, the other endocrines, is itself governed in part by blood levels of both pituitary secretions and other hormones, so that, for example, high blood levels of adrenalin will throttle back the hypothalamus, which slows the pituitary, which cuts down adrenalin output by the adrenal glands. This feedback system, of course, insures that hormone output does not rise too high or fall

---

* This fact, incidentally, suggests that to the extent dominant male monkeys engage in more sex acts than other males, part of the reason may be not their dominance as such but rather the high testosterone levels—and sexiness—which their dominance engenders.

too low, in very much the same way that a thermostat controls the heat output of a furnace.

But the hypothalamus is influenced not only by hormones, but also by nerve impulses from the brain, of which it is an integral part.* It is these impulses that shift our hormone output to meet the changing demands of our environment—which, of course, we perceive and evaluate through the brain—so that, for example, when we are angry or frightened our adrenalin output jumps as a way of preparing our bodies for fast and vigorous attack, defense, or evasive action (this is part of what physiologists call the "fight-or-flight" response). The sex hormones are subject to the same brain influences. Physicians have long known, for example, that a woman's menstrual cycle can be disrupted or even suspended, for weeks or months, simply by severe nervous tension or a nervous shock.

The influence of aggressiveness and dominance on hormones and sex reaches its peak in the case of some of the small tropical fish called "cleaners," which feed off parasites that they remove from the skin of other fish. One species, studied on the Australian Great Barrier Reef, lives in groups of one male with a harem of three to six females; the male dominates the females, and the larger, older females dominate the smaller, younger ones. If the male dies or is removed from the group, the largest of the females almost immediately begins to act like a male, carrying out typical male aggressive displays toward the other females. And within a couple of weeks *she actually turns into a male,* producing sperm instead of eggs! I am not suggesting, of course, that anything of the sort could occur in primates or other mammals; for one thing, most or all cleaner-fish females possess rudimentary testes, as mammalian females do not. Nonetheless, I find rather mind-blowing the fact that a female can change into a male simply by acting like one.

From all this evidence, it seems plausible that higher testosterone levels in male primates can be induced by aggressive activities, by dominance, by sexual stimulation, and quite possibly by other psychological causes—there is an enormous amount we still don't know about the relationship between the nervous system and the hypothalamus. Equally, it seems no less plausible that the increased testos-

---

* It is in fact composed of modified nerve cells, rather than of gland cells as are the pituitary and the other endocrines.

terone, depending on the individual and the situation, can stimulate aggression, or sexual activity, or perhaps other types of behavior. Given this appallingly complex set of relationships (even more complex, actually, than I have been able to show in this brief account), it would seem that though inherited differences in testosterone production among males doubtless exist, they can play only a minor role in determining which male will be most aggressive—or most dominant.

I might note in passing that the connection between aggression, testosterone, and sexual desire suggests one reason why conquering armies are prone to sexual promiscuity, not infrequently to the point of rape, which neatly combines both sex and aggression. It also suggests that women who succeed in dominating their mates are likely to find them unenthusiastic lovers. Finally—and here I am quite aware of treading on controversial and dangerous ground—it suggests that women who permit their mates a certain amount of domination, or at least the illusion of it, are likely to find them more passionate, other things being equal. I should add, however, that the particular interactions and relationships which men *perceive* as dominance, at least in the sexually stimulating sense, must surely vary enormously between one man and another, from the mere awareness of being larger and more powerful than a woman (which I personally find stimulating) to actively bullying her (which I do not). From my own experience, at any rate, dominance (or sex) has no necessary connection with who washes the dishes or diapers the baby; I have done my share of both, and did not find my sexual desires diminished thereby. At a minimum, I would say that a woman who conveys to her man that she finds him a strong, competent individual will not find herself sexually the loser.

Perhaps the strongest evidence that hereditary factors are of minimal importance in engendering dominance and aggression even among baboons (who with their relatives the rhesus monkeys are generally considered to be the most aggressive subhuman primates) is the fact that they are not found among all baboons—not even of the same species. In the olive baboon, for instance (a variety of the savanna baboon), aggressiveness and a dominance hierarchy are marked among groups living in open country—but, according to Thelma Rowell's observations, of minimal importance for groups living in forest country, just as with the forest-dwelling chimps. Conceivably, of course, Rowell's baboons might have been a hereditarily nonaggressive group—but she herself neatly disposed of that possibility. She put the animals into enclosures where they were more crowded and could not forage freely, so that they had to be fed regularly; this, as with Goodall's chimps, drew them together in large, hungry groups. Presto! The nonaggressive baboons straightway became aggressive and quarrelsome, and developed sharply marked dominance hierarchies.

I find it significant, in this connection, that the Walter Reed-Yerkes investigators found that testosterone levels in their rhesus males seemed to correspond most closely to the amount of "behavior interpreted as indicative of general tension." One might well conclude from this that baboons living in open country, like Rowell's baboons in cages, are in a state of generalized tension—here due, of course, to habitual awareness of possible danger. (This does not mean that the danger need be continuously present. Baboon attitudes toward particular features of their environment can evidently persist long after the incident that engendered the attitudes, as we saw from DeVore's account of the band which, after one of its number had been shot from a car, shunned cars for years afterward.) It is probably not coincidental that chimpanzees which have been observed crossing areas of open savanna appear to be under similar tension—with considerably more of a hierarchical structure than they normally show in the forest.

The same shifting relationship between dominance and tension induced by a particular situation appears to show up in food sharing among chimpanzees. As we noted in the last chapter, when a nondominant male chimp catches an animal, the dominant males will not attempt to seize it from him—indeed, he may even push them away when their "begging" for a share becomes too bothersome. When Jane Goodall first observed this, she was startled, since it was then generally believed that what a dominant male primate wants, he gets. Seeking an explanation, she concluded that a male chimp in possession of meat, a much-prized food, "may become more willing to fight for it"—that is, more tense. The dominant males then would "fail to detect those signals of apprehension which normally characterize their interactions with subordinates and instead meet very definite aggressive signals"—to the point where "they may feel hesitant in asserting their normal prerogatives."

All this evidence, it seems to me, clearly adds up to the conclusion that the dominance-aggression-hierarchy syndrome among primates is in no sense a genetically programmed compulsion, or even a strong innate preference; it is merely a potential: *one* way in which primates can organize themselves. The strength of the potential, moreover, must at all times have been held within limits by the fact that too much aggressiveness would have destroyed the group—and its members. In our own evolutionary line, "innate" aggressiveness, to the extent it existed at all, would probably have been held within even narrower limits by the need for cooperation among the group's males—first in dealing with predators, later in hunting big game, as we shall see in the next chapter. Even in baboons, as we have noted, a dominant male's ability to "aggress" successfully against subordinate males is often contingent on his ability to cooperate with—that is, to inhibit aggression against—the other dominant males of his band's power structure.

And whatever the primate (or human) potential for violence, the matter of whether it becomes expressed *in action,* and to what degree, is evidently determined not by heredity but by environment—particularly, it would appear, by how dangerous or how safe the environment is. Significantly, we find dominance and hierarchy most marked today in those human institutions specifically set up to deal with dangerous situations, real or imagined: the armed forces of any country you choose to name.

There is another bit of evidence supporting this view of human evolution. If some genetic tendency toward dominance and hierarchy did evolve and persist in our evolutionary line, we should expect it to show up most conspicuously in the simplest, most primitive human societies: peoples, that is, living in regions where food resources are sparse (relative, of course, to the tools and techniques for obtaining them) and the standard of living is correspondingly modest. The world of Australopithecus was like that, as was the world of all our ancestors up to a few tens of thousands of years ago. Yet it is precisely in such contemporary societies that dominance and hierarchy are virtually nonexistent. Thus Harold E. Driver's standard source book on the North American Indian tribes tells us that in the naturally poorer areas—covering the Great Basin, northeast Mexico, most of Alaska, and nearly all of Canada—"differences in status, other than those based on age and sex, were at the minimum. . . . Leadership, *weak as it was,* tended to be vested in the most capable man, regardless of ancestry, and this man was followed *only as long as he continued to demonstrate his superior skills and judgment"* (my emphasis).

Much the same can be said of comparable societies elsewhere in the world—the Yaghan of Tierra del Fuego, the Andamanese of the Indian Ocean, and the pygmies and Bushmen of Africa. Perhaps the outstanding case in point is that of the Tasaday, a hitherto unknown Stone Age tribe recently discovered in the depths of the Philippine jungle. In its safety from natural enemies, their rain-forest habitat resembles (or at least resembled) the world of the forest chimp—and the Tasaday, coincidentally or not, are quite as pacific as those apes. The few anthropologists who have observed them describe them as outstandingly gentle, uncompetitive, affectionate, and nonviolent. If, as Tiger, Fox, Ardrey and Company tell us, man is inherently prone to set up rigid hierarchies and dominate his fellows by force, somebody should tell the Tasaday and the Bushmen about it!

If an innate enjoyment of domination and aggression is not the source of human evil, neither is an innate enjoyment of killing. According to biotheology, this allegedly basic trait of human nature evolved over the past couple of million years, as man relied more and more on hunting as a major source of food. Acquiring an innate pleasure in killing animals, he also began to delight in killing his fellows.

There are so many things wrong with this theory that it is hard to know where to begin criticizing it. In the first place, it ignores the self-evident fact that hunting—using violence against animals—is psychologically an utterly different activity from using violence against man, and enjoyment of one has little if anything to do with enjoyment of the other. Both of them may on occasion involve a certain amount of vigorous, exciting physical activity—and this, as I have already noted, probably possesses a certain intrinsic attraction for most human males. But in other respects they are poles apart. In everyday life—disregarding, that is, such special and much more complicated phenomena as the pilot "wasting" a village or the gangster "hitting" a business rival—the man who deliberately kills or injures another is above all an angry man. This was the case with the archetypical homicide, in which Cain was angry because the Lord had accepted his brother's offering while rejecting his own; it has been the case ever since. But is a duck hunter angry at the ducks? Some primitive peoples, indeed, actually apologize to the animal they have killed or are about to kill, which is hardly the way of the murderer, or even the mugger, with his victim. If hunters enjoy hunting—and its popularity as a recreation argues pretty persuasively that they do—their pleasure comes from their skill in stalking and shooting, the expected praise from their fellows, and, perhaps, the prospect of a savory and unusual dish for dinner. The killing part is incidental. The same difference shows up clearly among such nonhuman hunters as dogs. Both a dog threatening another dog and a dog chasing (i.e., "hunting") a cat or squirrel may be excited, but the resemblance ends there. The first animal will hold its head low, lay back its ears, erect the fur on its shoulders, and growl; the second will display none of these threatening signs, but will rather bark or bay.

Indeed, when we examine the actual motives of killers in our society, we find that "love of killing" as such is irrelevant to nearly all of them. For many, it is "I kill you because you'll kill me if I don't" —for example, the combat soldier confronting the enemy or the cop confronting a robber—and, of course, the robber confronting the cop. For others, it's "I kill you to get something you have that I want" —the Syndicate "button man" knocking off a competitor, or occasionally the robber with his victim (police authorities tell us that robbers seldom kill unresisting victims; their liking is for loot, not homicide). For a few, it boils down to "I kill you because you have hurt/humiliated me and I am angry"—the Cain-Abel case or that of the man who shoots or knifes the woman who spurned him, or the man for whom she spurned him. Even here, it is not the killing per se that satisfies, but killing a particular person. And, again, criminologists tell us that in many such cases the killing is more or less unintentional. The aggressor wants to *injure* his victim but is drunk or spaced out on some drug so that his judgment is impaired, or happens to have available a weapon (such as a knife or a cheap pistol) that too easily produces fatal injuries. If we look for men who derive satisfaction from the act of killing itself, we find them only a tiny, tiny minority: such exceptional killers as Richard Speck, who butchered eight young women one bloody evening in Chicago. And the Specks are typically labeled "pathological killers"; that is, they are seen— quite rightly—*not* as normal human beings, killing for normal, human motives, but as cases of mental disease. Indeed, these rare killers- for-the-love-of-killing—who, according to biotheology, are simply displaying motives derived from a million years of big-game hunting and thus possessed by all men—are in fact utterly terrifying to the rest of us because their motives are so utterly alien and their actions so totally unexpected.

But let us for the sake of argument disregard all this evidence. Let us assume that man's long career as a hunter—on present evidence, several million years—somehow did endow him with some sort of innate, generalized delight in killing, evoked alike by the slaughter of a mastodon and the slaughter of a neighbor. It still doesn't add up. Because a man, or a tribe, that simply delighted in uninhibited killing would not have lived long—not, at least, once man had graduated out of the rabbit-and-prairie-dog grade of hunting and begun tackling really dangerous beasts. A prizefighter may enjoy slugging, but he courts an early knockout if he doesn't also know when to duck. Some of us may, as Tiger and Fox say, be "turned on" by violence, for whatever reasons, but most of us, when confronted by it, are, like Ardrey, timid souls—and for excellent evolutionary reasons: they that take the sword, or its equivalent, generally stand a good chance of perishing by it. Over nearly the whole of human prehistory, when one could not shoot one's enemy from a thousand yards or bomb him from thirty thousand feet, *killing inevitably involved the risk of being killed* —and any man, or ape-man, so enamored of violence that he failed to assess the risk and duck out when it was too great would have been gored or trampled to death in short order. Even DeVore's aggressive baboons, which were quite capable of ganging up on and facing down a leopard, turned tail when confronted by the more formidable lion; in other situations baboons have been observed to meet danger by hiding in long grass, if available, or of course by taking to the trees, if reachable.

The young Masai warrior is, or at any rate was, expected to prove his manhood by killing a lion single-handed, which he usually did sucessfully, with a spear designed for the purpose. But no Masai, whatever satisfaction he may have derived from killing "his" lion, then made a habit of it—for obvious reasons.

Today's nearest parallel to the primitive hunter is not the gangster or mugger, or the Nazi guard at an extermination camp, or the pilot bombing a target he often cannot see: it is the combat infantryman, who, like our ancestors, must risk his own life to kill efficiently. And his job, for all man's alleged "killer impulses," is never in great demand; the world's "grunts" and "dogfaces" are mostly poor men, for whom the alternative is poverty, or draftees, for whom the alternative is jail. An "innate impulse" that must be evoked by environmental or legal compulsion can't be much of an impulse. In contrast, when we turn to a really fundamental impulse, the impulse to copulate— which Tiger and Fox casually couple with "the impulse to kill"—we find that it seldom requires compulsion; at any rate I know of no case where men have had to be drafted for the purpose!

Neither by instinct nor inherited preference, then, is man a killer. He is, as we well know, *capable* of murder—even, to the extent his technology permits, of mass murder—but we can say with Horatio that "it needs no (Australopithecine) ghost come from the grave to tell us that." Yet if man is capable of violence—even, very occasionally, the old ultraviolence—he is no less capable of kindness and generosity.* The notion that he is an ignoble savage, *pace* Mr. Kubrick, is no less nonsensical than the more venerable notion that he is a noble savage. Man is man; he embodies all the potentialities he has inherited from his primate ancestors, plus many more he has evolved on his own, which we shall examine in Part II. And, as with the other primates, which of these potentialities he expresses in action depends on the environment he lives in—and especially on the customs of his group. If his group celebrates violence and rationalizes it with tendentious and unscientific reconstructions of human evolution, he may be violent; if it discourages violence as the negation, not the culmination, of humanity, he will for the most part follow his true innate impulses, preferring to make love, not war.

* Probably, as we shall see in a later chapter, a good deal more capable.

PART TWO

Man among Men

8

THE LAST
MILLION YEARS:
Evolution Since
Australopithecus

"What is this thing called a man?"
— L O R E N Z H A R T , Pal Joey

". . . the paragon of animals!"
— S H A K E S P E A R E , Hamlet

Australopithecus, whose psychological lineaments we have been sketching in earlier chapters, was, as already noted, clearly something more than an ape. He inhabited savannas and grasslands, as no ape does; he habitually stood and moved about on his hind legs, as no ape does; he used tools—both to get food and to defend himself—not occasionally but routinely, as no ape does; and he made some of these tools out of stone, as no ape does.

On the other hand, if he was clearly more than an ape he was equally clearly something much less than a man. To take merely the most obvious anatomical difference, his brain was no bigger than a chimp's, with a volume of five hundred cubic centimeters or less, making it only about two-fifths the size of ours. The difference is no less marked if we consider what that brain could and could not do. Most notably, Australopithecus could not speak. He undoubtedly used sounds, gestures, and facial expressions to communicate with his fellows, as all apes and monkeys do to one degree or another. We can even plausibly identify a few of the ways in which he communicated, since they appear to be more or less innate and to have originated before the human and ape evolutionary lines separated. Thus the hard, tight-lipped, level stare sometimes called a "dirty look" is an expression of anger and potential aggression in the chimp as it is in man, and probably served the same function in Australopithecus. But though Australopithecus could communicate anger and various other emotions, there is no reason to suppose that he was capable of speech in anything remotely approaching the human sense. (Since I do not want to get involved here in spelling out the difference between speech and other forms of animal communication, the reader must for the moment take my word for it that there *is* a difference—and an enormous one.) Australopithecus was a manlike ape, not an apelike man, and the fact that some prehistorians (on evidence that many people, including myself, consider dubious) have chosen to elevate some Australopithecines into the genus Homo should not be permitted to obscure that truth.

In any discussion of how the descendants of this manlike ape became first apelike men and then true men (and women) several important qualifications need to be kept in mind. First, the process was gradual and continuous, meaning that labels applied to particular steps in that process are bound to be somewhat arbitrary. For example, some fragmentary bones dug up near Modjokerto, Java, and dating from perhaps a million years ago,* have been described both as a late variety of Australopithecus and as a primitive variety of the species that succeeded him, Homo erectus—and both descriptions are "correct." Again, it is impossible to say whether the skull of "Tautavel man," found a few years ago beneath the floor of a French cave, is that of a late, advanced Homo erectus or of an early, primitive Neanderthaler; the skull's anatomy and presumed date (about two hundred thousand years ago) are equally consistent with either interpretation.**

The second qualification is that almost the entire period we shall be discussing—the last million years—is one in which methods for dating archeological finds are still very crude. Any date between about one million and fifty thousand years ago is not much better than an educated guess, and may be off by tens or even hundreds of thousands of years.***

---

*Not the famous "Java man," but a much older relative.

** The question of what species Neanderthal man should be assigned to, and of his place in human evolution, is a complicated one which we must defer until Chapter 11.

*** Readers interested in why this is so, or in dating methods generally, should consult Chapters 14 and 15 of my book *Climate, Man, and History.*

HUGO VAN LAWICK

The emotional life of all primates begins
with the bond between mother and child.

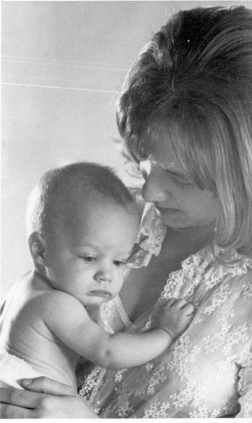

DEWYS, INC.

Infant primates do not live by milk alone; physical contact with something soft is at least as important.

Primate babies are interesting not just to their mothers but to other adults—always to females, but often (as here) to males as well.

At a very early age, the young primate begins to investigate the world around it. Its curiosity will last almost as long as its life.

Under deep stress, primates almost automatically seek physical contact for emotional reassurance.

The life-style of the dominant male baboon, sometimes depicted as the prototype of human violence and even criminality, also includes such activities as bodyguarding a mother and her infant,...

...grooming a favored female,...

...breaking up fights among other members of the group,...

...and befriending a sickly, orphaned infant.

IRVEN DEVORE

Male chimps will tolerate
a remarkable amount of
interference from juveniles
—even at life's most
intimate moments...

...and even dominant
males don't grab meat
from their "subordinates"
—they beg for it.

Mike's discovery that rattling kerosene tins could make him top chimp bears all the earmarks of what is called insight learning.

There is no mistaking when a female baboon is sexually receptive.

With human females, however, matters are considerably more ambiguous.

UPI

In nearly all primates, sex is an exciting but also casual encounter.

Only in man can it become intense and personal.

UPI

Deer Hunt
Castellón-Spain...

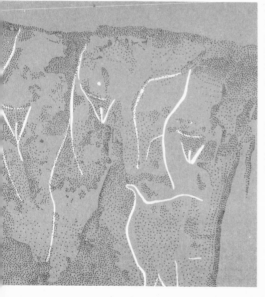

About 30,000 years ago, the rate of innovation in human cultures suddenly speeded up. This cave painting encompasses two notable innovations: the bow and arrow, and art itself.

Cave art also tells us that men have been looking at women in much the same way for more than 15,000 years—at least.

Primates are above all social—and sociable—animals.

The third qualification derives from the fact that we are dealing, by any estimate, with creatures whose existence covered long periods of time and increasingly large areas of geographical space. Homo erectus, though his time on earth was far shorter than that of Australopithecus (who lived in the African grasslands for close to five million years at least), still flourished for some seven hundred thousand years—nearly twenty times as long as modern man has been on the scene—and has left his relics at sites ranging from Spain to China; the Neanderthals, though their tenure was only about a tenth as long, were even more widely dispersed. Thus generalizations about what either creature looked like, or did, or was capable of, are at best approximations applicable more to certain times and places than to others.

For example, when we speak of Homo erectus as having a brain perhaps twice as big as that of Australopithecus we are actually talking about skulls whose capacity ranges from about seven hundred fifty to as much as fourteen hundred cubic centimeters, the latter well within the range of modern man. The main point to bear in mind is that, large or small, his brain *was* bigger (and better) than those of the African man-apes. His body was bigger, too though not in the same proportion: Australopithecus was no bigger than a modern African pygmy—four feet tall or less—while erectus was a five-footer, and rather burlier in build.* His anatomy had improved in other ways as well. His thumbs were longer in proportion to his hands, meaning that in addition to the "power grip" (the way you hold a hammer) which Australopithecus used to manipulate objects he could also employ the "precision grip" (the way you hold the nail) with a skill that Australopithecus probably could not. And his feet, pelvis, and hip joints had improved, so that in addition to trotting or shuffling about (which is how Australopithecus is thought to have moved) he could also walk with the long, swinging, heel-and-toe strides which, though slower than a trot, are unexcelled as a means of covering long distances with a minimum expenditure of energy.

But if "he" was a good walker, "she" was less so. Erectus's larger brain naturally meant a larger head, which of course had to squeeze through its mother's pelvis at birth. Evolution partially solved the

---

* Some Australopithecines were as large and robust as erectus, but for rather complicated reasons are generally considered to be side branches on man's family tree—great-aunts and uncles rather than great-grandparents.

difficulty by bringing the infant into the world with a relatively small and immature brain—in modern man, only 25 per cent of its adult size and in erectus probably not much more than that, as against an estimated 50 per cent in Australopithecus and 65 per cent in the chimp—but there was evidently a limit to how far that accommodation could go if the newborn infant was to have sufficient neurological equipment to survive. The only other solution was to broaden the female pelvis, and that is what happened. The result was the swelling hips and undulating gait we see in the modern woman, which are compromises between the demands of childbirth and the need for reasonably efficient locomotion. Unlike many compromises, they work pretty well most of the time, but not so well, in the locomotion department, as a man's legs and hips, which are uncompromisingly designed for walking and running.

The "pelvic compromise," taken together with the longer helpless period of the erectus infant—a consequence of the smaller, more immature brain it was born with—undoubtedly intensified the difference in life-styles between males and females. The males could range ever wider in search of game, and larger game; we know that erectus, though his main meat staples seem to have been such medium-sized animals as deer and horse, could and did kill rhinoceros and even elephant on occasion. Meanwhile the females remained at home—perhaps with a few older males as guards—tending their children, gathering nutritious nuts, roots, berries, and greens, and doubtless snaring or clubbing small game. "Home" was by this time a cave, when it was available and needed—as early as half a million years ago, erectus bands were living in caves near modern Peking; in warmer climates, it may have been merely a campsite surrounded by thorny branches, like a modern African kraal. As early as three hundred thousand years ago, some groups of erectus are thought to have built artificial shelters of branches and saplings near modern Nice on the French Riviera, though these seem to have been little more than windbreaks.

As I have already noted, erectus was a much more widespread creature than Australopithecus, who (apart from those ambiguous bones in Java) never seems to have moved out of Africa and certainly never out of the tropics. Erectus, by contrast, has turned up not only in Africa and Java but in Spain, southern France, Germany, Hungary, Syria, and two sites in China. Since winter temperatures in all these places are at best chilly, and in most of them outright cold, it is no surprise to find that erectus was the author of a really revolutionary invention: the controlled use of fire. The earliest known hearths (from France) date from perhaps three-quarters of a million years ago, and by half a million years ago fire was demonstrably being used in China and Hungary as well.

The geographical location of these early hearths argues quite persuasively that the original and main use of fire was to keep warm; in the tropics, the earliest hearths date from much later. But erectus was intelligent enough to devise other uses for this remarkable new tool. Charred bones in the Chinese caves and elsewhere show that he cooked his meat (and sometimes his fellows), thereby tenderizing it and partially breaking down its proteins, making them more nutritious to a creature whose teeth and digestive system had evolved to cope with a predominantly vegetarian diet. Of course erectus didn't know this, but the fact that he was unknowingly obtaining more nourishment per pound of meat, and expanding less energy in chewing it, nonetheless made his hunting more efficient. Fire also improved his hunting techniques in other ways. He learned to use it to harden the points of wooden spears (there is no evidence that he could make stone- or bone-tipped weapons) and also, it appears, as a way of driving game to a place where it could be conveniently killed. Excavations in central Spain have revealed what is thought to be the site of just such a drive, in which fires stampeded elephants into a swamp where, mired down, they could be dispatched with relative safety.

Like other and earlier weapons, fire could also be used for defense: to discourage predators from attacking the camp or cave. Although recent studies indicate that few if any animals have an instinctive fear of fire, it would not take many experiences with it—in the shape, say, of a burning branch thrust into the face of a hungry wolf or big cat—to implant a powerful learned fear of the flames, and of the two-legged creatures who wielded them.

Though erectus used fire in a variety of ways, there is no reason to think his technology had advanced to the point where he could make it at will. He must have depended on natural fires, set by lightning or (in a few places) by red-hot volcanic lava, and may well have used these natural fires a thousand times before he learned to carry them back to camp or cave and nourish them with sticks. Deposits of charcoal in the Chinese erectus caves reach a thickness of twenty-two feet, indicating that fires must have burned there for centuries.

Since erectus was now living in temperate climates with cold winters, he became increasingly dependent on hunting, at least in those regions. In the tropics, even in the dry season, there is usually some vegetation—roots or underground runners—that primates can consume; in China or Hungary there would be virtually no edible plant life for several months out of the year; even roots would be inaccessible when the ground froze. In those seasons, hunting would have been all that could keep the tribe from starving. On the evidence, erectus focused most of his efforts on herd animals such as red deer and horses, of which he could, with reasonable luck, kill several in a single hunt, as opposed to more solitary species which had to be sought out and killed one by one. But he clearly did not disdain such large, economy-size packages of protein as rhino and elephant.

In either case, he must have hunted systematically in groups; a herd of horses or an elephant are equally unpromising game for a single hunter. Even chimps do this in a very crude way; Goodall has described how different male chimps will "station themselves at the bases of trees offering escape routes to a cornered [monkey] victim." And group hunting is more efficient: studies of lions, for example, have shown that two of them hunting together will kill considerably more than they do hunting singly.

All of which adds up to the fact that the members of an erectus band were becoming far more dependent on one another than other primates, even including Australopithecus. Baboons, as we have seen, cooperate to avoid being eaten, but when it comes to eating it is every monkey for himself (or herself); the same is true of chimps, apart from the occasional sharing of meat described earlier. The social relationships of erectus were more complex. The females, kept to the vicinity of the home cave or camp by their helpless infants and limited walking speed, depended on the males to bring back meat from the hunt, which often must have taken place miles away from home. If the hunt was unsuccessful, the returning males would have depended on whatever plant foods and small game the females had rustled up in their absence, and would have relied on them at all times to literally keep the home fires burning. Women and men alike must also have begun relying on their fellows in injury or illness. In earlier models of protohuman society, this question did not arise, as it does not among today's monkeys and apes: a chimp that cannot feed itself will starve, and a baboon that, through injury, cannot keep up with the group will quickly be picked off by a predator. The existence of what prehistorians have called the "home base" meant that for the first time a sprained ankle or a fever need not be automatically fatal, as it would have been to erectus's ancestors.

The existence of these new forms of cooperation, no less than the improved technologies and techniques which erectus disposed of, almost certainly mean that these beetle-browed and still somewhat apelike creatures had already passed the threshold of true humanity: they could talk—not just communicate in the ways that other primates do, but speak to one another in some crude approximation of the way we do.

To understand this crucial step in human psychological and social evolution, we must now define the difference between primate communication (or animal communication generally) and human speech. It has been said that primates communicate only about their internal states, not about objects or actions in the outside world—messages along the lines of "I am angry" or "I am frightened" or "I am sexy." While there is a lot of truth in this, it is perhaps something of an oversimplification; some arboreal monkeys, for example, have different alarm calls for "danger from the air" (an eagle), "danger in the tree" (a snake), and "danger from the ground" (a leopard). A more useful way of defining the limitations of primate communication is to say that it deals *primarily* with the animals' internal states but *invariably* with the here and now, never the there and then. Of all the animals, only humans can communicate about the past or the future, or about objects or situations that are out of sight or hearing: to use the technical linguistic term, only human speech is capable of displacement. A no less important distinction is labeled "creativity." Human beings, that is, once they have learned a reasonable number of words and the rules for combining them—which occurs in the first few years of life—can put words together to produce new combinations *which they themselves have never heard,* and can, of course, understand similar, unfamiliar utterances. When Gelett Burgess remarked that "I never saw a purple cow, I never hope to see one," he was surely the first man in the world to make that observation; the rest of us routinely do the same thing, though our verbal creations for the most part deal with more mundane matters.

Over the years, a number of primatologists have attempted to teach chimpanzees to talk—since chimps, for obvious reasons, are the most promising primate students—but the animals learned no more than two or three words. The failure was chalked up to deficiencies in their brains, but this didn't explain very much, since little is known of the relationship between brain and speech even in humans. One basic problem, certainly, is that chimps have no propensity to imitate sounds as they frequently imitate the gestures and actions both of their fellows and of human trainers. But they turn out to have a quite remarkable capacity for dealing with visual symbols, as opposed to auditory symbols (i.e., words). A young chimp, Washoe, was taught to use one of the sign languages taught to deaf and dumb individuals, and in two years acquired a vocabulary of over thirty "words." Another, Sarah, was trained to use bits of cardboard of contrasting shapes and colors as symbols for some hundred and thirty different objects, colors, actions, and even grammatical concepts such as the "if-then" relationship between two ideas. She was then able to "understand" (i.e., respond appropriately to) simple sentences such as "Sarah take banana (if-then) Mary no give chocolate Sarah."

Two points are worth noting about Sarah's achievements. First, the symbols were "pure" symbols; none of them resembled the objects or ideas they symbolized. The symbol for "banana" looked nothing like a banana, and that for "red" was not red. Second, Sarah learned to deal with them *as* symbols. For example, she evidently developed a concept of "brown" quite apart from specific brown objects (such as chocolate, which she dearly loved), so that she could apply the correct symbol to a brown piece of cardboard, when asked the question "Color of?" (The interrogation sign was represented by another "concept" symbol.) Sarah's language—it is hard to think of any other term—thus involved something like displacement and also, since she could both understand simple unfamiliar combinations and construct new ones according to the rules she had learned, some degree of creativity.

The reason Sarah cannot speak (and never will) evidently has less to do with her brain than with her vocal apparatus. Philip Lieberman of the University of Connecticut has in fact made some detailed anatomic and computer studies of the sound-production apparatus of monkeys and apes, and finds them, as one would expect, much inferior to ours in terms of the variety of sounds they can produce.

The main problem seems to be with the tongue and the pharynx, the part of the respiratory tract lying above the larynx or voice box. In man, the pharynx is relatively deep, with the back surface of the tongue arching up to form its front wall, so that by moving the tongue the volume of the pharynx can be altered. These changes in the pharynx plus similar changes in the front part of the mouth (between the upper surface of the tongue and the palate) modify the sounds emanating from the voice box, to produce the different vowels. In monkeys and apes, by contrast, the tongue lies flat and cannot alter the volume of the pharynx, so that the number of different sounds the animals can produce is very limited. Since it *is* so limited, the animals have had no evolutionary incentive to learn to imitate sounds.

But granted that the chimp brain (though not its throat) has the capacity for speech, and that Homo erectus had a bigger and better brain than any chimp, how do we know that he had the necessary vocal apparatus? The answer is that we don't know—directly. But the activities he engaged in and the skills he acquired are of a kind that would have been impossible without speech of some sort. Organizing a drive of elephants, with or without the aid of fire, is not an activity that can be improvised on the spur of the moment (as is the case with hunting among chimps); it requires planning and an understanding of what the other man is going to do, at least on the level (to employ Sarah's language) of "I yell (if-then) you stand up wave arms." For that matter, fire itself requires some degree of planning and foresight; if you wait until your fire is down to smoldering embers before going out to pick up sticks, you'll be lucky if it isn't out altogether by the time you return with the fuel. And planning and foresight are one of the things that language is about. With the aid of its vocal symbols, which "stand for" objects and actions which may not be physically present, *we can think about these things when they are not present;* psychologists have long known that man characteristically thinks by means of silent ("subvocal") speech. With language, therefore, erectus could think about a fire going out while his actual fire was still blazing—and take steps to insure that it continued to blaze. He could make not just tools (which Australopithecus did), but tools to make tools, such as a notched blade of flint with which he could later round and smooth a wooden spear. And since erectus demonstrably did do these things, it follows he possessed speech of some sort.

But it was surely of a very crude sort. Lieberman has done some further studies in which he compares the pharynx of modern man, that of the modern newborn infant (which can produce only a very limited variety of sounds), and that of Neanderthal man, the latter reconstructed from casts of fossil skulls. The Neanderthals were, as we have noted, later than erectus, and in all respects more human; though they possessed apelike beetling brows and receding chins, their brains were as big as, or even bigger than, our own.* But their pharynxes, as Lieberman has reconstructed them, were at least as apelike as they were manlike—were, in fact, much like those of modern babies. They could not, for example, produce the vowel sounds of "boot," "beat," "boat," "bought," or "bah," though they could have managed "bit," "bet," "bat," "but," and "put." The implications Lieberman draws from these experiments are rather more complicated than I can follow, but what they seem to add up to is that the Neanderthals could not have communicated by sounds nearly as rapidly as we do—perhaps only a tenth as fast. And erectus would have been, if anything, worse off; he could speak, but just barely. And since silent speech, as we have noted, is the characteristic medium of human thought, it follows that he could think in the human sense, but just barely.

However, even this primitive level of speech and thought produced important, if very slow, changes in man's capacities, as we can see when we compare erectus with his Neanderthal descendants. The latter's tools were better, as well as more varied, than those of erectus, and now included not merely tools to make tools but "compound" tools such as spears composed of a sharp stone point lashed to a wooden shaft. Either the Neanderthals or their immediate ancestors also discovered a remarkably sophisticated tool-making technique— the so-called Levallois method. To make an Australopithecine chopper, or an erectus "hand axe," one need only secure an appropriate piece of stone and bang or chip away at it until it is the right shape. There is a certain amount of skill involved, but it is a skill constantly guided by the emerging shape of the tool. A Levallois point, by contrast, is produced by carefully chipping a lump of flint into a shape which looks nothing at all like a spear point. Then, by tapping the

---

* However, the not uncommon remark that "if a Neanderthal man were dressed in modern clothes, you wouldn't notice him on a bus" is perhaps an overstatement. At least one anthropologist has declared that personally he'd get off the bus!

"prepared core" gently at the proper place, a perfect point suddenly leaps from the unpromising-looking lump. What is involved is not simply skill but a certain power of imagination—the ability to "see" the point before it is even crudely in evidence, as sculptors can "see" a shape in a piece of stone which to the rest of us is just a boulder.

The Neanderthalers are believed to have made clothing of skins laced together, as contrasted with the simple belted hide or fur blankets which were the best erectus could do. They not only lived in caves, but apparently built sapling-and-hide tents inside them, carefully faced away from the entrance to minimize drafts. With the aid of these and other inventions they were able to survive not only in tropical and temperate climates, but in semipolar ones—Europe during the first stage of the last Ice Age, northern China, and southern Russia—in all of which winters must have been bitter and often long as well.

As language, and the thinking it made possible, became increasingly vital to human survival, it seems very likely that man must have acquired some sort of built-in incentive to learn this crucial skill. And in fact modern men and women appear to enjoy talking for its own sake, not simply as a device for planning or organizing their activities; they notoriously spend a good deal of time talking even when there is nothing much to talk about. Children, too, seem to enjoy learning to talk, and once they have acquired the essentials of speech begin to play games with words—combining them in nonsensical ways, twisting them into puns and riddles—in very much the same way that all young primates play games involving more physical skills or the young chimp plays at building a nest.

The growth of language, and of the psychological payoff involved in using it in new ways, must have opened up another dimension in the human mind. Once one has learned to use words—names—to think and talk about things that are not physically present ("displacement") one can begin using them to talk about things that have *never* been physically present, which exist only in dreams or the imagination: ghosts, spirits, and a life after death. Indeed, the very naming of some absent or imagined thing can magically make it real. Even today we employ all sorts of verbal evasions to avoid such words as "cancer" or "death" ("a growth, "passed away"), as if by not naming them we could thrust them further off, and to "speak of the devil" is to invite his infernal presence.

Already by Neanderthal times man's imagination had expanded to the point where people buried their dead, equipping the deceased with the food and weapons he would need in some future life that no one has ever seen but that everyone could imagine. They engaged in rituals, such as piling caches of cave-bear skulls in a "box" made of natural slabs of stone. What these rituals meant, and what they were supposed to accomplish, are beyond our knowledge, but there seems no doubt that they were magic of some sort.

We should also note, however, that if the development of language opened up new possibilities for human societies, it may also have opened up at least one ominous new problem for them: how does one human being recognize another? A chimp recognizes another of its species as a chimp (rather than, say, a baboon) because the animal looks like a chimp, and perhaps because it smells like one; Australopithecus doubtless recognized his fellows in the same way. But as our ancestors became capable of speech, it seems likely that their operational "definition" of a man expanded to include not just looking and smelling like a man, but talking like one. Which is to say, talking *intelligibly* rather than making the strange-sounding noises that "foreigners" are prone to utter. As Jim remarked to Huckleberry Finn, "If a Frenchman is a man, how come he don't *talk* like a man?"

Everything we know about the history of language makes clear that it changes over time, automatically. And when two groups of people speaking the same language become physically separated from one another, it can take no more than a few centuries before their tongues become mutually unintelligible, as when the Latin-speaking inhabitants of the Roman Empire developed into speakers of French, Italian, Spanish and so on as the empire disintegrated and regular contact between its various regions ceased. We can hardly doubt that the same principle operated in linguistic prehistory as well, meaning that widely separated groups of erectus, as and when their wanderings brought them into renewed contact, would have found themselves unable to communicate—and thus might have regarded one another as something other than, or less than, human. Thus even as language created a new potential for human cooperation, it also engendered one for human conflict; the legend of the Tower of Babel is evidently much more than a myth.

The growing elaboration and complexity of human cultures we have just been describing implies several very important changes in human society. First, man, even more than other primates, now survived or perished as part of a group. Dependent on his fellows, male and female—and they on him—as adults as well as in childhood, and engaged in cooperative activities not merely in emergencies (as was the case with Australopithecus) but routinely, whenever he hunted large or gregarious game, his individual capabilities, large or small, would be far less vital than the capabilities of his band or tribe. In confronting a wounded mammoth, a hunter's personal strength and skill, be they ever so great, could be of little weight compared with the collective skills of the hunting group, including most especially their ability to cooperate with and rely on one another.

These considerations were perhaps less central to the lives of the tribe's women, many of whose activities—child care and food gathering—were still carried out individually, though for the benefit of the group as a whole. Tiger and Fox have erected around this contrast a theory which as near as I can make out—their statement of it is less precise than it might be—holds that men have evolved some special tendency to "bond" with one another, which women possess to a lesser degree if at all.

Given the rather vague way in which the theory is stated, it is hard to criticize in detail, but one can at any rate point out that it involves a quite unnecessary assumption about human nature. Primates, after all, have been "bonding" in a rudimentary way ever since they began to live in groups—that is, for tens of millions of years. Female primates have been forming at least temporary emotional bonds with their young for almost as long—and on the evidence, were doing so millions of years before the *males* got around to becoming emotionally involved with infants (remember the indifferent langur male as contrasted with the solicitous female). If the chimpanzee is any guide, the formation of *long-term* bonds between parent and child must once have been a female monopoly, as it still is among chimps. And at some period in prehistory (probably in the time of erectus) females and males clearly began forming long-term bonds for sex, child raising, and companionship, since we find such arrangements, in one form or another, to be universal in modern human societies. Given all this bonding—the development of special relationships with a special emotional quality—between females and children and females and males, there seems no need to conjure up some special emotional capacity to explain the formation of bonds between male and male.

To be sure, in most modern societies, both primitive and otherwise, men do in fact tend to bond more than women; the phenomenon has been described in groups of hunters (for example, among the Eskimo and the former Plains Indians), athletic teams, and military squads or sections. Tiger himself has made much of the widespread existence of special male clubs or secret societies in a great variety of cultures —often including rituals that supposedly serve to strengthen bonds among the members—whose counterparts are rarely found among females. But all these facts, it seems to me, can be quite adequately explained by noting that most human activities which involve functioning as a group are also predominantly male activities, and for reasons having nothing to do with male bonding tendencies. Large-scale hunting is a male activity, and always has been, because males were and are anatomically better equipped to pursue game and to throw rocks or spears at it (and probably also, as noted in Chapter 6, because the vigorous and exciting physical activities involved are more congenial to the male temperament). Warfare, defensive or offensive, has always been a male activity for reasons too obvious to mention; so, for rather similar reasons, are most team sports in which strength or speed are important.

Moreover, when bonding develops among men engaged in these activities, it doesn't happen just like that; it grows. The mutual trust and concern, the capacity to sense and respond to the group's needs almost without words which we find in a smoothly working fishing-boat crew, athletic team, or combat infantry squad, develop only as the men who compose them work or play or fight together over months. Oddly enough, the same sort of wordless communication also develops over the months and years between many husbands and wives.

By contrast, when we examine the traditional activities of women— caring for infants, gathering plant foods, preparing food, and so on (traditional in the sense that they are "woman's work" in most modern societies, and *all* primitive ones)—we find that they are, *and in most cases must be,* done by individuals. A team of hunters attacking a herd of deer is demonstrably more efficient than the same number of men acting independently, but a group of women attempting to dig up the same root makes for less efficiency, not more; the same can be said for two or more women trying to feed or bathe one baby. And the observation that too many cooks spoil the dinner must surely date from shortly after the invention of cooking. Women often work *in* groups—from Hopi women grinding corn on their metates, to the accompaniment of song and gossip, to small-town Americans in the Ladies' Aid Sewing Circle—but they seldom have had occasion to work *as* groups.

In modern urbanized societies, of course, they do increasingly work in this way, running PTAs, organizing church suppers, or (as did my wife and her friends) carrying on a weekly vigil for peace over the seven bitter years from 1966 to 1973. And I know of no evidence whatever that in such situations they operate less efficiently, or with less "team spirit," than do groups of men, "male bonding" and all.* Indeed, if the capacity for teamwork reflects some special innate male quality, as Tiger appears to believe, it is hard to see why his male secret societies should have to work so hard at fostering it. In short, the male team—at work, at play, or at war—does not work smoothly together because it bonds together; it bonds together because it works together. So does the female team—at work, at play, or at peace.

What *can* be said about the growth of human cooperation and interdependence among Homo erectus and his descendants is that any evolutionary changes it wrought in the human psyche (that is, by giving certain types of personality a better chance of survival) would necessarily have been in the direction of more sociability and "bonding" in *both* sexes. If the men still enjoyed vigorous and exciting physical pursuits, perhaps even deriving a special kick if these were spiced with danger—as primate males had long done and men still do—any innate tendency for this enjoyment to express itself in domination of man by man, comparable to the domination scuffles of male grassland baboons, would have been weakened by the stern necessities of survival. An erectus or Neanderthal band whose males esteemed and trusted one another would have survived; one whose males habitually feared or intimidated one another would not. Human society was becoming, if anything, more equalitarian—and the male temperament was perhaps growing, if you like, more "feminine." As has been said by a distinguished prehistorian whose name now escapes me, the first animal domesticated by man was—himself.

The term "Neanderthal" is sometimes applied today to extreme conservatives by their liberal opponents, and though I approve the

* From my own observation, the same can be said of teams including *both* sexes, such as those working together on a magazine.

sentiment, the term itself is unfair to Neanderthals; the hard-nosed "rugged individualist" beloved of the conservative mind would not have lasted a week in a Neanderthal band. For these primitive men, slow-talking and slow-thinking though they may have been, the question was not "What can the government do for me?" (there was no government) or "What can I do for myself?" but "What can we do for one another?"

Another important implication of the increasingly elaborate human cultures (including language) is that there was much more to be learned. We can pretty safely guess, therefore, that this period saw the growth of new and more efficient forms of learning, in addition to the imitation, empathetic learning, and simple trial and error which man's ancestors had long employed.

The first of these has been called "insight learning." I first observed this phenomenon when my daughter Amanda was about eighteen months old. We were sitting on the sofa one day doing something or other when she, being a normal, manipulative young primate, picked a cigarette butt out of an ashtray, examined it, and then threw it on the floor. I of course said "No!" and returned the butt to the ashtray. Amanda then picked up the butt again, held it on the floor, and looked up at me with an expression that I had learned meant approximately "What are you going to do about it?" What I did was to say "No!" again—in the tone that Amanda had long known carried a strong undercurrent of "or else!" She was in a dilemma. To drop the butt on the floor the second time would, she knew, involve painful consequences, yet she was clearly reluctant to put it back in the ashtray (for reasons of pride, I suspect, but I can't prove this). She pondered for a moment—you could practically see the wheels going round—then lowered herself to the floor, trotted across the room to a wastebasket, and dropped the butt in it.

This was an action—actually, a series of actions—she had never done before, and had never seen done; one does not, after all, drop individual cigarette butts into a wastebasket. There was no conceivable way in which she could have learned to do it, by imitation, reinforcement, or whatever; she figured it out for herself. It was at about then that I began wondering whether behaviorist learning theory, which up to then had seemed to me pretty reasonable, really covered the facts. And the more I observed Amanda—and later her younger brother, Sam—the less credible the "atomic" theory of learning looked.

Subsequently, I learned that insight learning had been described in chimpanzees as long ago as World War I. The great German psychologist Wolfgang Köhler, finding himself interned as an enemy alien on the island of Tenerife in the Canaries, occupied his time by studying a colony of captive chimps established there. His subsequent account credited them with the ability to use insight to solve such problems as using a stick to get a piece of fruit outside the cage, stacking several boxes into a tower in order to reach a bunch of bananas, and so on. At about the same time, the great American primatologist, Robert M. Yerkes, for whom the Yerkes Laboratory is named, was reporting similar findings.

In the decades that followed, there was much dispute over just what Köhler had observed, and whether it indeed showed "insight." Eventually, however, careful experiments by psychologists such as the late Herbert Birch established that chimps were indeed capable of insightful behavior. This is generally described as an action that is (a) new, (b) "smooth" and continuous—i.e., with no preliminary fumbling around, (c) sudden, and (d) purposeful—i.e., directed toward some identifiable goal. Since all these criteria except perhaps the last could apply to actions imitated from another animal, we should perhaps add a fifth condition: the action must be one that the animal has never seen.*

The last qualification makes insight almost impossible to demonstrate unequivocally in wild chimps, since one can never be quite sure what the animal has or has not seen. Nonetheless, Mike's employment of kerosene tins as a new tool for establishing dominance, from Goodall's account, bears all the earmarks of insight; his chances of seeing it done previously seem virtually nil.

So far as I know, nobody in or out of the psychological profession has any but the most nebulous notions of how insight works. In part it seems to involve a shift in perception, whereby familiar objects or ideas are suddenly seen in a new relationship. Thus Mike was familiar with kerosene tins as a source of noise, and also with noisy displays

---

* The reader will note that all these criteria apply to Amanda's performance with the cigarette butt.

by his male fellows as a way of establishing dominance; his insight could have amounted to somehow establishing the mental connection tins-noise-dominance—and acting on it. But how such perceptual shifts take place—if they do—and why they occur in some animals and not in others are still mysterious; they will probably remain so until we learn a great deal more about the actual working of the brain.

Whatever its mechanisms, insight is an everyday reality of human experience. It is the bulb lighting up over the head of a comic-strip character, the feeling of "Aha!" that all of us have experienced when a tricky problem suddenly yields its solution. It is also the reason why man is unlikely to be soon replaced by the computer. A computer can learn after a fashion; it can be taught to do the equivalent of adding two and two (the actual numbers are of course much greater and the mathematical operations far more complicated); it can even "grasp" if-then relationships ("If A is greater than B, add C to D; if A is equal to or less than B, subtract D from E"). But it takes a man to combine two and two and two and two and realize that they add up to the animals marching into the ark. A computer, that is, can "perceive" those relationships that are programmed into it, but it takes a human being to program the computer—because only our brain has the insight to perceive the relationships in the first place.

The second new form of learning, unlike insight, is so far as I know a wholly human trait, with no parallels whatever even in our chimp cousins: the deliberate use of pleasure (or "positive reinforcement") as a teaching tool. Chimps, as well as baboons and langurs, use negative reinforcement to alter the behavior of their young—threats, grimaces, or cuffs to make the youngster stop doing something that annoys its elders, or that threatens to endanger it or to hurt a still younger animal. But they never employ positive reinforcement to get the youngster to do something, or to continue doing it. As we have seen, chimps learn a great deal, but they do not, except in a very limited and negative sense, teach. Our own species, by contrast, employs positive reinforcement routinely, from the simple pat on the head to the piece of candy promised "if you're a good boy." (It generally *is* a boy; girls seem to require less reinforcement in that direction.)

Nor does it stop at childhood; remove from our society such reinforcing "contingencies" as money, praise, and back-slapping and things would grind to a halt. Not long ago, I read an article by an industrial manager who enthusiastically reported his experience with B. F. Skinner's "behavioral engineering"—the systematic reinforcement techniques that Skinner and his disciples have been touting as a solution to social problems. Translated out of its professional gobbledygook, the article amounted to the statement that if you praise people when they've done a good job, you get more and better work out of them—a useful discovery, no doubt, but hardly an original one. We must, I suppose, be grateful to Skinner for supplying a "scientific" rationale that permitted this man to accept a principle which common sense—not to speak of simple humanity—should have taught him long before. One wonders what life was like in that factory before management discovered positive reinforcement!

We do not know, and probably never will, when men, or proto-men, began teaching their children, and each other, by this simple and effective technique. It seems not unlikely, however, that an early ingredient of even the primitive language of erectus was the command (or request) "Do this!"—and that when the individual in question did what was asked, some gesture of affection was a not uncommon sequel. Indeed, if Sarah could learn to act on such injunctions as "Sarah pick red color (if-then) Mary give Sarah chocolate" by picking the red carboard—and getting the chocolate—then similar verbal injunctions would very probably have become incorporated into erectus's crude language. But whenever it occurred, it was unquestionably an invaluable addition to man's repertoire of techniques for dealing with his fellows. Skinner's experiments have shown very clearly that "positive reinforcement" produces quicker and more efficient learning than "negative reinforcement" if what you are after is getting the animal to do something rather than refrain from doing something; in teaching children (and adults) new skills, praise is better than punishment. To be sure, his findings apply only to the very simple-minded varieties of learning which he has studied, but there seems every reason to believe that they are relevant to the other, more complex forms of learning we have been discussing. Parents, teachers, and industrial managers, please copy!

There is one more broad question we must ask about erectus and his descendants before we get on with some detailed specifics of their psychological evolution: were they—and are we—"territorial animals"? To Robert Ardrey and some others, of course, the answer is a loud and ringing "Yes!"; indeed Ardrey's book, *The Territorial*

Imperative, gave a new phrase to the English language. Regrettably, however, his discussion, when not simply confusing, is largely misleading.

Ardrey defines his imperative as "an inherent drive to gain and defend an exclusive property," and if we understand "property" in the sense of "real estate" (as against, say, stocks and bonds) the definition is a good one. Many animals do seem to possess just such an inherent drive—most notably the birds, among which it was first described and has been most extensively studied. During the nesting season, the males of many bird species stake out a particular patch of woodland or meadow from which they then drive away other males of their species. Moreover, their behavior seems to be essentially instinctive rather than learned, though as we noted much earlier, the same could be said of most bird behavior, due to the small size of the avian brain. The evolutionary function of this instinct seems to be to guarantee each male-female pair a foraging space containing sufficient food to nourish them and their nestlings; males who for one reason or another fail to establish a territory seldom if ever succeed in mating. And once the nestlings are grown, the imperative disappears, and birds of a feather begin flocking together. The extinct passenger pigeon migrated in flocks estimated at up to a billion birds, and even today such pests as the starling form aggregations of fifty thousand or more which show no regard for territorial boundaries, bird or human.

When we turn to our own zoological class, the mammals, territorial behavior turns out to be considerably less common, even during the breeding season. Many mammals are certainly territorial—though how much part instinct plays in it is arguable—but many are not. And among the latter are our chimpanzee cousins, whose bands range through their forest habitat without regard to "strangers"; if two groups of chimps meet the result may be casual indifference or friendly, sometimes excited, sociability—but never has a chimp band been seen to drive another band away from, say, its "own" grove of wild figs. The territorial drive is no more pressing among gorillas, our closest living relatives next to the chimps.

If territorialism is not imperative among our anatomic relatives, the great apes, what about our ecological relatives, the grassland baboons? These monkeys are certainly territorial in the sense that a particular band restricts itself to a particular stretch of country, but the reasons have little if anything to do with an inherent drive to defend it. As described by Irven DeVore, the motivating force is rather group tradition: the fact that they are intimately familiar with the few square miles of their home range, knowing "the best feeding places, the safest sleeping sites, the most dependable sources of water." As the group moves toward the boundaries of the familiar, "its members become progressively more tense, and beyond those limits, they never venture." Psychologist K. R. L. Hall and a coworker once tried to drive a group of baboons out of its range, says DeVore, "only to find that when the monkeys reached the boundary they turned and ran back, right past the two people who were driving them." There were no territorial defenders at the boundary forcing them to turn back—if anything, the force was in the other direction—yet turn back they did, because they found the unfamiliar too daunting.

Man is unquestionably a territorial animal in this sense: though we range far more widely than any other primate—occasionally even as far as the moon—nearly all of us are still most at ease in the community or neighborhood or stretch of country we know from long acquaintance. For man as for the baboon, there's no place like home. Like all primates, we are exploratory and curious, deriving stimulation and pleasure from new experiences often merely because they *are* new. But the new, because it is new, is necessarily unpredictable, and too much uncertainty in life places a strain on man or monkey; we find new experiences most acceptable when they are displayed against a background of the old familiar faces and places.

But this is a long way from saying that we therefore possess Ardrey's innate compulsion to exclude others from our home turf. Chimps don't do it nor, indeed, do baboons; bands of baboons with adjacent ranges (whose boundaries not infrequently overlap) appear to get along mainly through mutual avoidance, on the principal of "you stay on your side of the street and I'll stay on mine." And even the avoidance is far from absolute; according to DeVore, "two or more groups . . . will often come together to feed out of the same fruiting tree or to drink from the same water hole."

Even Ardrey concedes, indeed, that our primate relatives provide meager evidence for any human territorial imperative. Its genesis, he believes, dates rather from the period when man became a "predator" (a term whose ambiguities we have already noted), during which a predatory tendency to intrude on the territories of others, and to defend one's own, became grafted onto the older primate live-and-let-live biophilosophy. But when we examine the actual behavior of nonhuman predators, the evidence for this view turns out to be very thin. Wolves, for example, sometimes establish territories, but their response toward outsiders, as Ardrey himself describes it, has far more in common with the mutual avoidance and live-and-let-live attitudes of the baboon than with human aggression and defense at national borders: "Sniffing, nose rubbing, and tail wagging denoting friendly intentions are dutifully, even ceremoniously, exchanged. And the visitors in all hospitality are issued their visas." Nor do all wolf packs display even this pacific version of the territorial imperative; the difference seems to depend mainly on the food animals they prey on. Where the animals are resident in a given area—moose or deer— the wolves are resident, and territorial. Where the animals are migratory caribou, however, the wolves follow the herds, and of course are not territorial, since their territory is constantly changing.

Many of the same observations have been made of African predators, whose behavior has been summed up by George B. Schaller and Gordon R. Lowther with particular relevance to the probable behavior of early man. Of the six predators they surveyed, two—the cheetah and the wild dog—were definitely not territorial; for what it is worth, these are also the two species which regularly hunt by day rather than at twilight or at night, which was doubtless true of the early human hunters, as it is of most hunting peoples today. Of the remaining four animals, only one—the jackal—was unambiguously territorial in the Ardreyan sense. Leopards were found to be "probably" territorial, but only as regards the males, while lions and spotted hyenas resembled the wolf, being sometimes territorial and sometimes not, depending primarily on whether their prey was resident or migratory.

Schaller and Lowther's conclusion on the probable behavior of early human predators is worth quoting at length, since it injects some invaluable common sense into an area that has inspired much uncommon, if eloquent, nonsense: "If the early hominids relied predominantly on hunting for subsistence, they obviously had a choice of systems open to them. They could be resident, either territorial or nonterritorial. . . . Or they could be migratory, following the herds as the wild dogs do. Or they could be resident for part of the time and nomadic for the rest, depending on the season. We believe that all these systems were used, *that each species and population within a species adapted itself to local circumstances* just as the wolf and lion do" (my emphasis). Man, the most adaptable of animals, was no less adaptable in this sphere, and his very adaptability tells us that his hunting behavior could not have been heavily constrained by biological imperatives, territorial or otherwise. Man on occasion may act as a territorial animal—but there is nothing very imperative about it.

Man's long career as a predator, in short, does not seem to have begotten any very significant changes in his nature as regards either its aggressive impulses (as we noted in the previous chapter) or its territorial ones; we cannot seriously consider it as the evolutionary equivalent of original sin, as Ardrey often seems to do. We shall see in the next chapter that the hunting way of life did modify man's innate propensities in some important ways, but not those usually cited.

We should also be aware that if hunting was important in the life and evolution of primitive man, it was seldom all-important. Feminist writers in particular have quite reasonably complained that prehistorians' lengthy discussions of "man the hunter" ignores half the human race—"woman the gatherer." We can go further and point out that, judging from contemporary hunting-gathering peoples, primitive humans seldom subsisted even primarily on game. For these modern tribes, hunting typically supplies something like a third of the diet, the remainder consisting of plant foods plus, in some places, molluscs and/or fish. The exceptions, as we would expect, are those peoples living in climates that make plants a scanty and unreliable food source, the Eskimos being the extreme case. For prehistory, a similar exception would be regions just south of the great ice sheets, though the climate of Ice Age Europe was less severe than that of today's Eskimo country along the Arctic coast. At other times and places, by contrast, there is every reason to think that woman-the-gatherer contributed at least as much to the family dinner table as her hunting mate. Primitive man was undoubtedly a hunter, but he—and especially she—was doing a lot of other things as well.

9

THE GIFT RELATIONSHIP: Evolution and Altruism

"It is more blessed to give than to receive."
   —ACTS, 20:35

"Not as a ladder from earth to heaven,
Not as an altar to any creed,
But simple service, freely given
To their own kind in their common need."
     —KIPLING, The Sons of Martha

"In any society it is in the nature of the gift, in the end,
to be its own reward."
     —MARCEL MAUSS, The Gift

In science, as in most other areas of human activity, wisdom begins with asking the right questions: as we have noted several times already in this book, asking a silly question reliably begets a silly answer. To be sure, asking a sensible question does not guarantee a sensible answer, or indeed any answer at all, since the facts needed for an answer may not be available. Nonetheless, without the question, the chance of the answer making sense is small. The whole edifice of Newtonian physics (which, though it has been superseded in certain areas by Einstein's discoveries, remains the foundation of modern physics and mechanics) resulted in part from Newton's realization that the key question to ask about moving bodies was not "Why do they move?" but "Why do they stop?"

As we saw in the last chapter, the question "Why is man a killer?" is a silly question, since man—considered in terms of his actual behavior—is typically *not* a killer. A far more sensible question, though it has escaped the attention of the biotheologians, is "Why is man an altruist?" We feed and clothe our children, bandage their hurts, soothe their fears—and this despite the fact that even the best-behaved kids can at times be little monsters. If a friend goes broke for reasons beyond his control, we are more likely than not to offer a loan if we can spare the cash. If a woman is disabled by injury or illness, her relatives and neighbors turn out to lend a hand with the kids and household chores. If a blind man asks help in negotiating a busy intersection, he is not often disappointed. And beyond these direct and personal services to our fellows, millions of us contribute tens of millions each year to help people we have never seen and almost certainly never will—starving Bengalis, earthquake-shocked Nicaraguans, hurricane refugees along our own southern coasts. And we do all these things for other members of our species far, far oftener than we kill (or even injure) them.

I am not, to be sure, claiming that we do not sometimes perform generous acts under social compulsion, as some of us kill under compulsion, still less that all of us are generous all the time. Yet it seems incontestable that nearly all of us do act generously at least some of the time. In fact it can be argued—and I shall so argue—that without this pervasive web of mutual help and concern no human society, past or present, could long endure, and that for this reason if no other we must seek the roots of altruism among the built-in incentives which evolution has implanted in us.

Altruism, like the use of positive reinforcement as a teaching tool, and unlike most of the other traits we have been discussing hitherto, is a peculiarly human kind of behavior. The other primates, as we have seen, gather food, mate, squabble among themselves, engage in mutual back-scratching, and band together for mutual defense, even as we do. But almost none of them *give* to their adult fellows, as most of us do fairly regularly, whether in the form of material assistance or of psychological aid and comfort. Nonetheless, we find the beginnings of altruism far back in our family tree, in the shape of the primate mother's concern for her infant.

As we saw in Chapter 5, this concern, which exists to some extent among all mammals, is powerful and universal among primates, as a necessary consequence of the prolonged helplessness of the primate infant. To the degree that a young animal is unable to meet its own needs—and in the young primate that degree is at the beginning almost total—some adult animal must be motivated to meet those needs. The langur female, as Phyllis Jay describes her, is clearly so motivated; we saw how even when the baby is quietly resting "she grooms and strokes it softly," and how, when one of a group of female langurs is holding a baby, "at the first sign of discomfort" another female will reach for it. From evidence of this sort we credited the femal langur with an unlearned, built-in capacity to sense the needs of another creature, and an equally built-in desire to satisfy those needs—and that is, in essence, what altruism is about. As we also noted, given the increasingly prolonged period of infant helplessness as we move up the primate family tree, there is every reason to think that these innate propensities have persisted in our own evolutionary line, up to and including the females of our own species.

In the same chapter and the following one we noted the capacity of the baboon male—in sharp contrast with the langur male—to become physically and emotionally involved with the group's infants, a trait stemming, according to Irven DeVore, from the male's role as a group defender who may have to take risks to defend the infants in question. The aggressive activities of these male baboons have been repeatedly portrayed as the prototypes of human violence, oppression, and war—and so, in a very remote sense, they may be. What has somehow escaped the attention of most commentators on human evolution is that they are much more certainly the prototypes of other human activities generally considered rather more admirable: defense of the weak, and self-sacrifice. The dominant baboon male moving out ahead of the band to confront a predator, while the females and young draw back, may not be able to verbalize the principle of "women and children first," but he is acting on it. Indeed, one need not be overimaginative, I think, to see in these hairy cousins of ours, prepared to defend their band at the risk of their own lives, a foreshadowing of those tribal kings in the ancient Mediterranean world whose duty, in dire emergency, was to sacrifice themselves ritually for their people, or even of that King of the Jews who, many believe, gave His life that mankind might live eternally. Greater love hath no man—or baboon.

One can, to be sure, argue that the male baboon does not *know* he is risking his life, and doubtless he doesn't. But his whole mien and posture show at the very least his awareness that he is confronting danger, a danger that under other circumstances he would flee from. The fact that the many men throughout history and prehistory who have emulated the male baboon were, thanks to their greater intelligence and imagination, far more clearly aware of the risks they were running, yet ran it anyway, is less a slur on the baboon than a compliment to our own species.

We saw how in the chimp the female's concern for her offspring can persist into adolescence and even adult life, so that if her half-grown son is attacked by an older male she may come to his aid, or at least make threatening noises if she dares not confront the attacker directly. Male chimps, too, though they seem less involved with their juniors than do the females, certainly show a certain capacity to sense the needs of adolescents and respond to them. Goodall several times observed male adolescents, frightened by the presence of a mature male, being reassured by a pat from the older animal. The same sort of reassurance also shows up in relationships between adults, as indeed it does in our own species.

Precisely why behavior of this sort evolved among chimps is not easy to figure out. In part it is doubtless connected with the much slower growth of the young chimp, which makes maternal protection necessary for a longer period than in either the langur or the baboon. But this can hardly be the whole explanation, since the special mother-child bond persists well beyond the time when it could play any significant role in the child's survival. Goodall has described the extraordinary case of a female, Flo, and her grown son, Flint, who were, it appears, unusually close. When Flo died—probably of old age—Flint showed signs of acute distress and depression and within a few weeks died himself, apparently of what in man would be called a broken heart; at any rate, an autopsy failed to reveal any other cause of death.

An additional reason for mutual concern among chimps may be simply that they are more intelligent, and therefore more complex, creatures than any monkey, capable of much more varied interactions with their fellows. Among other indications of this is their enlarged vocabulary of communicative noises, gestures, and grimaces, implying that they have more different things to "say" to one another—and, by the same token, more to understand. It seems not unlikely that, given an animal of this complexity, an enhanced sensitivity to the actions and moods of other members of the group may be a necessity if conflict within the group is not to reach disruptive levels.

But there is, I suspect, yet another and perhaps even more important evolutionary reason for the chimpanzee's capacity for empathy, having to do with the animal's capacity for empathetic learning. In imitation learning pure and simple—a process that is especially common among the primates—the animal does something simply because it has seen another animal do it, and continues to perform the action because the results are reinforcing. Examples are the young monkey or ape eating a plant that it sees its mother eat, and continuing to eat it because the plant tastes good or satisfies its hunger, or the young male chimp copulating because it has seen others copulate, and continuing to do so for obvious reasons.

Empathetic learning is what we saw in Darby and Riopelle's monkeys and John's and Chesler's cats, described in Chapter 3. Here the animal may eventually imitate, or at least parallel, the action of another animal, but often performs a quite different action; Darby and Riopelle found that their observer monkeys seemed if anything to learn most rapidly from the other animal's mistakes—that is, they then chose the (rewarded) object which the other had *not* chosen. Even more important, the learning, as we noted, did not involve reinforcement in any traditional sense, since the animals clearly learned a good deal without performing any action that *could* be reinforced. What seems to have happened in these experiments was that the observer animals were deriving some form of satisfaction (or dissatisfaction) simply from watching another animal being reinforced, were able to form a mental connection between their own satisfaction and the other animal's actions, and then themselves perform an action which would yield the same satisfaction. They were, in short, learning from the other animal simply by observing it, and, by observing, sharing its emotions.

Empathy in its simplest and crudest form must have originated far back on the mammalian family tree. The ability to "sound the alarm" which we find in all primates and many other mammals certainly involves the communication of an emotion—alarm or fear—from one animal to another. Less certainly, but very plausibly, something of the sort may be involved in the maternal behavior of primate and other mammalian females: the mother senses the alarm or distress of her infant, becomes distressed herself, and alleviates her own distress by alleviating the infant's. At the beginning, no doubt, empathy operated only in one (or both) of these specific and limited areas, but it evidently expanded and grew, first into the basis of a new way of learning and eventually (in the chimp and probably some other primates) into a means of enhancing group solidarity. The history of life is full of instances where anatomic structures evolved for one purpose ultimately turned out to serve quite different purposes. Those fearsome offensive weapons, the lion's claws, got their start as the protective scales of some primitive fish; the delicate bones that amplify sounds within our middle ear were once part of the jaw structure of an ancestral reptile. And we saw in Chapter 4 how the primate eye, brain, and grasping hand, evolved to meet the specific necessities of life in the trees, turned out to be no less useful for life on the ground. If anatomic features can prove so protean, psychologic ones can hardly be less so.

The chimp's relatively high capacity for empathy, then, would represent a sort of by-product from its obvious high capacity for learning—specifically, for empathetic learning. And we can with reasonable confidence ascribe at least the same degree of empathy, and of altruistic behavior based on it, to our Australopithecine ancestors of some five million years back. The females would be much involved in ministering to the needs of their infants and younger children, but would retain close ties of mutual aid and affection with their grown sons and daughters. The adult males would also have concerned themselves with the needs of the young, at least by romping and playing with them. In addition, however, they must—given their grassland habitat—have evolved a considerable capacity for what much later men would call self-sacrifice, fighting against predators to defend their females and young—if need be, to the death. And both males and females doubtless made considerable use of the little reassurances and gestures of affection that are still the lubricant of life among their descendants.

But all this, while impressive enough for five million years ago, is still a long way from the systematic and continued mutual aid, comfort, and concern which we see today within human groups, and often enough even among different groups. These ancestors of ours doubtless possessed the altruistic capacities of chimps—but chimps, as Goodall remarks, "usually show a lack of consideration for each other's feelings which in some ways may represent the deepest part of the gulf between them and us."

What bridged that gulf (as I have already intimated) was hunting. Far from turning our ancestors into cold-blooded killers, as the bio-theologians allege, a life-style based on meat eating much more probably speeded their conversion into altruists.

This would have come about in two ways. First, our ancestors perhaps as early as Australopithecine times and certainly by the time of Homo erectus were hunting cooperatively, in groups; as we have seen, even chimps occasionally do this. There can be no doubt that group hunting survived as a cultural trait because, as noted earlier, it is more efficient. But Australopithecus, or even erectus, can hardly have had any conception of efficiency, or much (if any) capacity to rationally compare the results of different techniques. Efficiency, in short, can explain why group hunting survived, but not how it developed in the first place. Very probably it developed, like so many other forms of human behavior, because it involved a direct psychological payoff to its practitioners: all members of the group must have been able to share in the rewards of their joint activities.

We can see how this could have come about from reports on hunting among baboons and chimps, both of which hunt, though neither depends on meat for any substantial portion of its diet. Baboons are strictly individual hunters, with each animal pursuing its own chosen prey. The payoff is equally individual: each animal consumes what it catches—if some higher-ranking animal doesn't grab it. Chimps, however, hunting cooperatively, enjoy a no less cooperative payoff. According to Geza Teleki, an associate of Goodall's, as soon as the prey has been seized all the chimps within reach "are free to grab a part of the carcass without risk of retaliation from the . . . captors." Obviously, sharing of this sort in chimps did not develop for logical reasons, along the lines of "if I don't give him a share now, he won't help me hunt next time." Rather, it must have been the other way around: without a willingness to share, there would have been no payoff to any but the actual captors of the prey—and therefore no group hunting. A chimp, that is, does not share because he hunts cooperatively; he hunts cooperatively because he is capable of sharing, and has learned from experience that he can expect a share of what the group catches.

But as hunting became a major source of food, as it perhaps was for Australopithecus and unquestionably was for his more advanced descendants, it must have promoted altruism in another way. Game —especially larger animals—must often have been tracked and killed miles away from the campsite or cave where the women and children were based. And if these weaker members of the band relied on meat as an essential portion of their diet, as they must have done at least in the colder regions and seasons, the hunters could not simply have shared out and consumed their kill on the spot; some of it would have had to be carried back home. Which is to say that the hunters must have evolved at least a rudimentary awareness of the needs of those they had left behind *and a desire to meet those needs*—even at the price of eating less meat themselves. Meanwhile, back at the camp, the women would have been under no less of a compulsion to reserve some of the berries and roots they had gathered and the small game they had clubbed or snared against the possibility that their men would return with empty hands—and stomachs.

We find a very crude prototype of this sort of altruistic behavior among animals far removed from our own family tree: wolves and other wild dogs. Typically they hunt in packs, as did our ancestors (though not exclusively male packs); typically, one or two of the pack remain at home as puppy sitters. And the returning hunters regurgitate part of their kill for the benefit of those who stayed behind. What motivates wild dogs to do this is not known; it may well be an essentially automatic, "instinctive" reaction. But this could hardly have been the case with our own ancestors. One could, indeed, argue that if (as Ardrey has alleged) man possesses an "instinct to kill" because he occasionally kills his fellows, he must possess a far more powerful "instinct to share" because he typically shares with his fellows. A more plausible explanation, I think, is man's capacity for empathy, coupled with his increasing capacity for "displacement" —in speech and in action. Erectus, that is, did not merely respond to the needs of his (or her) fellows when they were present, as with the langur female responding to the needs of her infant, or the male chimp reaching out to give a reassuring pat to a frightened infant; he could also imagine, and respond to, the needs of those not present.

As with so many other varieties of human behavior, we find the prototype of this human pattern among chimps, who not only share the kill among the hunters (regardless of who actually killed the animal) but also share it *among those who took no part in the hunt.*

After the initial share-out of the prey among the (male) hunters, all the chimps in the neighborhood, male and female, gather in "sharing clusters" around those who have seized a chunk of meat and "beg" for a piece of the much-valued food. As often as not, they get it; eventually most or all of the animals end up with at least a taste. And there is, I must stress, no "practical" reason why this type of behavior evolved, in terms of the group's nutritional needs; the sharers share out of what Teleki calls "social considerations": because they evidently derive some satisfaction from responding to the begging requests of their fellows.*

This sort of sharing, from reasons of what must be called good fellowship, is not exceptional among chimps, but typical: Teleki says categorically that "no chimpanzee . . . has ever been observed to capture and privately consume a mammal, however small, if other adult chimpanzees were present to form a sharing cluster." And if this is true of chimps, how much more true must it have been of our hunting ancestors, for whom sharing food must have been not merely a matter of sociability (though it doubtless was that as well) but often a stark necessity. Thus we, their descendants, routinely respond to and satisfy the needs of others—sometimes, indeed, in the hope of some tangible reward, sometimes in fear of what people will say if we don't, but often because satisfying the needs of others, and thereby sharing their satisfaction, *is intrinsically rewarding.* Humans, by evolutionary necessity, have acquired altruistic impulses adding up to the principle that it is at least as blessed to give as to receive.

So far as Homo erectus is concerned, this reconstruction of their behavior is admittedly hypothetical; we believe they shared because there seems no way they could have survived if they didn't. When we reach Neanderthal times, however, we find considerably more direct evidence of altruism.

The first physical descriptions of the Neanderthals portrayed them as hunched, shambling figures more like apes than humans, a picture derived primarily from studies of the first complete Neanderthal skeleton to be unearthed. Much later, however, more careful examination of these bones made clear that what ailed their owner was not

---

* Social occasions centering on the sharing of food—particularly much-valued food, such as a large roast or barbecued chunk of meat—are not unknown among our own species.

apishness but arthritis.* The skeleton was that of a man about sixty, who at his death and for some years before it has been so crippled by disease that he could not stand upright, let alone move about with any ease. He could not, that is, conceivably have hunted game with his fellows or made any other very significant contribution to the physical needs of his tribe or family. Simply as a matter of tribal economics, they should have killed and eaten him. In fact, however, for all those years they had supplied him with food and whatever else he needed for survival. Similar evidence has been found at other sites: fifty thousand years ago, these creatures which, as we have seen, may have lacked even the ability to speak in more than semiarticulate grunts, were looking after their own.

Let us now, for the moment, abandon evolution and take a look at some up-to-date, laboratory evidence on the nature of altruism. It demonstrates, by the most unimpeachable "objective" techniques, that satisfying the needs of other human beings is rewarding in itself.

In 1971, a group of researchers at the University of Oklahoma wished to determine whether altruism could function as a reinforcement in B. F. Skinner's classic "instrumental conditioning." They recognized, however, that they could not test the effect of altruistic reinforcement openly, since the subjects' responses could be biased by the general conviction that altruism is praiseworthy. Accordingly they engaged in a bit of deception. The subjects were not told that they were expected to learn anything; instead they were given to understand that they were evaluating the responses under stress of another individual. This person—actually a confederate of the experimenters—had the task of holding a metal stylus steady in a tunnel while supposedly receiving a painful electric shock, during which process he visibly "suffered." The subject was told to evaluate the confederate's performance by setting pointers on three dials; at a signal he then pressed a button to record his evaluations on tape, at which point the confederate received a ten-second break from his stressful task and heaved a loud sigh of "relief." Control experiments were run in the same way, except that the confederate received no "shock" and showed no signs of either suffering or relief.

What the experimenters were interested in was not, of course, the

---

* Why the original mistake was made is an interesting story which the reader will find in George Constable's book, cited in the bibliography.

subject's evaluation of the confederate's theatrics, but rather his unconscious response to them, as measured by how quickly he pressed the button after receiving the "record" signal. From the very beginning, there was a significant difference between the experimental and control subjects; the former, confronted by the confederate's apparent suffering, averaged 1.06 seconds between the signal and pressing the button that ended the "shock," while the latter averaged a more leisurely 1.3 seconds. Moreover, the experimental subjects showed much more improvement in performance than did the controls; their response, motivated by the cessation of the confederate's "suffering," speeded up by more than a third, while the controls improved only slightly, so that the difference between the two groups was even wider at the end than at the beginning.

Other experiments under slightly varied conditions established that altruism functioned in all respects like ordinary nonaltruistic reinforcement. The experimenters concluded that "the roots of altruistic behavior are so deep that people not only help others" without any reward—which earlier experiments had shown—but find the help rewarding in itself.

Of course this experiment, taken by itself, does not prove that the psychological payoff of altruism is innate rather than learned; the fact that most of us find money rewarding is hardly evidence that we are born with an appreciation of its value. But taken together with the facts cited earlier it makes the case for an innate human propensity to help others very convincing indeed. We *know* that female langurs —and baboons and chimps—are from an early age interested in babies and concerned with their needs. And if this prototypical impulse toward altruism is learned rather than innate, it must be learned in such a way that the males acquire it to a far less marked degree, or not at all—which seems ridiculous. We *know* that a male chimp will pat a frightened adolescent for no apparent reason other than that the youngster *is* frightened. (Were it simply a matter of the frightened adolescent being a nuisance, the elder animal would simply chase it away, as male chimps often do and male langurs almost invariably do.) We *know* that our hunting male ancestors must have shared their kills, no matter which of them did the actual killing, and also carried meat back to the women, kids, and old folks at home, from the relatively direct evidence of Neanderthal skeletons and from the fact that we, their descendants, are here to argue the point.

No doubt the specific actions by which our ancestors met the needs of their fellows were learned, just as the female langur learns to meet her infant's needs—by watching and imitating others, and by practice.* But the *motivation* to learn, like the motivations for learning other actions vital to survival, must have been innate. If the primate mother's impulse to satisfy her infant's needs is essential to its survival —as it is—and if our ancestors' willingness to share food was vital to *their* survival—as it was—then we should expect to find in this area, as in so many comparable ones, a built-in payoff that would encourage the learning of these things. And from all the evidence, that is exactly what we do find, in the shape of empathy—the ability to laugh when others laugh, rejoice when they rejoice, suffer when they suffer. Empathy exists to one degree or another in very nearly every human being and in every human culture that has been described (with one problematic exception that I shall discuss in a moment). It exists because we could not survive, as infants or as adults, without it.

Let us now examine how the biotheologians, who as we have seen manage to credit our species—often on the flimsiest evidence—with all sorts of discreditable motives, deal with man's more generous impulses. Tiger and Fox, in *The Imperial Animal,* correctly see the act of giving as "perhaps the most basic step on the road to truly human social relationships." But they find its prototype not in the relationship between the primate mother and child, but in that between debtor and creditor. Giving "implies an obligation to return the gift." "If a human being gives something, real or incorporeal, to another, something will be given back. Even the Spanish beggar gives his blessing in return for alms."

One might expect that a generalization this far-reaching would be supported by pretty comprehensive evidence. In fact, the authors cite only a single study, dating from 1923, the salad days of anthropology; presumably no further light has been shed on the question in the succeeding half century.** And when one digs into their argument

---

* The link between mother-child altruism and adult-adult altruism is not mere conjecture; it shows up quite clearly in the chimp. Older infants "beg" for plant food from their mothers, and often get it, in very much the same way that, as adolescents or adults, they will beg for meat from adult males.

** I have assumed for the sake of argument that the work in question actually supports the Tiger and Fox view of human giving; in fact, the quotation from it at the beginning of this chapter strongly suggests that it doesn't.

a bit further, one finds it based on a false premise: that other adult primates do not share. As we have seen, this is false. (As noted earlier, the authors knew, or ought to have known, it was false when they wrote it.) And giving among chimps, as Goodall and Teleki have described it, obviously does not involve any "obligation" to return the gift; the animals are incapable of this kind of bookkeeping. Even less is any obligation involved in the female chimp's response to her infant's begging for a piece of fruit, or the langur female's soothing of her fractious baby. On all the evidence, our ancestors were giving —first to their young, later to their fellows—long, long before they became capable of the sort of wheeling and dealing our two imperial anthropologists see as basic to human gift giving.

Beyond this, Tiger and Fox simply duck the question of motive— the payoff we have discussed above. They appear to see gift giving (or gift exchanging) as somehow built into human psychology—part of what they call our "biogrammar"—but on how it actually works they are silent, apart from intimating that it is somehow concerned with paying off (no pun intended) an obligation, if at times with nothing more substantial than a thank you or a blessing.

Instead of further belaboring the unlikelihood of this in evolutionary terms, let us take a look at some actual givers: thirty-eight hundred unpaid British blood donors, studies of which were reported by the late Richard Titmuss in his book *The Gift Relationship*. Asked why they gave blood, they naturally gave varied answers. But if we group the answers by type, we find that nearly two-thirds of the reasons must be classed as altruistic, while only about one donor in twelve gave blood for "selfish" reasons, or to repay an obligation (for example, a transfusion to a member of their family).*

A young woman factory worker was eloquent on the subject. On her questionnaire she wrote, "You cant get blood from supermarkets and chaine stores. People them selves must come forword, sick people cant get out of bed to ask you for a pint to save thier life so I came forword in hope to help somebody who needs blood." A more literate factory foreman was more succinct: "No man is an island." And these donors, I must stress, were no gallery of English eccentrics; the British blood-bank system depends entirely on such voluntary gifts, involving

* The remaining answers did not fit neatly into either group, though my impression is that more of them fell into the altruistic camp.

well over a million donors a year. (To further point the moral, I might just add that according to Titmuss's account the voluntary, altruistic British system yields more reliable supplies of blood, and of better quality, than the predominantly nonaltruistic and heavily commercialized blood-bank systems of the United States.)

Technically, of course, the British donors fell within Tiger and Fox's "reciprocity arrangement," for all of them received—or at least were offered—a cup of tea for their trouble, thereby presumably entering into a "deal" along the lines of "I give blood, they give tea, and we're all square." Personally, I find "I came forword in hope to help somebody" far more credible. If you have ever watched a child on Christmas morning, ask yourself: was *your* payoff the perfunctory "thank you"—which, indeed, was probably forgotten in the excitement—or the way the kid's face lit up when he saw what Santa Claus had brought? Do people cry at the movies because they have paid admission?

A more recent biotheological assault on altruism has been leveled by the anthropologist Colin Turnbull in his hair-raising book *The Mountain People*, an account of the Ik tribe of eastern Uganda. The Ik, says Turnbull, are "as unfriendly, uncharitable, inhospitable, and generally mean as any people can be," and if his account of them is accurate this is an understatement. Instead of caring for their children, they toss them out of the hut at the age of three to survive as best they can; instead of caring for the aged and feeble, they literally snatch food from their mouths; instead of distress at the misfortunes of their fellows, they show amusement.

So far, so good—or so bad. But Turnbull then makes this tribe of near-monsters the text for an elaborate sermon on human nature; the Ik, he claims, prove that altruism is a "myth," that "our much-vaunted human values are not inherent in humanity at all"; their dog-eat-dog society shows "how shallow is man's potential for goodness." And here he has abandoned science for theology.

Had Turnbull been less shell-shocked by his encounter with the Ik, he might have spent less paper recounting their present nastiness and more in discussing how they got that way. In fact, though he is quite vague on a number of points, one can reconstruct from his account the main lines of what turns out to be an appalling story of bureaucratic stupidity. The Ik were originally seminomadic hunters who roamed the borderland between Uganda, Kenya, and the Sudan. As such, it appears, they were quite as honest, generous, and compassion-ate as hunting peoples (according to Turnbull's own statement) gener-ally are. Subsequently, their wandering existence was first circum-scribed by the national boundaries set up among the new East African states and then destroyed by the Ugandan government, which con-verted their prime hunting ground into a national park—and told the Ik to quit hunting and become farmers, just like that.

This was bad enough; even worse was that the available "farm" land to which they were shunted was in fact steep, rocky, and, even in a good year, rather dry. And Turnbull did not visit them in a good year: he met them in the midst of a drought when crops withered in the ground and even drinking water sometimes had to be fetched from scummy water holes five miles away. Though it took him some months to grasp the fact, very nearly all the people he found so repugnant were either suffering the pangs of hunger—and sometimes thirst—or, literally, dying of it. And this state of affairs lasted for not one year but two. Turnbull gives no figures, but I would guess that at least half the tribe must have slowly starved to death.*

The Ik, in other words, were suffering the combined effects of acute culture shock, in which their whole traditional way of life had been destroyed at one stroke of a bureaucratic pen, and acute famine, in which—as Turnbull himself repeatedly says—a policy of every man (or woman, or child) for himself *was the only conceivable way that any of them could have survived at all.* What the Ik prove, in other words, is that when people are forced to live under grossly abnormal and dehumanizing conditions they are likely to behave in grossly abnormal and dehumanized ways—which, while a distressing thought, is hardly a startling one. But their tragic story proves nothing about the nature of altruism, except, indeed, that how altruistic men are at a particular time is likely to depend quite heavily on circum-stances. One is tempted to inquire "And what else is new?" But apparently it *is* new to Turnbull. When one analyzes his arguments,

---

* An interesting sidelight on Turnbull's conception of anthropological research is the fact that he did not, so far as I can gather, make any effort to bring this horrible situation to the attention of the Ugandan government or anyone else who might have done something about it. When the government finally—and too late—got around to distributing food to the Ik, Turnbull did try to have the food given to those who needed it most rather than (as actually happened) to the most skillful and unscrupulous connivers. But if he himself played any role in initially prodding the government into doing something, he has kept very quiet about it.

they amount to saying that man cannot be credited with altruistic impulses unless they show up *under any circumstances.* Which is nonsense. Man incontestably possesses sexual impulses, but they don't make us sexy all the time. Turnbull, like some other biotheologians, is arguing in effect that if man isn't a Good Guy—everywhere and all the time—he must be a Bad Guy, a view more relevant to soap opera than science.

The story of the Ik, read with somewhat more detachment than the author brought to writing it, actually proves rather more than he realizes. To me, at least, the most extraordinary thing about them, given the appalling experiences they had undergone, is not that they lost most of their humanity but that they still retained traces of it. Though the Ik cheated and robbed their parents and friends (and everyone else) for food, they never killed for it—which does not say much, incidentally, for the allegedly innate human impulse to kill. Though Ik parents abandoned their children at age three, the mother still cared for them up to that point, albeit grudgingly, and with the father's grudging acquiescence—even though it would have been easy enough, as Turnbull notes, simply to have left the baby somewhere for a leopard to carry off. Selfish, treacherous, and mean-minded they became, but not to the point where they lost the ancient primate compulsion to tolerate and care for the young. Finally, as Turnbull notes with some wonderment, they would go to considerable trouble simply to be with others of their kind. They exchanged no gestures of affection, seldom even conversed, yet appeared to derive some comfort or pleasure from the mere presence of their fellows, as primates have been doing for tens of millions of years.

The Ik's story proves something else, too. Turnbull's tribe of near-monsters is also, as he himself intimates, a vanishing tribe. If the wages of sin is death, the Ik are getting paid off; within a generation or so they seem doomed to disappear as a people. Precisely as I have been arguing, in fact, human societies cannot survive—could never have survived—without the generous impulses of mutual concern and help. And human nature, as it has evolved over the past few million years, necessarily reflects this fact.

I myself, let me emphasize, am not claiming that man is "innately good" or any such oversimplified and romantic folderol. If a chimp is a complex creature compared with a langur, man is inconceivably complex as compared with a chimp—meaning that his actions are governed by the most intricate and variable combinations of motives, along with myths, ideologies, and rationalizations. All I have argued is that among those motives is a capacity to empathize with other men, to share their pleasures and pains—and therefore a capacity to derive satisfaction from meeting their needs.

Obviously the same evolutionary processes that have endowed humans with this capacity have also endowed them with the capacity to derive even more powerful satisfactions from meeting their own needs—and if the two come into conflict, as must sometimes happen, self-interest is more likely than not to come out on top, as it did among the Ik. But the fact that certain motives are, under certain circumstances, less powerful than other motives does not make them less real; if on a blistering August afternoon a ditch digger reaches for a glass of beer in preference to a beautiful woman, this is no reflection on his virility.

Whether our behavior at a given moment is governed by our concern for our fellows or our concern for ourselves is obviously going to depend heavily on the alternative choices open to us, and on the rewards attached to those choices. Titmuss, in discussing the implications of his blood-bank study, emphasizes that the altruism of British blood donors, as compared with those in most other countries, is not due to any inherent moral superiority, but to the fact that in this area British society has institutionalized generosity. Set up a social framework in which men are permitted to be altruistic and most of them will rise to the occasion; set up one which encourages them to be selfish and most of them will sink to it. If a society offers special rewards to those who pursue the strategies of dog eat dog and "I'm all right, Jack," then many people are going to pursue those strategies, at whatever cost to the altruistic, "do-gooder" side of their natures. For that matter, if a society, or its leaders, can succeed in defining people of a different language, or color, or religion, or ideology, as not really human, then those of us who have swallowed the definition may well cease to respond to them as fellow humans, surveying their misfortunes unmoved, or even ourselves encompassing their destruction.

But if we find such manifestations of human nature distressing, the remedy is not to belabor human nature, misrepresenting human beings as something less than animals, with no ingrained concern for anything but their own personal comfort. The soured romantics who proclaim humans basically selfish are no less childish than the romantics who proclaim them basically altruistic; nature has made them both. And nature also seems to have arranged matters so that societies which, through tradition or necessity, systematically foster selfishness as against altruism have a short life expectancy: along with the obscure Ik, we have the example of a much better-known society which, having deliberately institutionalized inhumanity, expired in a Berlin bunker after twelve years, though advertised to last for a thousand. If, then, we are concerned with the survival of *our* society, we might well inquire whether in fact its institutions foster our selfish impulses as against our altruistic ones—and if so, how they can be changed to give the latter greater scope. "We crave to be more kindly than we are," wrote Bertholt Brecht; given the chance, we will be.

10

THE SEX RELATIONSHIP: Who Does What to Whom, and Why

"In man sexual intercourse has ceased to be simply a biological necessity and has in addition become a cultural distraction."
— JOHN NAPIER

"Is Sex Necessary?"
— JAMES THURBER

There is something to be said for an author who begins his book with a really obvious bit of hokum: at least you know what to expect in the following pages. Thus when Desmond Morris titled his well-known work on evolution and human nature *The Naked Ape,* it figured he was throwing the reader a curve. Morris's justification of his title was the claim that "naked ape" is how the proverbial zoologist from Mars would classify our species—"ape" because of our obvious similarity to the other large, tailless primates, and "naked" because we have almost no hair. This explanation was hokum, and Morris—who is clearly a literate chap—knew it. "Naked," in my dictionary and I am sure in his, means primarily without clothing, a description which applies to all the apes *except* man. If one is talking about an animal lacking not clothes but hair, one says "hairless"; did anybody ever hear of a breed of dog called the Mexican Naked?

The point of the hokum, of course, was that "naked" is a lot sexier than "hairless"—and sexy sells books. That Morris was well aware of this is shown by the fact that his chapter on sex accounts for more than a fifth of his book, not to mention glancing references in other chapters. His discussion of the subject includes such titillating items as the fact that men have larger penises, in proportion to their body size, than do any other primates. No doubt this is true, but it tells us very little about human nature. That the size of the male organ has something to do with virility is, indeed, a superstition held by many teenage boys and quite a few of their elders, but Morris, who is a professional zoologist as well as an author, certainly knows that this is nonsense.* If one is looking for a "supervirile" animal, on the basis of penis size, the prime example is the jackass, whose erect penis—I have seen this—may actually touch the ground beneath its belly. This fact perhaps supplies an appropriate commentary on men who take pride in possessing oversized equipment.

Be all that as it may, Morris for various reasons characterizes his naked ape as "the sexiest primate alive." So far as the males of our species are concerned, there is little if any truth in this. Most male primates appear to copulate as often as they get the opportunity, which is more than can be said of some human males. K. R. L. Hall, observing a baboon band in South Africa, ticked off twenty-one copulations in a ten-hour day for the number-one male, while number three on one occasion was clocked at ten in a a little over two hours—possibly the all-time primate record.** To be sure, Hall found it "obvious" that these chain-copulating male baboons did not ejaculate every time, but concedes that he was quite unable to tell which copulations ended with ejaculation and which did not. Perhaps what seemed so obvious to the human scientist would have appeared less obvious to a baboon observer. On the other hand, Irven DeVore's Kenya baboons ejaculated nearly every time—and copulated much less often.*** The highest frequency he cites is five times in three and a half hours, which is much closer to the human scale; some men have

* The superstition has also made its special contribution to the mythology of American race relations. Black men are widely reputed to have larger penises, on the average, than white men. So far as I have been able to discover, this is true, at least as regards the flaccid organ; erect may be another story. But this putative fact has then been taken to mean that black men are more virile and/or more attractive to women (black or white) than white men, a supposition which has become a source of pride for some blacks and a source of anxiety for some whites—though there is not a shred of evidence supporting it.

** The Roman poet Catullus, with his *novem consecutivas futationes,* would have approached this figure, except that his claim probably represents poetic license—in both senses.

*** DeVore judged that the males had ejaculated when copulation ended in "a pause of from two to four seconds during which the male's whole body remains rigidly fixed." Most men—and women—will find this very plausible.

probably equaled or even surpassed this figure during their best years. Jane Goodall is less specific concerning the sexual capacities of male chimps, but her account leaves little doubt that any time a female chimp is willing, all the males gather round eagerly for the fun.

Where the human male has it over the male baboon or chimp is not in sexiness but in the availability of the female. Female apes and monkeys are receptive, at best, for less than half their (approximately) monthly cycle,* and not at all when they are pregnant, or for several months at least thereafter. The human female, by contrast, is receptive—in theory, anyway—virtually all the time. Whether this makes her "sexier" than other female primates is perhaps a matter of semantics; certainly when the latter *are* sexy they seem to be sexier, in purely quantitative terms, than most women. Hall's baboon chain-copulations all involved a single female as well as a single male, and Goodall describes one occasion—apparently not particularly unusual—in which a single female chimp copulated with seven males in succession; one of them even managed a second turn at bat. Few if any women would care for such an experience, apart from professionals, and their motive is money, not sex. But "sexier" or not, the human female is potentially much more available than her primate sisters.

What made the human female a woman for all seasons—and times —is not wholly clear. Years ago, when drive reduction (and also Freudianism) was all the rage among psychologists, it was generally believed that sex was the motivation for the long-term associations among groups of men and women that we call tribes or societies. But this theory died a natural death when it was noted that other primates could and did maintain groups quite as stable regardless of how frequently sex came into the picture. As we have several times noted, primates live in groups because they like being in groups, sex or no sex; some species form all-male as well as male-female groups. A more recent and more plausible conjecture has come from DeVore, who relates the expansion of women's receptivity to the growing importance of hunting for man. He notes that in baboons, for example, sexual frustration can lead to considerable friction among the group's males. In one instance, the group contained six full-grown males and seven mature females, but only one of the latter was in heat at any

---

* DeVore says "only a few days," but this seems true only of certain species.

given time. Since all six of the males were turned on by the single female, the result was marked tension "expressed in almost continuous harassing and fighting for her possession." Later on, four of the females came into heat simultaneously, and tension was much reduced; indeed the animals formed "consort pairs"—temporary pairings-off of a male and a female—for several days at a time. Among hunters, DeVore notes, "any fights over sex would have impaired both their ability and their desire to cooperate while out hunting." This would have been even more certain if, as I have suggested earlier, the "aggressive" activity of hunting stimulated the men's sex hormones; had they returned from the hunt in a state of intense expectation to find only one or two females receptive, the result might well have been a turning of their spears and clubs against one another—and a fatal reduction in the number of hunters.

This theory is of course very much in line with what we noted in an earlier chapter: as humans evolved beyond the Australopithecine stage, they increasingly survived or perished as groups, not as individuals. That is, expanded sexual receptivity would have given no evolutionary advantage to any individual woman or man, but *groups* in which the women were receptive more of the time would have had a better chance of survival. Plausible though this theory is, however, there is no direct evidence that male conflicts over sex, and their resolution, actually played a role in human evolution. As we have noted, chimpanzee males never show such conflicts; it is rare for a male even to show impatience while waiting his turn, and outright attacks on other males in these circumstances have never been observed. Sexual jealousy among males seems to be pretty common in human cultures, but there is little evidence that inherited propensities have much to do with it.

What may well have turned the balance toward greater female receptivity is that sex among humans is—or at any rate can be—a far more complex and profound experience than it is among other primates. The most obvious indication of this is time. For the baboon or chimp, copulation lasts only a dozen seconds or so, with perhaps half a dozen thrusts by the male, while in man it is likely to be measured in minutes, not seconds. But this is the least of the differences; sex in man is not only quantitatively different but qualitatively as well—and to a degree that can be called, without exaggeration, revolutionary.

What began this revolution in primate sexuality was our ancestors' assumption of the upright posture as part of their adaptation to grassland life; the profound shift from quadrupedal to bipedal locomotion involved an equally profound shift in methods of copulation. Earlier members of our line must have done it in the same fashion as virtually all other quadrupeds: the female on all fours, with the male approaching her from the rear. But the remodeling of the pelvis and the lengthening of the legs which we find already marked in Australopithecus would have made this increasingly impractical for the female. Nor would a hands-and-knees position have been much of an improvement, since it would have forced the female to support most of the male's weight (and her own) on her knees, which are not designed for this purpose.* In the female baboon or chimp, the weight during copulation rests primarily on the padded and toughened soles of the feet; the human knee, by contrast, is both bony and tender-skinned.

The obvious consequence was a shift from rear-entry sex to face-to-face sex, which enabled the female to carry much of the weight on her buttocks. These are, indeed, no tougher-skinned than the knees, but are of course much broader, thereby spreading the weight over a larger area, and also heavily padded. Part of the padding is composed of the gluteus maximus muscle, whose marked development in humans is an inevitable part of bipedalism: it serves to pull the leg backward during locomotion and also helps hold the body in an upright position. In modern women, at least, the padding is thickened by a layer of fat beneath the skin. This subcutaneous fat, though present in both men and women, is considerably thicker in the latter, giving their bodies the relatively rounded contour that contrasts with the angularity of the male. In both sexes it covers most of the body, but in women tends to be especially thick over the buttocks; in a few ethnic groups, such as the Bushman and Hottentot, it forms almost a shelf protruding from the lower back. All sorts of explanations have been put forward for woman's special padding, none of them notably convincing; personally, I find sexual cushioning at least as plausible as any other theory. The subcutaneous fat, incidentally, also pads

---

* We are talking, remember, about a time long before the invention of beds, or even the fur rugs that Homo erectus may have slept—and copulated—on; in Australopithecus, copulation undoubtedly took place on the ground.

women across the shoulders, which carry most of the remaining weight during copulation.

We are talking, of course, about the face-to-face, man-on-top posture sometimes called, by would-be sexual sophisticates, "the missionary position." The term was supposedly coined by an African tribe which had never heard of the position until they were advised by a missionary that that was the only proper way to do it. Alas for sophistication: both the missionary and the tribe are mythical. The missionary position is by all odds the most common sexual posture the world around. Most other positions, according to the anthropologist Paul S. Gebhard, are usually employed only in special circumstances—notably "where speed or secrecy is paramount."* Gebhard specifically warns against what he calls the "Kama Sutra fallacy"— the notion that there are an enormous number of different coital positions. The definitive comment on this was provided by that splendid fictional rogue and cad, Harry Flashman, when he observed that number 36 in the Kama Sutra "is the same as number 74, but with the fingers crossed." To this I would add a further warning against what might be called the "Lo, the poor Anglo-Saxon fallacy": the notion, widely held among both British and Americans, that non-Anglo-Saxons are more experimental in sex and have a generally better time in bed—especially if their skins are dark—than do Anglo-Saxons. The peoples of the world of course vary enormously in their customs, including their sexual customs, but sexual postures happen to be among the *least* variable.

Face-to-face sex—whichever party (if either) happened to be on top—had profound psychological implications for Australopithecus and his descendants. In the first place, it is potentially a much more personal relationship. A male baboon or chimp advancing on a female for amorous purposes sees mainly her backside; a man sees the woman's face, and she his. And whatever may be said about the esthetic qualities of the female backside as opposed to the face, there can be no doubt that the latter is a far more expressive object; it can convey emotions and reactions far more intense and varied than can even the most callipygian rump.

Face-to-face sex is not merely a more personal relationship, it is

---

* This would apply to the aptly named "knee-trembler," in which the participants stand face to face.

also a more all-embracing one, figuratively and literally. A male baboon copulates by gripping the female's ankles with his feet, thereby raising himself off the ground and into position, and steadies himself by gripping her back or side fur with his hands. The male chimp is if anything even more casual; he may rest one or both hands on the female's back, but sometimes balances himself by gripping a branch.*
In both cases, there is little physical contact between male and female except for the genitals. Face-to-face sex, by contrast, implies, if it does not demand, that the participants embrace one another; they are in contact not just with their genitals but also with their chests, bellies, hands, and the inner surfaces of their arms and legs. It makes possible stimulation of the lips, tongues, and nipples of the participants, all of them richly supplied with nerve ends.** Simply in terms of the amount and kind of skin being stimulated, human face-to-face sex is almost inevitably a more exciting experience than ape or monkey sex.

The stimulation would have been further enhanced as and when our ancestors lost the body hair possessed by all other primates. Nobody is certain when this occurred, and nobody has explained, at least to my satisfaction, why. The usual explanation is that the loss of hair occurred when man became a hunter, as a way of facilitating elimination of excess body heat generated in the pursuit of game. As against this we have the fact that no other predator has found such an adaptation necessary, not even the lion and tiger, which because of their size eliminate heat more slowly, other things being equal, than would a hairy animal the size of man.*** To be sure, lions and tigers do not do much running; like most cats, their hunting technique is primarily a matter of stalk and pounce, and is therefore less likely to lead to overheating. But both cheetahs and wild dogs *do* run down

* Orangutangs are reported to sometimes do it face to face with *both* parties hanging from branches, which is, I believe, something that even the authors of the Kama Sutra never thought of.

** The touch sensitivity of the lips and tongue probably evolved much earlier, as an extra means of appraising objects before chewing and swallowing them; nipple sensitivity was, of course, an incentive to females to suckle their young. Anyone who has ever watched, say, a female cat feeding her kittens can have little doubt that she enjoys the process quite as much as they do.

*** This is a consequence of something called the square-cube law, which amounts to saying that in larger animals the area of body and lung surface, through which heat is eliminated, is smaller in proportion to the mass of body tissues, in which heat is generated.

their prey—and are just as hairy as the lion. At least as plausible, it seems to me, is that hairless (*not* "naked") was not so much cooler as sexier for hominids, and that those who were least hairy were more satisfying partners in face-to-face sex, hence were more likely to find mates. Readers who have experienced sex both naked and clothed will no doubt be able to form their own opinions.

But no less important than the increased quantity of stimulation during sex was the *kind* of stimulation. For the sensations of warmth and pressure on the front of the body and the inner surfaces of the arms *are precisely the sensations which every young primate first experiences in its mother's arms.* They are, as we saw in Chapter 5, the original and prime source of comfort, reassurance, and security, of the young primate's first important "positive" emotional experience —of love, in fact. Other primates can experience sexual excitement and release, and most or all of them can experience some degree of love, as infants and—in the case of the chimp, at least—probably as adults, but the two experiences are separate, evoked on different occasions by different situations and individuals. Only man can fuse them into the superpowerful emotion of sexual love.

In recent years, not a few women have complained that their men treat them like mothers. Perhaps so, but the mistake, if such it be, is understandable. When a man and a woman embrace she *is,* psychologically, his mother—and he, hers.

But we are still not done with the human sexual revolution, for our ancestors brought yet another dimension to sexual intercourse: empathy. As we saw in the preceding chapter, growing human interdependence implied, as one of its basic conditions, a growing capacity to sense and share the emotions of others, and there is no reason to suppose that this capacity did not include sharing sexual excitement. Thus in men and women the excitement of "pure" sex—itself no trivial emotion in any primate—plus the added emotional force of contact comfort-security, could achieve still greater heights through mutual awareness of the other's emotions, her fire adding fire to his and vice versa.* If sex means much more to human beings than to other primates—and I think it undoubtedly does—the reason is not

* It hardly needs saying that the embrace of face-to-face sex would have been especially favorable to this development. The closer you are to someone physically the more easily and intensely you sense his or her emotions.

that we are, in Morris's terms, "sexier," but that we are human, able to combine our primate sexiness with our distinctively human postures and emotional capacities.

Had human sex not become human but remained on the chimpanzee level, with its peculiar combination of excitement and casualness, it is quite conceivable that women might have retained the female chimp's limited receptivity to sex; the men of the band, returning from the hunt, would have been quite content to line up like male chimps for a turn with whatever female, or females, happened to be receptive. Even in modern times, impersonal sex is not something that men are likely to fight about; they take turns amiably, like miners in the Old West lining up at the town whorehouse on payday. But to the degree that sex did *not* remain at that level, becoming personal, intense, and mutual, it also became something that men were unwilling to wait for. To use an economic metaphor, masculine demand for sex had increased—become more intense; if human society was to remain viable, supply—feminine availability—had to increase comparably. The alternative would have been "sexual inflation," an increasingly high value placed on sex by men, and ultimately the social disruption which extreme inflation almost automatically produces.*

The human sexual revolution typifies a process that was becoming increasingly important in human evolution: the transfer or spread of psychological and physical capacities and tendencies which had originally served one evolutionary purpose into quite different areas, with results that could not have been predicted from their initial functions. An early example of this was the hand, which having originally evolved as a means of locomotion in the trees became a device for holding tools and other things on the ground. The sexual revolution was brought about by a combination of human traits all of which had evolved earlier for nonsexual reasons: upright posture (a means of combining locomotion with tool using), contact comfort (a safety device for the airborne infant primate), and empathy (originally a way of alerting the group to danger and encouraging child care, later the basis for observation learning). The more diverse capabilities man developed, in short, the more these capabilities could—and did— combine in quite unexpected ways. Man is not only the most adaptable of animals but also the least predictable.

* Acute disproportion between supply and demand in *food* is of course what destroyed Ik society.

The sexual revolution did more than change the mechanics and quality of sex; it also involved some degree of change in the motivations for sex. This may sound odd, since "everyone knows" what the motivation for sex is—at least everyone who has ever experienced it. But when we take a closer look it turns out that things are not quite that simple. To be sure, once the male has inserted himself in the female, things take their course more or less automatically —and males, at least, are unlikely to require more than a single experience of this sort to convince them that inserting themselves in a female is something very much worth doing. The really fundamental question, however, is why the male inserts himself in the first place.

There can be no doubt that in chimps—and almost certainly in man as well—the mechanics of copulation are learned, not instinctive. As we noted earlier, a male chimp raised in captivity, with no opportunity to observe copulation, doesn't know how to go about it. The Yerkes Primate Laboratory, which breeds as well as studies chimps, at one time used an experienced young female as an "educator" for backward males; according to Geoffrey H. Bourne, she "rapidly seduced them by showing them the right thing to do and then helping them to do it." Of course sex is seldom if ever a problem among wild chimps, since by the time a young male has reached puberty he has observed scores or hundreds of copulations among the adults of his group. Nor is it a problem for humans, though in few human cultures do children have the opportunity to observe their elders *in flagrante;* as the possessors of language, we can to a large extent substitute words for direct observation, so that it is a rare boy who, by the time sex comes around, has not learned from his friends (nowadays, sometimes from books or sex-education classes) at least the basics of who does what to whom when the lights are out.

But knowledge, observational or verbal, is still, for the male, not enough. For copulation to take place, both parties must be willing* —but the male must also be able. And the former, as most men have on occasion learned to their embarrassment, does not necessarily imply the latter. Something must turn on the male to the point where he achieves an erection, otherwise all the sexual know-how in the world is worthless.

---

* Except, of course, in the case of rape—though even here the female may be "willing" simply in the sense that she is too terrified of her attacker to resist.

In our culture, among others, the things that turn on men are—as was said of the activities of the young Persian named Darius—many and various, from commonplaces like tight jeans, bikinis, and black lingerie to such curiosa as chains and rubber raincoats. And the sexual properties of most of these things—including most of those I have just enumerated—are obviously learned; the notion that men could be *innately* excited by black lingerie (let alone rubber raincoats) is too grotesque for discussion. All these and many other objects, evidently, must in some way or another have become associated with sexual excitement to the point where they themselves induce that excitement.

But where does the excitement come from in the first place? Not, obviously, from copulation, since we have just seen that without strong initial excitement on the male's part there won't *be* any copulation. From an evolutionary standpoint, the answer is obvious: what turns on men must be women—and, of course, vice versa. Women, that is, must very probably be objects of intrinsic interest to men—as babies almost certainly are to women—and must unquestionably possess some intrinsic quality or qualities that excite men sexually. The late Paul Goodman, in an interview a few years before his death, put the matter very well: "To fuck the female, the male has got to have an erection. . . . He has to put his penis in the right hole. It is a very complicated maneuver and unless it is done just right, the species will not survive. Well, our species has been around for a million years*—obviously there was a very strong heterosexual drive among the great majority of people."

Because it is so difficult to disentangle the intrinsically exciting qualities of women from their cultural trappings (what we might call the "black lingerie factor"), we had best begin our inquiry with some of our primate cousins. For the primate male, females are exciting because of the way they smell and the way they look. Females in heat smell different than at other times and also look different; specifically, the skin around their vulvas (which is generally hairless) turns various gaudy colors and/or swells up; in the female chimp, the pink "sexual swelling" may far exceed the size of a man's clenched fist. And confronted with these interesting sights and odors, the males promptly become ready for action.

Among the monkeys (and probably in most other mammals) the

---

* The original interview said "billion," presumably a typographical error.

chief sexual trigger seems to be odor. A group of English primatologists actually analyzed the sexual secretion of female rhesus monkeys, and found it rich in half a dozen simple, volatile organic acids such as acetic acid (the stuff that makes vinegar sour). They then mixed up a batch of acids from their laboratory shelves, sprayed it on several castrated females, who under normal circumstances evoke no interest in males, and found that the males became excited just as they would have with normal females. The clinching evidence came from another research group testing a new type of birth-control pill on rhesus monkeys. The pill did not prevent the females from coming into heat normally or "presenting" themselves to the males, but it deranged their internal chemistry just enough to make them smell different, so that the males who were supposed to participate in the experiment promptly and unanimously became impotent.*

So far as I know, similar experiments have not been performed on chimps, but Goodall's observations leave little doubt that both sight and smell play a part. The sexual swellings of what she calls the "pink ladies" are objects of immediate male interest, but the males also sniff the swellings, apparently in search of whatever stimulus the odor may provide.

And it is here that the human line, from Australopithecus on down, diverges from the other primates. An animal that habitually walks on its hind legs cannot—there is no way of putting this delicately —easily go around sniffing female genitals. It has been suggested, indeed, that the pubic hair in women (and quite possibly men as well) serves—or served—to collect and concentrate sexually arousing odors, and there is very likely some truth in this. But in our culture, at least, females often go to great lengths to eliminate or disguise their natural odors, by means of daily baths, deodorants, and perfumes, with no apparent effect on male interest. Whatever role odor plays in human sexuality, it must be a minor and dispensable one.

* For readers curious as to what these remarkably, well, potent chemicals smell like, I might note that my handy index of chemical compounds describes them variously as "vinegary," "sweatlike," "rancid," and "like rancid cheese." What they smell like in combination is something the reader had best imagine for himself, but on the face of it—or the nose of it—the odor doesn't sound like anything that would make the perfume industry rich. Still, it is just possible that adding small quantities of these sexy acids to perfumes might enable those costly substances to do in reality what their advertisers say they do. Any interested perfumer can get the details from me for a small commission.

We are then left with visual stimuli as the sexual trigger, but evidently stimuli rather subtler than the obvious sexual colors and swelling of the other primate females, since women show no such changes. Nor, of course, is there any reason they should; the function of these changes in the other primates is to convey the message "It's time!" and for a woman it is—always in theory—time all the time. What we should expect to find instead is some permanent, not temporary, change in the female's appearance at puberty which attracts and stimulates male interest. Of course there are several such changes, most notably involving the hips, breasts, and buttocks. Desmond Morris has specifically focused on the breasts as the female sexual trigger, on the ground that there is no other reason for them to exist. Other primate females, he notes, have breasts that remain unobtrusive except when they are nursing an infant, while human breasts are generally rather obtrusive all the time.*

While there is probably something to the theory of the female breast as a sexual trigger, it's not a theory I would carry too far. Though breasts undoubtedly have an enormous sexual significane in our own culture, an important reason is that until very recently they were the only distinctive portion of the female body that could be publicly commercialized without courting jail. In many other cultures, women habitually leave their breasts uncovered, yet the men do not become sexually excited more often than other men.**

We can perhaps get further clues from the Cro-Magnons, relatively recent ancestors of ours dating from perhaps forty thousand to twelve thousand years ago. Unlike Homo erectus or the Neanderthals, they were men of wholly modern type, and were also, as most people know, the first artists. Their sculptures and paintings—notably those found in dozens of caves in southern France and northern Spain—are mostly devoted to animals, but occasionally include human figures, giving us our first glimpse of what our ancestors actually looked like, mainly our female ancestors, since the male figure seldom appears. Some of the female figures, indeed, are distorted, with certain features grossly exaggerated (perhaps for magical purposes), but others seem to be as naturalistic as the much more common animal drawings. (They are

* This has drawn the fire of a few women's liberationists, who find the notion repellant that some parts of women serve specifically to attract men.

** Thus to the Polynesian, says one authority, the female breast is "of interest only to a hungry baby."

not unlike some drawings found in such modern caves as men's washrooms, though the latter are much cruder in every sense.)*

From these drawings, we can judge which aspects of women the artists found particularly important or meaningful—that is, which parts they exaggerated (when they did) and, if some parts were omitted (as they often were), which parts were left. The answer turns out to be the hips, thighs, buttocks, and—most especially—the mons veneris and vulva. We do not, to be sure, have any direct evidence that the artists in question were men. On the other hand, we have very clear evidence that somebody twenty thousand years ago was interested in womens hips, thighs, etc.; if anybody wants to argue that the interested parties were women rather than men—well, I wish her luck!

Most men who remember their own adolescence will recall, as I certainly do, that at some point they began to look at women in a new way. The women were shaped no differently than they had ever been, but the shapes were interesting as they had never been. Not because we had had erotic experience with women (most of us hadn't), or because we had suddenly learned that one *could* have such experiences (we had known that long before), but because the shape of a woman *had somehow become interesting and stimulating to us in itself.*

On the evidence of the cave drawings, men have been looking at women in much the same way, and for the same reasons, for two hundred centuries—and doubtless much longer. They have, in short, been "ogling" women, "giving them the old up-and-down," for a long, long time, and not, as some fanatic feminists would have it, because they have always been male chauvinist pigs but because an interest in female anatomy is built into the male genes. In this sense, men have always viewed women as "sex objects," and always will; if they ever quit, the human race will be ripe for extinction.** Nor is there, I

* The naturalistic female figures, incidentally, dispose of one of the sillier feminist accounts of evolution, put forward by Mary Jane Sherfey. She theorizes that during the Ice Ages women, unable to perform their usual tasks of gathering plant food, simply sat around the family cave getting fat. This fantasy not only ignores the existence of slender, "sexy" cave drawings but also the fact that Eskimo women, who do even less plant gathering than did Cro-Magnon women, are not notably stout.

** One should, however, distinguish sharply between girl-watching, which is innate, and girl-groping, which is not—and which women, quite understandably, find infuriating. In my younger days I was myself occasionally groped by strange men, and I didn't much care for it.

think, any rooted female objection to this sort of attention. My daughter at sixteen put the matter very sensibly: "Actually, I like being a sex object—so long as I'm not *just* a sex object."

But if feminine contours are intrinsically a focus of male sexual interest, they are clearly not the cause of acute male sexual excitement; otherwise a large proportion of the men on a bathing beach, or even a city street in summer, would be walking about in an embarrassingly erect posture. Exactly what intrinsic properties of the female turn male interest into male readiness can only be guessed at; my own guess would be the sight of the mons veneris and vulva, and/or the female's own indications that she is interested.

So far as the vulva is concerned, women cover it in public in virtually all cultures, including those in which the male genitals are uncovered, though among a few tropical peoples the covering is barely symbolic: a narrow strip of cloth or fiber. And exposure of the vulva —actually or symbolically—by spreading the legs is almost as universally deemed a sexual invitation. Given our species' capacity for dealing in symbols, any female actions or words that clearly convey her sexual readiness would presumably do as well. One bit of evidence confirming this theory is found among the products of the pornography industry. I am not, indeed, such a fool as to credit pornographers with any great insight into human psychology, let alone human evolution, but I do credit them with knowing their own business. And that, as numbers of our courts have noted, is appealing to prurient interest —male prurient interest. Well, a virtually universal feature of prurient fiction is that the female characters in it are visibly and vocally ready and eager for sex. Even in sadomasochistic porno, involving scenes of flagellation and sometimes torture, the author as often as not indicates, directly or by inference, that the women in question find these activities sexually exciting. Women's expression of their sexual interest, by word or action, would then amount to the human counterpart of "presenting" by other female primates—which, indeed, often seems to play a part in initiating male activity.

It is not impossible, however, that men also retain traces of much older primate patterns of sexual response. I should not like to swear that a young woman walking along the street wiggling her bottom does not affect men in the same way that a female chimp "presenting" her rump affects a male chimp.

But if we take it that some expression of female readiness is necessary to produce male readiness, what produces female readiness? Here studies of other primates are virtually useless, since their females seem to be turned on simply by the state of their hormones at a certain time in their sexual cycle, and this is obviously not the case with women. It seems not unlikely that the distinctive features of the male body play some part, as the female body does with men, but what these are remains to be determined. The problem has not been simplified by the fact that until fairly recently it was widely assumed in our culture that women—at least decent women—didn't have sexual desires. The inevitable result, of course, was that a lot of women didn't, and those who did were discouraged from thinking about, let alone analyzing, them. Thus the task of disentangling innate from cultural factors in sex is far more difficult with women than with men.

It is worth noting, however, that even in other primates female sexual response is not *simply* a matter of hormones. Though females in heat are for the most part ready to accept all comers, they do show clear preferences among the available males, in that they present much more often to some than others. In part, this seems to reflect the males' dominance status, but the relationship between dominance and sex appeal is anything but clear-cut. In one of Phyllis Jay's langur groups, containing six adult males, the one *most* often solicited by females was ranked either number four or (by my figuring) number five, yet he was more popular than number one, half again as attractive as number two, and nearly three times as appealing as number three. In frequency of actual copulation, he was outranked by number one, but still ranked equal to number two and outranked all the others. The same sort of pattern was observed by DeVore in one of his baboon groups, also containing six adult males; though sexual popularity tended to go with dominance status, the second most popular male was also the *lowest* in the hierarchy.

Exactly what it was about these nondominant males that made them so popular among the females is unknown; presumably only a female langur or baboon could tell us. The implication for our species would seem to be that men ranking high in one or another "dominance hierarchy" are likely to be popular with women, other things being equal—but that you don't *have* to be dominant to have sex appeal.*

* We might note in passing that monkey and ape males also show sex preferences. Thus Jane Goodall's Flo—old (her teeth were almost worn away), bulbous-nosed (apparently due to a fungus infection), and with half an ear missing—was still by all odds the most popular with the males. Nor was this a matter of experience, as Goodall

There is one more point about the evolution of female sexuality that is worth considering: the nature of the female response to copulation. Some zoologists—Morris is one of them—allege that monkey and ape females do not experience orgasm, and then theorize extensively as to how and why that capacity developed in our species. I do not myself feel that these theories are worth much discussion, because the basic premise is far too fragile. If, as we saw earlier, it is not always possible to say whether a *male* monkey has had an orgasm, I would say that the chances of determining whether or not a female monkey has had one are virtually nonexistent. Certainly there seems no doubt that these females enjoy sex and dislike sexual frustration. Geoffrey Bourne tells an amusing story of an experienced female chimp at Yerkes who was introduced to a young male. As he came into the cage, he got an erection, and she immediately presented. Being inexperienced, however, he didn't know what to do next, and commenced to masturbate—whereupon the female, peering through her legs and seeing what was going on, turned and attacked him in a rage. Hell hath no fury . . .

Speculations on the subject are not helped by the fact that there is still a great deal of confusion as to how and why women do—or don't—have orgasms. Freud, as most people know, laid great stress on the superiority of the "vaginal" orgasm to the "clitoral" variety, for reasons which reflect his own preconceptions about women rather than any comprehension of their sexuality. Much more recently, some feminists have alleged that there is in fact no such thing as a vaginal orgasm (as one flippant commentator has put it, clit is it); this doctrine of "clitoral supremacy" is allegedly based on the famous Masters-Johnson study of human sexual response. Even more recently, two male anthropologists have declared that there is no such thing as a *clitoral* orgasm, likewise citing the Masters-Johnson study. When one turns to what Masters and Johnson actually said, however, it turns out that they contradict both sides: what they found was that there was *no detectable physiologic difference between clitoral and vaginal orgasms.*

About all one can do at this point is to sum up the situation in a few brief statements. First, there is a vaginal orgasm, Virginia; the women of the Turu tribe in east Africa, whose clitorises are removed

---

originally suspected; other experienced females were much less appealing than Flo, or than some young, inexperienced ones.

at age ten, enjoy active and orgasmic sex lives, not only in marriage but especially in their semi-institutionalized adulteries called *mbuya*. Second, there is also such a thing as a clitoral orgasm, as thousands of women—and men—can testify. Third, there is—if we can believe Masters and Johnson—no physiologic difference between the two, at least not in our culture. Fourth, and finally, doctors disagree on whether there is any psychologic, subjective difference, and so do women. The most reasonable conclusion seems to be: every woman to her own orgasm. We can hardly doubt that, since it has always taken two to tango, first or last, female primates must always have been provided with some sort of innate incentive for copulation more or less comparable to that possessed by males. But of what that incentive consists among the other primates, and how—or whether —it was modified during human evolution, we can, for the moment, do no more than shrug our shoulders.*

Matters are not much clearer when we consider the probable evolution of another aspect of human sexuality, the family. In all human societies, without exception, we find more or less stable relationships between a man and a woman (sometimes, a man and several women; rarely, a woman and several men) which involve sex, the production and rearing of children, and some sort of economic interdependence.** But of the three, sex seems in some ways to be the least important element, in the sense that though marriage universally implies sex, sex does not necessarily imply marriage—nor, for that matter, does marriage necessarily imply exclusive sex. Paul H. Gebhard, of the Institute for Sex Research, estimates that premarital sex for females is explicitly allowed in 40 to 50 per cent of preliterate societies, and if one adds those which publicly condemn but secretly tolerate it, the percentage rises to 70; as regards males, the percentage is even higher. For extramarital sex, the percentages are somewhat lower, but it is at least tolerated for women in something like half the societies studied, though most of them place certain restrictions on person, time, and place. (Often, for example, the husband's permis-

---

* For what it is worth, a recent study at Harvard found that in female students the length and (less certainly) the duration of the menstrual cycle decreased when the women were in contact with men—and not sexual contact, merely social. Evidently just being around men can do something to the female hormones, but exactly what this is, and what relationship (if any) it has to female sex impulses, remains to be determined.

** The man who works at a job while his wife keeps house and looks after the kids is obviously just as dependent on her as she is on him.

sion is required.) Again, the percentages are probably higher for men. In other societies, such as our own, extramarital sex, though formally condemned, is still practiced to a degree that has made it one of the prime ingredients of literature, from Aeschylus to Jacqueline Susann.

Matters become somewhat clearer when we note that "family" in most societies is a much larger entity than merely two sexual partners and their children; it includes brothers, sisters, aunts, uncles, and grandparents in bewilderingly varied combinations. As is said even in our own society, "You're not just marrying her, you're marrying her relatives." And this, as it turns out, is very much in the primate tradition.

As recently as fifteen years ago, many primatologists would probably have scoffed at the notion that the concept of "family" is relevant to any species but our own. As now appears, however, the concept was irrelevant merely to the type of research that had been done up to that point. To determine with certainty which of a group of wild primates is related to which necessitates—since they cannot themselves tell us—observation extending over many years, so that infants known to have been born to a particular mother can be followed into maturity and their relationships with their mother and siblings studied. As such studies—notably, for instance, Goodall's on chimps and the Japanese work with macaques—have increased both in number and duration, it has become apparent that monkeys and apes do have families, and fairly stable ones.

The "generalized" primate family consists of a female, her daughters and granddaughters, and (among chimps at least) her and their sons, though the latter seem to be rather more loosely attached to the family. It is this long-term matriarchy-sisterhood that forms the stable nucleus of many smaller primate bands; larger groups may be composed of several such subgroups. Males, in most species, not infrequently shift from one band to another; females seldom do so, and once they have produced their first infant, almost never. Thus in primates, as in so many human societies, the family depends primarily on genetic relationships, not on sex relationships.

What our evolutionary line added to this, of course, was father. From what we have already seen of ape and monkey sex habits, it is clear that even if these primates could somehow formulate the concept of fatherhood, their promiscuity would make it meaningless. How this situation changed, and why, is anyone's guess. One likely ingredient was a tendency of a particular male and a particular female to pair off. As we have noted, other primates do this, but the "consort pairs" seldom if ever last for more than a few days. Lengthier pairings could have developed out of such relationships quite naturally, as a result of man's (and woman's) growing intellectual and emotional complexity, leading to a more marked preference for one partner as against another. And in a consort pair extending over years, not days, the male would almost automatically have fallen into a special emotional relationship with his consort's children, simply from prolonged association with them—quite apart from whether or not he was biologically their father, though in most cases he would have been. (In a number of "permissive" societies today, a man is deemed the father of all his wife's children, even those known to have been fathered by another.)

But wherever and however this happened, we can be pretty certain that it could have happened only to the degree that the females had become more or less continuously receptive to sex. In most modern societies, long-term man-woman relationships have their problems even so; that such relationships could have survived a long period of sexual disinterest on the part of the female, *plus* active sexual interest by other females, seems unlikely in the extreme. If DeVore is right in seeing the hunting way of life as decisive in changing the pattern of female sexuality, we can place the beginnings of the modern family at some time during the period of Homo erectus, or later.

There is, however, an alternative—or supplementary—explanation for the rise of the fully human family: simple survival. It may well be that societies embodying these stable relationships developed less friction in sexual matters and/or provided a better environment for raising infants to maturity, and therefore were more likely to succeed and persist than those which did not. The universality of the family today may reflect merely a long period of natural selection between cultures in which those with the more primitive, primate type of family were weeded out.

But whatever its origins, whether in genetically transmitted preferences or in efficient cultural patterns, the persistence and universality of the family argues powerfully that it answers some deep-rooted need of our species. Which is why I, for one, view with considerable skepticism suggestions that the family is dispensable—notably, in the matter of child rearing. Every bit of evidence we have, evolutionary, sociological, or anthropological, tells us that the young of our species is an animal whose nature is geared to growing up in a stable group of adults—that is, familiar and predictable people; we ignore this evidence at our, or our children's, peril. To slightly paraphrase the Declaration of Independence, prudence would dictate that institutions long established be not overthrown for light and transient causes.

By the same token, however, I also doubt whether the family as an institution will in fact be abolished anything like as easily or quickly as some of its critics seem to think; reports of its death appear to be considerably exaggerated. Human nature, flexible though it is in many ways, is basically a very tough fabric (as we saw, traces of it cropped up even among the psychologically devastated Ik) and those who propose to tailor it to a radically new pattern may find the job a lot harder than they expect.

Up to this point, we have confined ourselves pretty well to "normal" sex. But what about the evolution of "abnormal" sex—masturbation, incest, homosexuality, and the like?

So far as masturbation is concerned, we can forget the "abnormal." In our own culture, it is more the rule than the exception; according to Kinsey at least half the females and 90 per cent of the males have done it at one time or another. So, according to various observers, have other species, ranging from captive lions (using their paws) to zoo elephants (using their trunks) to captive dolphins (using a convenient jet of water spurting into their tank). And so have innumerable apes and monkeys, not just in captivity but in the wild, though its prevalence among primates probably has more to do with their possession of tool-manipulating hands than with any special sexiness or "perversity." (Similarly, its much greater prevalence among male primates probably reflects the fact that the receptive female seldom lacks for male company, whereas the turned-on male may find the receptive female or females monopolized by another.) Thus the notion that masturbation causes insanity, "softening of the brain," and similar dire consequences, which until fairly recently loomed large in popular—and even medical—folklore, is pure myth; if there were any truth in it, our species and several others would long ago have flipped out entirely.

Incest is quite another matter. It is undoubtedly "abnormal," in that every human society places restrictions on which relatives are permitted to copulate with which, and the closer the relationship, generally speaking, the more widespread the taboo. On the other hand, such restrictions do not seem to reflect any very powerful innate tendencies in man. One indication of this is the very strength of the taboo itself in most societies; over the long run, human groups are unlikely to invest much thought or emotion in forbidding something that people have little interest in doing anyway. (Thus the Eskimo and other far-northern peoples have no stringent taboos against appearing naked in public; climate exercises its own prohibitions in this area.) Another indication is that despite taboos, incest continues to exist in many societies, though how widely it is difficult to say, since there are few if any reliable figures. For what these are worth, however, the practice seems to be rare at best even among the most sexually permissive peoples.

Nonetheless there seem to be precedents for the incest taboo among the other primates. Long-term studies of monkeys and apes such as we have already cited indicate that sons seldom if ever copulate with their mothers; perhaps significantly, mother-son intercourse seems by all odds the rarest type of human incest. Nobody is quite sure why primates should observe this "taboo"; one suggestion is that a male primate must "dominate" a female (whatever that means) in order to copulate with her, and he always retains sufficient "awe" of his mother to make domination impossible. Be that as it may, the dominance theory would hardly explain the further fact that copulation between brother and sister is also rare, though apparently less so than mother-son couplings. Father-daughter copulation is, of course, quite another story, since it takes a sapient primate to know his own child; again, it is perhaps significant that this seems to be the most common form of human incest.

The transformation of the primates' rather loose and variable "anti-incest impulse" into the powerful taboos found in our own species probably came about through a combination of biological and cultural selection. As most people know, incest is biologically counterproductive, in the sense that offspring of it have a far higher than average chance of being born with a disabling or lethal genetic defect. It is estimated that every one of us carries dozens and perhaps hundreds of such genes—none of which, however, will damage our offspring unless they happen to get the same "bad" gene from their other parent as well. Obviously the chances of this happening in tribes where matings between close relatives were common would have been far greater than in those observing an incest taboo, with the result that the former would have been both less fertile and, on the average, less physically and mentally fit than the latter. For that matter, I would not put it past the intellectual capacities of the Cro-Magnons, and perhaps even the Neanderthals, to take conscious note of the low fertility and plentiful defective offspring of, say, father-daughter and brother-sister unions, to then conclude that such unions were displeasing to the spirits, and on that basis to forbid them.

Homosexuality is, of course, equally "abnormal" in the sense that it is rare in most human societies and totally absent in some. Tiger and Fox, to be sure, have cited homosexuality as one of the "universals" of human societies, but as usual they are careless with the facts. The anthropologist Donald S. Marshall, in his study of sex on the Polynesian island of Mangaia, states flatly that "there is no trace whatever of the active practice of homosexuality or of homosexual relationships," despite the fact that "in such a permissive society . . . there would appear to be ample opportunity for innate homosexuality to flower unopposed." And the Mangaians *are* permissive; sex begins at puberty, is practiced frequently and ingeniously for as long as it remains physically possible, and is for all ages one of the chief foci of existence. Christian ministers among the native population are much more likely to employ sexual and scatological proverbs than biblical ones; the islanders' vocabulary of terms concerning sex and sexual anatomy must be one of the most extensive in the world outside a medical dictionary—and, incidentally, contains no word for virgin.

The absence of homosexuality in this easy-going culture is the more notable in that a few Mangaian men (much less than 1 per cent), possibly for hormonal or other physiologic reasons, assume the social role and dress of women; they enjoy, and often excel at, "women's work" such as cooking or sewing, and delight in women's company (on Mangaia, oddly enough, social—as opposed to sexual—relations between the sexes are meager outside the family). And they are fully accepted as people, playing "an active role in the social life of the island, both . . . religious and . . . secular." By our standards they are certainly effeminate, yet they are *not* homosexual.*

---

* Such transvestite and/or effeminate males are found in not a few primitive societies, though they are never numerous; among the Plains Indians they were known as *berdache*; among the Basongye, a Congolese tribe, they are called *bitesha* (plural,

Homosexuality is also "unnatural" in the sense that it is nonexistent, or virtually so, among other primates, and that there is no credible evolutionary reason for any innate homosexual drive in man comparable to the innate heterosexual drive noted by Paul Goodman in the interview cited earlier. Goodman's testimony is the more impressive in that he himself was bisexual all his life; he married twice and produced several children, yet at the same time engaged in periodic homosexual "adventures." Homosexual activity, by either males or females, is in fact a product of human ingenuity rather than human evolution, in much the same way as are many variations of heterosexual activity—or tennis, or golf.

A majority of Americans, of course, are not content to regard homosexuality as abnormal and evolutionarily unnatural; for them it is also a "perversion," to be rooted out of the body politic by legal, or at least medical, measures. Even Donald Marshall and Robert C. Suggs, in their otherwise enlightening anthropological discussion of sex around the world, declare that "social toleration of active homosexuality as [an] openly accepted pattern of behavior cannot be justified under the present state of medical and scientific knowledge." They go so far as to intimate that the continued spread of this "disturbing behavior pattern" would threaten the survival of society, though they stop short of explaining why. For them, homosexuality is abnormal, a "deviation"—and as such is immediately lumped with such other deviations as sexual abuse of children (by homosexuals *and* heterosexuals), rape, and even the murderous activities of the Manson "family"—who were, however, heterosexual. Though they don't say it in so many words, their basic premise appears to be that any sexual deviant is at least potentially a criminal—not merely the perpetrator of a technical, victimless crime, as are all active male homosexuals, but a likely practitioner of sexual violence against some veritable victim.

But what, in that case, of such no less "deviant," no less "unnatural" activities as the various forms of oral-genital sex, which are indulged in by hundreds of thousands, perhaps millions, of Americans, most of them as impeccably heterosexual as I am myself or as (I assume) Marshall and Suggs are? In many American states these

_____

kitesha). The *berdache* were sometimes homosexual and sometimes not; the *kitesha* are rumored to be but deny it—and some of them are certainly married (to female *kitesha*). In our own society, contrary to popular belief, not all transvestites are homosexuals.

practices are just as illegal as homosexuality—even, if you can believe it, when carried on between husband and wife! If all these Americans are also potentially violent sex criminals, we'd better start building more jails.

So far as I am concerned, to suggest that all homosexuals are potential child molesters is as fantastic as to suggest that all heterosexuals are potential rapists—or to allege, as many homosexuals do, that all antihomosexuals are, at bottom, closet queens. The fact that homosexuality, along with several dozen other human sexual inventions, is a "deviation" or a "perversion" is neither here nor there. Perversion, in fact, is a concept that eludes scientific precision; the only sensible definition of it that I know of was given me some years ago by a young woman of my acquaintance, who observed on one occasion that perversion "is any kind of sex I don't like doing." This, I think, translates as "one man's perversion is another man's diversion," and so long as nobody is being exploited, violated, or annoyed, to each his (or her, or its) own. My own modest acquaintance with homosexuals leads me to the conclusion that as a class they are neither more nor less likable than heterosexuals; I would say of them what has been said of many other kinds of sinners, real and alleged: by their fruits ye shall know them. As Rudyard Kipling observed in a somewhat different connection:

> There are nine and sixty ways of constructing tribal lays,
> And every single one of them is right.

Nonetheless, the perennial and widespread attempts at regulating sex, normal or deviant, among so many and diverse peoples points up the very basic fact about human nature that we noted earlier: thanks to the convergence of several unrelated evolutionary developments, human sexual excitement is an extraordinarily powerful emotion, and therefore a potentially frightening one. Even among permissive peoples such as the Mangaians (and many others in Polynesia), sex is regulated to some degree—and is, moreover, the subject of much joking and laughter. And laughter (another uniquely human trait) is, among other things, our prime way of relieving tension, of deflating situations (and people) we would otherwise find too threatening to bear. We joke, openly or surreptitiously, about our rulers and our bosses; soldiers joke about death, as the poor joke about their poverty. And everyone jokes about sex, thereby paying tribute to the power that evolution has given it over us; the alert reader will note that I have done so repeatedly in this chapter. The suggestion by some psychologists that sexual humor is actually a product of sexual inhibition and frustration clashes with the anthropological facts: "dirty stories" among Polynesians and many other thoroughly uninhibited peoples would make an old-time burlesque comic blush.

On the wall of a Cro-Magnon cave in the French Pyrenees is a small, lumpy stalagmite. Next to it, crudely drawn in red ocher mixed with animal fat, is the figure of a little man, arranged in such a way that the protruding stalagmite . . . but you get the picture. This drawing, I am convinced, was—must have been—intended as a joke, the first known joke in man's long history. And it was a dirty joke.

11

THE CREATIVE IMPULSE: Language, Art, and Innovation

"In the beginning God created the heaven and the earth. . . ."
—GENESIS, 1:1

"Art is the imposing of a pattern on experience, and our esthetic enjoyment in recognition of the pattern."
—ALFRED NORTH WHITEHEAD

As we survey the long tale of human evolution, we can see that it is punctuated by at least two crucial transitions. The first, occurring (at a guess) some seven million years back, was when the earliest Australopithecines turned their backs on the forest and their faces toward the grassland, permanently abandoning part-time life in the trees for full-time life on the ground. The second, dated at a million years ago, give or take, was when more advanced hominids began using noises to refer to things that were not present, thereby achieving the first crude version of human speech. Obviously, neither of these transitions occurred in any such short, simple fashion as this account suggests; the former took hundreds of thousands and the latter tens of thousands of years. Nevertheless, fast or slow, they *did* occur, and with consequences important enough to be reflected in scientific nomenclature. Transition One saw the evolution of some variety of Ramapithecine ape into Australopithecine ape-man; Transition Two, the transmutation of the Australopithecines into full-fledged Hominines of our own genus.*

---

* As noted previously, some prehistorians place the emergence of genus Homo considerably earlier. My own feeling, however, is that the achievement of speech is a

The existence of both these key transitions will evoke little argument from any prehistorian. Far more controversial, by contrast, is the question of whether and, especially, when there occurred a third marked transition in human evolution. Bound up with it is another and even more controversial problem: who and what was Neanderthal man? Was he, as the majority of prehistorians currently believe, merely a variety or subspecies of modern man—in technical terms, Homo sapiens neanderthalensis (modern man being classified as Homo sapiens sapiens)—or was he, rather, a different species altogether, properly labeled Homo neanderthalensis, or was he conceivably no more than a variety of Homo erectus?

At first glance, this sort of terminological dispute seems of the most minimal importance to anyone but the specialist in prehistory. As we shall see, however, its resolution is intimately connected with some key questions about evolution and human nature.

Prehistorians have attempted to resolve the relationship between the Neanderthals and ourselves on essentially anatomic grounds, and that is where the trouble starts. For anatomy, as zoologists have long recognized, can be a treacherous guide. It is generally agreed, to be sure, that members of the same species must be more similar to one another anatomically than they are to any other species (though there are exceptions even here)—but how similar is similar? Putting it another way, how different must two animals be from each other for us to be certain that they are indeed of different species? A horse and a pig are obviously different species, but what about a horse and a zebra? Or a domestic horse and the wild Przewalski's horse of Central Asia? Or, for that matter, a Shetland pony and one of the great Percherons or Clydesdales that once hauled our brewery wagons? In fact, the horse and zebra are indeed of different species, the domestic and Przewalski's horses probably so, while the Shetland and Percheron are of the same species—though their anatomy differs considerably more than that of the other two pairs.

Given these and innumerable other anatomic ambiguities, modern zoologists have adopted behavioral and genetic criteria along with anatomic ones: two animals, or populations of animals, are deemed of the same species if, under natural conditions, they freely interbreed

---

considerably more meaningful criterion for separating Hominine from Australopithecine than the rather ambiguous anatomical features cited by these experts.

and produce fertile offspring.* By these criteria, the various races of modern man are clearly of the same species, despite their marked differences in color and (less markedly) in anatomy—differences which, in many animal groups, would be prima facie evidence of species difference. All modern races interbreed, and have done so wherever different racial populations have lived adjacent to or mixed with one another.

But the interbreeding criterion, valuable as it is for dealing with existing animals, hardly serves when we are considering the relationships of fossils. Obviously there is no way of telling whether the last Neanderthals could or did interbreed with the first modern men (usually called Cro-Magnons). Or—is there? Though we cannot, certainly, step back in time and observe the mating habits of these primitive humans, are there, perhaps, ways in which we can infer those habits, in somewhat the same way we inferred that Homo erectus could talk even though nobody has even heard one do so? I believe there are.

Before beginning to draw inferences, however, let us first examine the anatomical evidence, for whatever it may be worth. To begin with, the Neanderthals were clearly different from modern man, notably in the form of their faces.** Their foreheads sloped backward more than ours do, their eyesockets were topped with heavy bone ridges, and their chins were flat or backward-sloping rather than pointed as ours are. Taken as a group, all of them—with the exception of some skulls found in Palestine, about which we shall have more to say later—resembled one another more than any of them did modern man; by the same token, the various varieties of modern man resemble one another more closely than they do any Neanderthal (with the same Palestinian exception).

There is also the matter of the Neanderthal pharynx, already alluded to in Chapter 8, which—as reconstructed by Philip Lieberman—was shallower and less flexible than the modern pharynx and

---

* The final qualification, of course, separates such close relatives as the horse and donkey, whose offspring, the mule, is notoriously "without pride of ancestry or hope of posterity."

** For simplicity, I include among the Neanderthals not merely the "classic" Neanderthals of western Europe but other populations contemporary with them, including "Rhodesian man" of southern Africa and "Solo man" of Java, technically classified as Neanderthal*oids.*

therefore, by his reasoning, considerably less adequate for speech. But this anatomic difference, since it involves the long-vanished flesh of the Neanderthals rather than their tangible bones, which can be examined and measured, is to some extent inferential, and as such is not accepted by all prehistorians.

All that anatomy tells us, in short, is that the Neanderthals *could* represent a different species, not that they do. There is, however, one more faint anatomical clue. In cases where modern varieties of man interbreed, they produce not merely a blend of racial traits but a very diverse blend. Thus among any sizable group of American or West Indian "blacks" one will find intermixture with whites reflected in skins ranging from purplish dark brown to cream, hair ranging from kinky through wooly to wavy, and features ranging from "pure African" to European.* Moreover, these various racial traits are by no means neatly assorted; one sees light-skinned blacks with kinky hair and "Negroid" features, medium-skinned ones with wavy hair and/or European features, and so on.

If the Neanderthals and Cro-Magnons did indeed interbreed, one would expect similar results: "mixed" populations, in which, say, a Neanderthal brow was combined with a modern chin, and vice versa. And no such populations have turned up. But this is of course purely negative evidence; the failure to find such skeletons may mean merely that none of them has survived or that we have not looked long enough. The theory of evolution was long attacked on the ground that nobody had even found a skeleton of the so-called Missing Link connecting man with the apes, until the discovery of the Australopithecines in the 1920s and '30s settled the argument.**

Let us now abandon anatomy and take a broader look at the "Neanderthal problem." To begin with, "sapient" or not, they were around

---

* "Pure African" features are actually something of a myth; even the purest Africans show considerable variation in feature.

** Or settled it as much as any argument with antievolutionists is ever settled. Even today, many of them still attack the teaching of evolution in schools, on the ground, among others, that many "transitional forms" between one group of animals and another have never been unearthed. The fact that in some evolutionary lines—notably, for example, that of the horse—transitional forms have established the animal's evolution in detail for fifty million years back is ignored, as is the further fact that increasing numbers of such forms (for example, Australopithecus) continue to turn up in our own line. Basically, these people simply don't *want* to believe in evolution—and any argument, or no argument, will serve to convince them they are right.

for a good long time—from at least one hundred thousand to perhaps thirty-five thousand years ago. Moreover, they covered a lot of territory: their remains have turned up in China as well as in Java, Africa, and Europe. During nearly all this period, so far as we can tell, they were the only variety of man on earth; no Cro-Magnon types of skulls have been dated even provisionally at earlier than about 40,000 B.P. (Before Present), and most are thought to date from 30,000 B.P. or, usually, later.* Likewise, no Neanderthal skulls have been firmly dated at later than 35,000 B.P. In other words, after successfully populating most of the eastern hemisphere** for some sixty thousand years, they apparently vanished in only five thousand—and did so, moreover, at just the point where modern man appeared on the scene. Which is at least an odd coincidence.

The sudden disappearance of the Neanderthals and the more or less simultaneous appearance of modern man can be explained in at least four different ways:

1. All the Neanderthalers evolved very rapidly into Cro-Magnon types. Few prehistorians believe this. Even those who contend that *most* Neanderthalers evolved into modern man generally concede that this could hardly have happened to the "classic" Neanderthalers of western Europe; they are simply too different. To me it seems unlikely even if we exclude these Neanderthalers. To place all the other Neanderthalers among the ancestors of modern man implies that their widely scattered populations all evolved, independently, at the same rate *and in the same way*. The Rhodesian Neanderthaloids, that is, would have evolved into the ancestors of the Bushman,*** the Javans into ancestral Australoids such as today populate Australia and most of New Guinea, the Chinese into ancestral East Asians perhaps resembling American Indians, and so on—all of whom, as we have previously noted, ended up looking more like one another than any of them did like their Neanderthal forebears. This seems to me to involve an incredible degree of coincidence in timing as well as in genetics.

2. None of the Neanderthalers evolved into modern man. I don't

---

* One should bear in mind, however, that since the majority of Cro-Magnon remains were unearthed before modern radiometric dating methods were available, their dates are at best approximate.

** The western hemisphere was uninhabited.

*** The Negro is a relative newcomer to southern Africa.

know of anybody who believes this, nor any reason why they should. If Neanderthalers were the only type of man on earth fifty thousand years ago—which seems virtually certain—then some of them, surely, must be numbered among our own ancestors.

3. Some Neanderthalers evolved into modern man, whose expanding and spreading populations then interbred with and absorbed the remaining Neanderthalers. This involves other implausible assumptions. Modern man, as we have seen, seems to have been around since 40,000 B.P., and his appearance has not changed notably since that time; that is, he did not look any more Neanderthal then than he does now. If, then, we theorize that these early moderns were a blend of Neanderthals and a population of some other type, we face a dilemma. On the one hand, if the two populations were roughly equal in numbers, those of the "other type" would have to have had a "supermodern" anatomy; otherwise we would look a great deal more Neanderthaloid than we do. But no trace of such ultramod skulls has ever turned up, and indeed it is hard to imagine what they could have looked like. Alternatively, if modern men absorbed the Neanderthalers with few or no anatomic traces, we must assume that they markedly outnumbered the Neanderthalers—by at least four or five to one—and I know of no reason why this should have been so. Population density, then and now, is largely a matter of technology, particularly the technology for getting food. And while there are, as we shall see, reasons for thinking that Cro-Magnon technology rapidly became better than Neanderthal technology, there is no evidence that it was all that much better thirty-five to forty thousand years ago, when the intermixture would have taken place.

4. Some—probably a rather small number—of Neanderthalers evolved into modern man, whose expanding populations thereupon displaced or physically exterminated the remaining Neanderthalers. This seems to me most consistent with the evidence. The evolving Neanderthal population would presumably be represented by the Palestinian skulls already cited, whose features, though not fully modern, are by no means wholly Neanderthaloid. Significantly, these skulls appear to date from fairly late in the Neanderthal era. Even more significantly, these skulls are reported to have fully modern vocal tracts, indicating that the linguistic abilities of their owners were little if at all inferior to those of modern man.

And these same linguistic abilities would have made the first mod-

ern men—presumably descended from these ancient Palestinians—
formidable competitors for the Neanderthals. Speech, as we have
noted, is the vehicle for human cooperation, and the more efficient
the speech, the more efficient the cooperation. Modern man, then,
would from the beginning have been better at cooperative hunting
than his slower-witted Neanderthal contemporaries, meaning that in
any given region he would have obtained a lion's share of the available
game, thereby increasing his own numbers and, perhaps, decreasing
those of the Neanderthals through malnutrition.

One must not, to be sure, exaggerate the intellectual differences
between Cro-Magnons and Neanderthals, visualizing the latter as a
bunch of "village idiots" who characteristically stood about wondering vaguely what to do next. Slow thinking does not by any means
imply slow acting, as a glance at any group of monkeys will make
clear. For that matter, the Neanderthals are known to have successfully hunted such game as the mammoth, an animal sufficiently formidable to make fast reactions by its hunters the price of success and,
indeed, survival. So long as they were dealing with relatively familiar
situations such as their culture had already evolved techniques to cope
with, they would have operated quite as efficiently as any group of
modern hunters; where they would have been at a disadvantage would
have been in rapidly devising new techniques for coping with the
unfamiliar, especially to the extent that these techniques necessitated
rapid communication among the members of the hunting band.

Simply as hunters, then, the Cro-Magnons might have pre-empted
enough of the game to starve out their Neanderthal neighbors. They
might have done more: unpleasant though the thought is, there are
hints that they may not have confined their hunting to four-legged
game but may on occasion have butchered and eaten the Neanderthals. In 1899, at Krapina in Yugoslavia, there were unearthed the
remains of what may have been an entire Neanderthal band—some
twenty individuals of all ages and both sexes. The skulls were smashed
and the limb bones split, perhaps to get at the marrow, and there were
enough traces of charring to suggest that the human meat had been
cooked. The find has, of course, never been dated accurately, but it
is thought to date from *very* late in the Neanderthal era—between
45,000 and 35,000 B.P. Which is to say, at about the time that the
Cro-Magnons would have been moving into eastern Europe from
their (presumed) Palestinian birthplace. And in 1965 a find of similar

grisly Neanderthal relics was unearthed near Hortus in southern France, apparently (no radiocarbon dates are yet available) dating from the same period or even a little later.

Certainly if the Cro-Magnons had an advantage over the Neanderthals in ordinary (animal) hunting they would have had even more of an advantage in warfare, genocidal or otherwise: with quicker wits and better "communication capability" their tactics would have been far more flexible. And military history, from Braddock's defeat by the Indians at Fort Pitt to the French defeat by the Vietnamese at Dienbienphu, testifies to the superiority of the adaptable, flexible warrior to the fighter whose tactics are fettered by the chains of habit or military doctrine.

But of course this entire line of argument rests on the assumption that the Neanderthals *were* slow thinkers and poor communicators, that Lieberman's controversial reconstructions of Neanderthal vocal tracts, and his conclusions about Neanderthal linguistic capacities, are in fact correct. Before buying the theory, therefore, we might prudently inquire whether there is some independent line of inquiry, some category of evidence apart from anatomy, that would tend to substantiate—or disprove—Lieberman.

As it happens, there is. If the Neanderthals were slow to evolve ways of dealing with new situations, as Lieberman's theory implies, they would be no less inept at devising new ways of dealing with old situations. That is to say, we should expect their culture, taken as a whole, to be notably less innovative than that of their Cro-Magnon successors. *And that is precisely what we find.* The Neanderthals were unquestionably able and successful hunters and gatherers, but great innovators they were not. They may have invented the "flake" technique for making stone tools, in which knives, scrapers, and the like are made of flakes chipped off a lump of stone instead of from the lump itself (its importance lies in the fact that the flakes are generally sharper than the shaped lump, and also that a given weight of stone will yield something like five times as much cutting edge as with the older technique). They very probably invented laced clothing, which, taken with improved forms of shelter, enabled them to survive in both Europe and East Asia in glacial or near-glacial times. They may have invented the "compound," stone-pointed spear, but this, while an improvement over the simple wooden spear, was hardly a revolutionary improvement. They were also the first men to make bone tools, but only occasionally. On the evidence we have, these innovations are about all they have to show for their sixty thousand years on earth—a period, let us remember, half again as long as modern man has been on the scene.

When we turn to the Cro-Magnons and their descendants, innovation suddenly becomes not the exception but almost the rule. By around thirty thousand years ago, men had reached Australia, and they were men of essentially modern type,* which means that some innovator had discovered how to make a canoe or raft. Both the Neanderthals and Homo erectus, as we know, reached Java, but they could have traveled on foot during any Ice Age, when the mass of water locked up in the great continental glaciers lowered sea level by three hundred feet or more—quite enough to dry up the Straits of Malacca and Sunda which separate Java from the Asian mainland. Beyond Java, however, the straits grow far deeper and, since they are rather too wide for swimming, could have been crossed only in some sort of watercraft.

At just about the same time as modern men were paddling to Australia, others were wandering across the dry bed of the Bering Sea into North America; a skull of modern type unearthed near Los Angeles has been dated at about 23,000 B.P., and a piece of worked bone from the Yukon at several thousand years earlier. This extraordinary trip, through eastern Siberia and the Alaskan and Canadian Arctic, would have been impossible unless someone had invented improved clothing (probably sewn rather than laced) and improved shelter (probably the semisubterranean "pit house" still constructed by some Eskimos and Indians) with which they could survive the frigid blasts of a northern winter.**

Still at about the same time, or even earlier, somebody—almost certainly the Cro-Magnons of Europe—had invented the "blade" technique of tool making, which yields ten times as much cutting edge per pound of stone as the "flake" technique, and a cutting edge sharp

* The earliest Australoid skulls, though more primitive than those of other races (notably in their heavy brow ridges) are less primitive than Neanderthal skulls, none of which have been found anywhere near Australia. The original settlers of Australia can plausibly be seen as a group of very early Cro-Magnons, primitive in some features but with fully modern vocal tracts.

** Readers seeking more information on the discovery of America should consult my book *The First Americans* (see bibliography).

enough to shave with. Modern prehistorians who have mastered this technique sufficiently to demonstrate it in public warn their audiences not to handle the blades struck off a piece of flint or obsidian lest they cut themselves. A few thousand years later, the Cro-Magnons had invented the atlatl, or spear thrower, a device by which a projectile can be hurled far harder, or farther, than with the hunter's unaided arm. By 15,000 B.P. or so, the expanding Cro-Magnon tool kit included not merely the scrapers and knives of earlier days but needles, saws, barbed harpoons, skillfully sharpened burins for working bone, drills for piercing it, and stone and bone projectile points of a dozen different shapes and sizes.

Nor were all Cro-Magnon man's innovations purely utilitarian. He—or she—decked himself or herself with necklaces of ivory, shell, and animal teeth, and pendants carved from bone and stone. Most extraordinary of all, the Cro-Magnons invented art. By 25,000 B.P. or earlier, they were engraving crude drawings of animals on the walls of caves in southwest France; by 15,000 B.P. they had added to engraving the artist's techniques of drawing, painting, carving in both low and high relief, and—on a small scale, at least—sculpture in the round.

Prehistorians have debated at length over why the Cro-Magnons produced their diverse and beautiful *objets d'art*; the most prevalent view is that they did so for magical reasons, painting animals to insure plentiful game, and drawing and carving figures of women—sometimes, as we have seen, quite sexy ones—as a way of evoking the forces of fertility in animals, plants, and (very likely) people, which woman personified. However, anthropologists who have studied the artistic activities of such modern primitives as the Australian aborigines (who along with their very crude subsistence techniques possess a rich and vivid artistic tradition) note that they paint pictures for all sorts of reasons—sometimes to work magic, sometimes to record a notable happening, and sometimes simply because they feel like it.* But whatever the reason, or reasons, for Cro-Magnon art, it clearly

---

* Ucko and Rosenfeld (see bibliography) have written an excellent and hard-headed survey of Cro-Magnon art and the theories "explaining" it, including very convincing evidence that some of the theorizers have bolstered their theories by omitting and misstating facts—a phenomenon we have already noted in this book. Their dry comment on the erotic cave drawings is typical: these, they declare, may well have been drawn not for magical but simply for erotic purposes.

represents not merely an important innovation but a whole new category of human invention: the fabrication of objects with no discernible relationship to the "practical" activities of survival and reproduction. Man the toolmaker had begun producing tools—artifacts—to meet not just his physical needs but also his spiritual ones.

There are, as we noted in Chapter 8, indications that the Neanderthalers possessed a spiritual life of some sort, and that they used natural objects as "tools" for this purpose. For example, close studies of a Neanderthal burial found in the Middle East suggests that they—or some of them—may have buried their dead with flowers. But there is, I think, all the difference in the world between *using* natural objects for spiritual or esthetic purposes and fabricating objects for those purposes—as much as between tool using, which is not uncommon among chimps, and tool making.

Taking the innovations of modern man a bit further, we find that by about 12,000 B.P. he was using the bow and arrow in Europe, while by 10,000 B.P. he was making pottery in Japan, keeping dogs as scavengers, hunting assistants, and (sometimes) food in North America, and herding domesticated sheep in the Near East; within a few centuries he would begin raising his first crops. In another five thousand years he invented the ox-drawn plow, stones for grinding grain, weaving, irrigation, monumental architecture in both brick and stone, metalworking, the wheel, and writing.

But even disregarding this later period, in which man—thanks to the invention of agriculture and stock raising—had become both more numerous and more settled, we must conclude that modern man, in a mere thirty thousand years, had far surpassed the innovations achieved by the Neanderthals in a period twice as long; the rate of innovation must have increased by something like ten times. Quite as significant, I think, is the fact that the innovations tended to repeat themselves *independently* in different parts of the world. The atlatl, first invented in Europe perhaps twenty thousand years ago, was almost certainly reinvented in North America some ten thousand years ago. Agriculture was discovered independently in at least three places—the Near East, Southeast Asia, and Middle America—and may have been rediscovered in three more—China, West Africa, and South America. Pottery was invented twice in the Old World—in Japan and the Near East—and almost certainly at least once in

America. Writing was invented in Mesopotamia, may have been reinvented in China, and was certainly reinvented in Middle America, and much the same can be said of metalworking.

In passing from the Neanderthal to the Cro-Magnon stage of evolution, in short, man had—quite suddenly—become creative in a way and to a degree that he had never been before. And creativity, let us recall, is one of the key attributes of human speech; with words, and the rules for combining them, every one of us routinely generates new utterances, establishes new relationships, begets new ideas. If, then, human creative capacities underwent a rapid expansion about forty thousand years ago, it is very hard indeed to believe that this expansion did not reflect a similar expansion in linguistic capacities, which would mean that Lieberman, quite apart from his anatomic deductions concerning the Neanderthal and Cro-Magnon vocal tracts, is right. The Neanderthals must indeed have been slow speakers and slow thinkers, able to cope efficiently enough with a known and more or less predictable environment, but fatally disadvantaged in dealing with the unexpected—most especially, we can believe, the unexpected appearance in their world of bands of people who were not so handicapped.

We can now ask once more the question with which we began this inquest: given the circumstances, is it likely that Neanderthals and Cro-Magnons would have behaved toward one another like members of the same species—that is, would have regularly interbred? Surely not! If two populations are to fuse into one, they must sooner or later end up talking the same language, meaning that one or the other must learn a new language. Doubtless any Cro-Magnon could have learned to speak "Neanderthal" (which is to say, whatever language the local Neanderthals spoke; their tongues must have differed radically in, say, Europe and Rhodesia), but it would have hardly been worth the trouble. Even a slight acquaintance with the language would have made clear that it was not a very expressive or efficient vehicle for communication, and that its native speakers, by Cro-Magnon standards, didn't have very much to say for themselves. And if the Cro-Magnons wouldn't learn "Neanderthal," the Neanderthals *couldn't* learn "Cro-Magnon"; they simply didn't have the vocal equipment. Thus a Cro-Magnon man mated to a Neanderthal woman would have found her dull company indeed compared to the women of his own tribe; a Cro-Magnon woman mated to a Neanderthal man would

quickly have begun complaining: "Honey, you never *talk* to me!"
—and with full justice.

We should also note that for two populations to fuse, each must
regard the other as human beings. The fact that American blacks and
white have not fused into a single population in some three hundred
and fifty years is due in large measure to the refusal of most whites
to accept the Negro as fully human, in part because he doesn't, by
their standards, *look* human.* And in scores of other instances, one
or another group of men has excluded other groups from the human
race because they didn't *talk* human. The Greeks referred to all
non-Greek speakers as *barbaros,* meaning something like "babbling,"
but with many of the connotations bound up in our own "barba-
rous,"** and the various language groups of modern India perennially
riot against and massacre those of their neighbors who speak different
tongues.

Given these capacities of modern humans, what would the Cro-
Magnons have thought of the Neanderthals, who probably didn't look
altogether human,*** certainly didn't talk human—*and couldn't
learn?* The probability is that they would have seen their beetle-
browed neighbors as un-persons, perhaps as game to be hunted down
when more accustomed fare was lacking, perhaps merely as animal
competitors, comparable to the wolf or hyena, to be tolerated if they
were not too annoying but driven out with clubs, stones, and fire if
their depredations on the game herds became too onerous. We can
thus visualize the Neanderthals in various parts of the world as being
progressively forced into the poorest and least attractive regions,
much as the rapid expansion of Negroes into central and southern
Africa would much later push the aboriginal Bushmen into the semi-
desert of the African southwest. And the Neanderthals, slow-thinking
as they were, would have lacked the adaptability which has enabled
the Bushman to survive and thrive in an environment where most
Europeans (and many Africans) would perish of hunger and thirst.

But however one visualizes the process, whether as violent, even
cannibalistic extermination or relatively peaceful pre-emption of the

* More recently, the Black Muslims have returned the compliment by defining
whites as devils, not men.
** Significantly, the original, pre-Greek root of *barbaros* has also begotten such
words as "baboon" and "bobby."
*** The differences may not have been marked, but were certainly noticeable.

earth, humanity had clearly achieved a third major evolutionary leap: man the toolmaker had given way to man the creator.

To specify in any precise way what this step meant for human nature is not easy; creativity is hard to define and even harder to study, in or out of the laboratory. My own feeling is that, like human sexuality, it is compounded of several different ingredients, some of them dating far back in human evolution, others much more recent. One element, certainly, is the intrinsic satisfaction generated by new experiences. Curiosity, as we noted in the early chapters of this book, is characteristic of many, perhaps most, mammals, and is especially characteristic of the primates; it is the drive to amass new information which any animal with a high "information-processing capability" is almost bound to evolve. Another element is the pleasure that monkeys, apes, and men obtain from manipulating their environment, something closely allied in its nature and evolutionary roots to curiosity itself, since by manipulating things one can obtain more new and varied experiences from them—which is to say, of course, more information.

Yet another element, probably, is the incentive attached to insight learning discussed in Chapter 8. If, that is, the achievement of new insights—the perceptions of new relationships among objects in one's surroundings—came to play an increasingly important role in human learning (and as we saw there are strong reasons for believing that it did), then it is very likely that the achievement of such an insight would have come to carry with it some inherent satisfaction, quite apart from any subsequent "reinforcing" consequences. And given man's developing capacity to deal with objects symbolically, by means of words, it would not have been much of a step to obtaining satisfaction or pleasure from perceiving new *verbal* relationships—from getting new ideas.

All these elements in creativity might well have existed in fairly well-developed form among the Neanderthals or even earlier. What modern man added with his greatly enhanced linguistic capacities was a mechanism for generating in abundance the new ideas that gave him such satisfaction.

The excitement of creation is the first Cro-Magnon scratching idly with a twig in a smooth patch of earth, perceiving that his scratches looked vaguely like the horse he had killed the day before—and realizing that with more scratches he could "make" a horse! It is his five-hundred-times-great-granddaughter examining a clay-plastered basket (used, perhaps, for gathering seeds) that someone had left too close to the fire and noting that the clay had turned hard, so hard that it did not melt away in the rain as ordinary clay did. It is Archimedes shouting "Eureka!" as he leaped from the overflowing bath in which he had just discovered the First Law of Hydrostatics. It is Keats's "watcher of the skies when a new planet swims into his ken." It is every man or woman who has ever made an invention, solved a puzzle, painted a picture, composed a poem, contrived a recipe, designed a dress, built a bookcase—or a book. It is a major component of what my old professor, Edwin Berry Burgum, called the Esthetic Experience, "the perception of efficient activity": the awareness that something new has been added, that reality has been shaped into a new and more meaningful pattern. It is no coincidence that the ancient Hebrews opened their scriptures with the creative act in which God imposed shape and meaning on the formless, empty universe, thereby setting creativity first among the attributes of divinity. Creation is man's most distinctively human activity and experience and therefore, if you will, the moment at which he feels himself most like a god—most powerful, most knowledgeable—and least like a beast. Not for nothing is it sometimes called "the divine fire."

I must emphasize that the pleasure, the reinforcement with which the creative act endows us is something separate and apart from the results of the act. Creating a new or more perfect pattern can obviously entrain various pleasant consequences—money, sex, the admiration and praise of our families, friends, and associates, But it also engenders an immediate and special satisfaction of its own even without any such consequences—even, indeed, if the consequences are expectably *un*pleasant. The junior executive who conceives a new way of doing business will be pleased with himself even though he knows he must keep the idea *to* himself, on pain of offending a boss who dislikes innovations.

We find suggestions of this special excitement in creating newer and better patterns as far back as Homo erectus, who several hundred thousand years back was shaping "hand axes" with rather more symmetry and precision than would seem to have been required by any practical uses of the tools. However, this is problematic, since we are far from certain just what those uses may have been. We find a comparable esthetic sense much more certainly among the Solutreans, a Cro-Magnon culture of perhaps eighteen thousand years ago, whose famous "laurel leaf" and "willow leaf" points, shaped with the most exact symmetry and carefully thinned and finished by an elaborate technique called pressure flaking, involve an amount of human labor quite out of proportion to their practical value as spear points or daggers (some, indeed, are so large and delicate that prehistorians doubt they could have served *any* practical purpose).

How widely the creative impulse is dispersed among the human race is arguable. Some people—including not a few artists and intellectuals—tend to see it as the more or less exclusive property of artists and intellectuals, but their view seems to me far too narrow. Throughout nearly all of human history, and in large portions of the world even today, the mass of mankind has been too preoccupied with keeping breath in their bodies to have much time or energy for creation, if they were not actively discouraged from concerning themselves with it. Imagine, for example, the reception an Egyptian serf would have gotten had he suggested even a minor improvement in pyramid-building techniques. I myself have seen factory workers devise quicker and easier ways of doing a job that the time-and-motion engineers, with their clipboards and stopwatches, had not thought of, but they kept these innovations to themselves since they were convinced (not without reason) that to bring the innovation to the attention of their bosses would result in their doing more work for the same money, or in somebody being laid off because fewer men were needed. And if we include in the creative impulse Veblen's "instinct of workmanship"—the satisfaction from doing a job exactly right—we must, I think, conclude that at least a spark of the divine fire resides in the majority of our fellow men and women. Unfortunately, the instinct of workmanship too has suffered from social and institutional "negative reinforcement"; today especially, doing the job quickly, cheaply, and sloppily is more likely to be rewarded than doing it skillfully: if the car later breaks down or the washing machine quits working, that's the owner's, not the manufacturer's, problem.

Certainly creativity is not the monopoly of any racial or ethnic group; art—painting, carving, music, the dance—is a human universal, and there is no people so primitive that they do not create in at least some of these areas. One might argue, to be sure, that innovation must surely be at a low ebb among, say, the aboriginal Australians, whose culture, so far as we can tell, has changed less in the past twenty thousand years than any other in the world; their stone tools, for example, are often as crude as those of the Neanderthals, or cruder. A closer look, however, reveals that Australia is almost completely devoid of the free-flaking, tough minerals that lend themselves to precise toolmaking, such as the glassy flint that has inspired so many expert stonesmiths in other continents. When Australians have managed to get hold of more tractable materials, such as heavy glass insulators from a telephone pole, they have proceeded to shape them into "stone" implements equal in workmanship to those found anywhere, and to collect these "innovative" stones with sufficient enthusiasm to bring them into conflict with the Australian government. If the Australian natives are "backward" in comparison with nearly all other peoples, the reason probably has less to do with any inherent lack of ingenuity and imagination than with a certain cultural bias in favor of clinging to old, traditional ways. If some cultures discourage man's expression and enjoyment of his sex impulses, as they certainly do, then others could equally discourage his enjoyment of innovation in some or most areas.

More certainly we can say that certain cultures at certain periods, for reasons still obscure, encourage creativity in certain areas far more than others. England has not produced a major composer since the seventeeth century, while Germany begot a dozen; meantime, the English far outclassed the Germans in their own creative "specialty," poetry and the novel. Painting was successively dominated by the Italians, Dutch, and French; technology by the English, Germans, Americans, and—most recently—the Japanese; popular music by the Germans, Italians, and especially the Afro-Americans. The Romans were superb engineers but indifferent scientists, the Greeks were pioneering scientists and mathematicians but had little interest in engineering. Meanwhile, an obscure people in the hill country of Palestine was specializing in creative morality and ethics, to the point where its sacred writings became the foundation of three great religions.* The human creative impulse is a universal, but where and when and what people create are very much governed by the culture (or subculture) of which they are a part.

In our own culture we have the curious situation that whereas the

* The Jewish scriptures are of course, sacred also to both Christians and Moslems.

generality of men and women are little encouraged to be creative (and often, as we have seen, actively discouraged), large numbers of people make a profession of innovation. Their work is, of course, mainly concerned with designing new—or seemingly new—commodities for sale to the generality, or with contriving entertainments and stratagems whereby the generality can be induced to buy. The result has been the hypertrophy of innovation that Alvin Toffler described in *Future Shock* (a very superficial book built around an incisive concept) which at times threatens to overwhelm us psychologically. But it is innovation, as Toffler failed to note, of a special kind—trendy, superficial, and cheap—and thus perverts as much as it expresses human creativity.

A similarly perverse creativity is, I think, one of the main and most insidious components of that love of power which, though it is by no means a primate or human universal as the biotheologians claim, is unquestionably an outstanding feature of many human societies past and present, including our own. Power, of course, normally carries with it plenty of tangible rewards; Rank Has Its Privileges—tastier food, fancier raiment, more commodious housing, more complaisant women, and all the other amenities which can make life pleasant and interesting. Power can also represent, perhaps, a sadistic enjoyment of domination for its own sake, which is how George Orwell saw it in *1984* (though I must say I never found that part of the book really convincing). But power at what one might call its purest is something much more, for it enables its possessors, by dominating and directing the activities of others, to create through them—*and thereby to create on a scale that no individual creator or innovator can hope to equal.* To preside over the affairs of a corporation or a great university, a political campaign or a nation, means to impose one's own pattern, one's own conception of order, on tens and hundreds of people, and through them, on thousands and millions.

In itself, there is nothing wrong with this. The trouble comes when—as all too often occurs in our world—these hundreds and thousands become merely the raw materials of creation, the equivalent of the potter's clay or the cave painter's pigments mixed with animal fat, so that the creations of their powerful rulers take place without reference to—and often in contradiction to—their own human needs and qualities. Given opportunity and a little encouragement, man the creator, the tinkerer, the shaper of patterns, can become man the conniver and manipulator. Which is rather a daunting thought. One can, at least in theory, abolish the material rewards that encourage men to dominate their fellows. One can, still in theory, alleviate the interior hate and anger that are the wellspring of sadistic domination. But one cannot, even in theory, abolish man's inherent delight in reshaping and restructuring his world to the maximum extent his circumstances permit. It is in this sense, I think, that power truly tends to corrupt—not because it enables its possessors to live in luxury, though it often does, nor because it permits them to express instead of repressing their hates and hostilities, though it can do that too, but because it enables them to be as gods: to re-create the world, or a piece of it, after their own image.

12

A MIRROR TO MAN:
The Politics of Evolution

"The partisan, when he is engaged in a dispute, cares nothing about the rights of the question, but is anxious only to convince the hearers of his own assertions."
— SOCRATES

"Though this be madness, yet there's method in it."
— SHAKESPEARE

"Oh well," said Mr. Hennessey, *"we are as th' Lord made us."*
"No," said Mr. Dooley, *"lave us be fair. Lave us take some iv th' blame oursilves."*
— FINLEY PETER DUNNE

When an otherwise intelligent man suddenly starts talking nonsense, it's reasonable to ask what's bugging him. Likewise, when a literate, educated man or woman produces a book in which evidence, logic, and sense are alike set at nought, we are entitled to wonder why. Since he or she is evidently not getting at the rights of the question, just what *is* he getting at? What deep-rooted prejudices is he ventilating, what axe, and whose, is he grinding? And in no area of current writing are these questions more appropriate than in what we might call pop evolution, where—as we have repeatedly noted in earlier chapters—nonsense is more the rule than the exception.

In some cases, undoubtedly, the reason is no more complicated than the common desire to make a fast buck. Such was the case, I suspect, with Elaine Morgan when she sat down to write *The Descent of Women,* and this is rather a pity. She started with a great idea: to tell the story of human evolution from the female rather than, as almost invariably happens, the male viewpoint. Moreover, her book testifies that she is bright, witty and—so long as she is dealing with modern rather than prehistoric man and woman—well endowed with good, down-to-earth feminine common sense.* This is particularly noticeable when she is dealing with modern male writers on evolution, and her remarks on Ardrey, Morris, Tiger, and Fox are almost worth the price of admission. But when it comes to prehistory, alas, Morgan is trendy, superficial, well endowed with good old feminine cuteness —and very poorly endowed with the sort of background needed to write a useful book on evolution. I was not at all surprised to learn, for example, that her Oxford education was in English literature, not in any of the sciences or even in anthropology, fields which would have given her a much sharper critical sense about scientific evidence, and a much clearer notion about how to put it together.

As it is, she has constructed her theory of human evolution out of a mixture of fact, folklore, and fiction. In particular, she has based the whole thing on a fantasy of Sir Alister Hardy, who some years ago suggested that man might have spent a crucial stage of his evolution as a semiaquatic inhabitant of the seashore. Sir Alister is, indeed, a scientist—but a marine biologist, not a prehistorian, anthropologist, or paleontologist; his theory is one that nobody with any expertise in any of these fields takes seriously.

Even when she gets hold of an undoubted fact, Morgan often fails to realize that facts which apply to one group of humans don't necessarily apply to all. Thus her account of the supposed evolution of female sexuality involves repeated reference to the fact that human females often don't have orgasms. So far as British and American women are concerned, there seems to be a good deal of truth in this, but they are not, after all, the only women in the world. In fact, women in many cultures have no problems whatever with the orgasm. The ladies of Mangaia, for example—thanks to their culture's uninhibited and experimental attitude toward sex—routinely experience orgasm virtually every time, and indeed are likely to think themselves short-changed if they don't have two or three. Morgan's provincial attitude toward female sexuality is probably not unconnected with the notion, quite widespread among Britishers, that God is an Englishman (or, in her case, an Englishwoman)—and man (or woman) is made in God's image. But I suspect it is also not unconnected with

* I use the term "feminine" for a very simple reason: I have observed this type of intelligence much more frequently in women than in men, who seem to me as a class considerably more driven by fantasies and undefinable abstractions than their mates.

another notion, this one quite widespread among writers of all nationalities, that plausibility and readability are more important in a book than logic and sense.

Another likely entry in the fast-buck—or fast-pound—stakes is Desmond Morris. *His* discussion of evolutionary sex—which, as noted earlier, takes up a sizable portion of his first and most famous book, *The Naked Ape*—begins by conceding that generalization about human sexual behavior is difficult "because of the great variability that exists, both between and within societies." The only solution, he says, "is to take average results from large samples of the most successful societies. The small, backward, and unsuccessful societies can largely be ignored. They may have fascinating and bizarre sexual customs, but biologically speaking they no longer represent the mainstream of evolution." Speaking as a long-time professional writer and editor who has both made and listened to his fair share of writers' excuses, I would translate all this as "I didn't want to be bothered doing the research."

But Morris is more than a lazy writer; he is also at times a rather obnoxiously ethnocentric if not racist one. Speaking of his "backward and unsuccessful societies," he opines that "their unusual sexual behavior [may have] helped to turn them into biological failures as social groups." And this is the Missionary Position with a vengeance: the "native" seen as a self-indulgent, licentious heathen whose domination by more "successful"—and more inhibited—peoples is only natural. God is not only an Englishman, He is also engaged in punishing (evolutionarily speaking) those peoples whose "bizarre" sexual customs offend against Anglo-American middle-class morality. As Nero Wolfe is fond of observing, pfui!

Morris's pseudoscientific apologia for Euro-American domination of "backward and unsuccessful" societies typifies an all-too-common trait of pop evolutionists: their misuse of evolutionary theory as political ideology. Any account of man's past psychological evolution inevitably embodies certain conclusions about present-day human nature —which is to say, about human society: why it is the way it is, and what (if anything) can and should be done about it. And to the extent that these accounts disregard or misinterpret the facts, they become ideology, not science—and, like virtually all ideologies, from Mithraism to establishment Marxism, serve, like Morris's remarks on "bizarre" sexual customs, as apologia for some version of the status quo. As such, they fall into that category of popular literature I have elsewhere labeled Schlock Sociology, a modern literary genre whose function is to supply fake solutions to real problems. This is not to say that the fakery is necessarily deliberate or conscious, merely that it exists and, because it exists, is dangerous. If we are to treat effectively the ills of our society, we must first diagnose them, and a wrong diagnosis, as physicians well know, is worse than none at all, since it leads to both the withholding of needed treatment and the administration of therapy that will not make the patient "better" and may well make him worse.

In earlier chapters we have seen some of the ways in which the biotheologians Ardrey, Tiger, and Fox have ignored both fact and logic in their accounts of human evolution. It is now time to examine more closely what they are really getting at—the ideological method in their evolutionary madness.

Tiger and Fox, of course, view man as the "imperial animal," whose evolutionary nature, as summed up in their final chapter, is "to create hierarchies . . . to attempt to dominate and coerce others, to resort to violence either systematic or lunatic . . . to connive, to seduce, to exploit." In Chapter 7, I have shown at length just how far this picture is from the evolutionary realities of human nature, but as ideology its implications are obvious: men are going to continue to oppress and dominate one another ad infinitum, and nothing, or nothing very much, can be done about it. Thus the authors equate modern social and political elites, which they personify as "the people in the black limousines," with the groups of dominant males which are (supposedly) universal in primate societies. Therefore, "there will always be black limousines; it is only the people in the limousines who change." No less inevitable, evidently, is the conquest of the weak by the strong. "How," our authors inquire rhetorically, "can a reply be framed to the proposal that only powerful countries are proof against attack; that to rely on the goodwill of powerful neighbors is charming but hopeless and indeed perilous?" Were I to frame such a reply, I should begin by consulting the Canadians, Swedes, and Swiss, all of whom have for some generations relied—successfully—on the goodwill, or at least the tolerance, of powerful neighbors. So, for half a century, have the Irish of Eire, who despite their proximity to far more powerful nations have managed to maintain a resolute neutrality in world affairs, though their own military forces are of the most exiguous.

Tiger and Fox make extensive use of a rhetorical staple of Schlock Sociology which I have chosen to call the Evasive We. Thus they say, "We . . . create out of the stuff of a local hierarchy the basis of an imperial apparatus. . . . We strive to control huge areas of land and large groups of people." The political purpose of the Evasive We is, of course, to shift the responsibility for social evil from somebody to everybody—which means nobody. To expose its fraudulence, however, one need only substitute "my friends and I" for "we." And I can assure the reader that my friends and I have not the least desire to create an imperial apparatus or to control large areas of land and large groups of people; we keep busy enough trying to cope with the people in black limousines, who do. Nor, to be fair, do I think the alleged evolutionary impulse toward imperialism is much more powerful among Tiger, Fox, and *their* friends.

Let us consider some recent examples of efforts "to control large groups of people," powered, if we are to believe our two imperial anthropologists, by man's sempiternal impulse "to dominate and coerce others . . . to connive, to seduce, to exploit." The Bay of Pigs was connived at by the CIA and the Pentagon; neither I nor my friends were consulted, and indeed the Kennedy administration went to some pains to conceal from us—and the rest of the American public—the preparations being made for it.* The war in Southeast Asia was, as we now know, surreptitiously escalated by "the best and the brightest" in American public life, to the accompaniment of large-scale, systematic lying about what we were doing and why we were doing it. Neither my friends nor I were encouraged to say yea or nay to these activities, and in fact a couple of my friends spent some time in jail for saying nay too vigorously. Nor, to move to another part of the forest, were Mr. Khrushchev's activities in Hungary or Mr. Brezhnev's in Czechoslovakia cleared in advance—or afterward—with the Soviet equivalent of my friends and me; rather, some of *them* ended up either in jail or in certain specialized "mental institutions" which the Soviet authorities maintain for those of their citizens with "unnatural" feelings about dominating and coercing others.

If any of these activities were criminal—and I, for one, am con-

---

* Subsequently, President Kennedy told Clifton Daniel of *The New York Times* that had the *Times* published these preparations (which it could have done) it would have saved America from a major blunder.

vinced they all were—then the identity of the criminals is a matter of public record. To intimate, as Tiger and Fox do, that "we" did, or at least desired, these things is to file a spurious verdict of "murder by person or persons unknown," which under the circumstances amounts to acting as accessory after the fact.

Ardrey, too, relies heavily on that Evasive We. In his most recent book, *The Social Contract,* he more or less abandons his original contention that man is "instinctively" a killer, but still insists that "we enjoy the violent" (my friends and I don't) and that "we applaud the violent" (neither my friends nor I do). Speaking of political demonstrations, he alleges that "the peaceful march no longer excites us"; ergo, we "must incite police to violent confrontation." As it happens, I—and also my friends—have over the years participated in quite a number of demonstrations, peaceful and otherwise, and therefore have a certain amount of firsthand information on how "we" feel about them—which Ardrey, I strongly suspect, does not. Well, I can testify that the notion of inciting cops to violent confrontation does not "excite" me but rather scares the bejeezus out of me. You can get hurt that way, and I, being afflicted with neither masochism nor machismo, derive absolutely no satisfaction from getting hurt.

I would not want to mislead the reader: I do not have conscientious objections against any and every form of violence, though some of my friends do. Like the Mikado, I have my own little list of people whose disappearance would, in my judgment, leave the world better off. But even here I would infinitely prefer that they be removed peacefully from public life rather than violently from physical life. The only situations in which I can in any sense *enjoy* violence, even in fantasy, are in relation to people who terrify and/or enrage me beyond measure—and here, of course, the real enjoyment comes not from the violence as such but from the cessation of rage and/or terror. Much the same, I would wager, could be said about Ardrey himself; much the same could equally be said of 95 per cent or more of his readers, even as they wag their heads in agreement over his horrifying picture of man's "evolutionary" violent impulses run amok. For such people, the Evasive We easily translates into a still-more-evasive They: "they" are naturally violent, while "we, we precious few," are not.

Even more revealing on the nature of Ardrey's political platform are the particular kinds of violent people he chooses to view with alarm. These include delinquents and rioters in our slums and ghettos, students in America, strikers in Italy, and demonstrators almost anywhere who "provoke" the police to violence.* Fair enough. But he remains remarkably blind to the violence of, for example, police who provoke demonstrators (I have seen this), police and hardhats who attack them unprovoked (my friends have seen this), and police who in dozens of cities club and sometimes shoot ghetto dwellers (*not* rioters) with little or no excuse. Most startling of all is his evaluation of our war in Southeast Asia, which over a period of thirteen years managed to destroy something like a hundred times as many human beings—including large numbers of women and children—as all the concurrent strikes, riots, demonstrations, and trigger-happy cops put together. Of this appalling outbreak of violence, Ardrey can say only that it was "unpopular, unreal [!], purposeless, *and, above all, unwinnable*" (my emphasis). If the English language means what I think it does, Ardrey is here saying that the most important thing about the recent events in Southeast Asia is not that they were hideously, devastatingly violent but that their violence didn't work.

Yet the main political target of Ardrey's polemics is not, I think, the various (selected) violent groups he cites but rather a particular scientific view of violence: that its existence, prevalence, and nature are in large measure determined by culture and environment. In dealing with this view, which he calls environmental sociology, Ardrey spares neither epithets nor—I regret to say—rhetorical tricks. At one point, for instance, he manages in just two successive sentences to misdefine the environmental view in three different ways. First he ascribes to environmentalists the view that "riot and arson" are due *"only* to environmental *deprivation, neglect, or injustice"* (my emphasis), though the most dogmatic environmentalist would recognize, indeed insist, that there is a lot more to any environment than deprivation, neglect, and injustice. He then equates this view with one that "seeks wholly in the actions of the majority the motivations of the minority," which is not the same thing at all, and ends by equating both views with "presenting greater sympathy for the violator than

---

* In fact, a whole series of investigations and trials has now made clear that much American political violence in recent years was provoked not by the dissidents who were blamed for it but by professional provocateurs and "plumbers" hired by police departments and other "law enforcement" agencies.

the violated"—which is something different again. (I pass over his implication that the rioting minority is always the "violator," never the "violated.")

There is nothing about the environmental view as I, along with most environmentalists, would define it that excludes a biological, evolutionary component in human violence. As I have several times noted, evolution has indeed given man the potential for violence, chiefly because during his five-million-year residence in open country he was often confronted with predators—animal and sometimes human—whose threat to himself, his females, and his young could only be met by violence. But to recognize this potential is merely to say that man is sometimes violent, which we knew anyway. What we also know, however, is that he is clearly much *more* violent in some cultures, in some environments, and at some times. A thousand years ago, homicide was almost a weekly occurrence among the Viking settlers of Iceland; today, among the biological descendants of those same settlers, it is a rarity. The Pueblo tribes of the American Southwest were basically pacific, their Navaho and Apache neighbors were anything but; white Americans kill one another considerably oftener than white Englishmen, despite the two nations' shared heritage of language, law, and literature. And one could continue to list such contrasts almost indefinitely.

If, then, we—meaning my friends and I, among many others—are concerned about the increasing violence in our world and want to do something about it, our only rational approach is to take man's evolutionary nature, violent potential and all, as given, and go on from there. Human nature, millions of years in the making, is not going to change in our lifetime, or our grandchildren's. What we must inquire is why that nature expresses itself in violent actions so much more often at some times and places than at others. As always, wisdom begins with asking the right questions. If we ask "How can we eliminate violence from human affairs?" the answer is very probably "No way!"; man's evolutionary nature, if nothing else, will take care of that. But if we ask rather "How can we *minimize* violence?" the chances are that we can find an answer, since a number of cultures have, by accident or design, done so.

We have already seen how aggression and violence in baboons can vary enormously in different environments. Ardrey describes the baboon as "a born bully, a born criminal, a born candidate for the hangman's noose [!]. . . . He is ugly. He has the yellow-to-amber eyes that one associates with the riverboat gambler [!!]." And while we need not take this anthropomorphic fantasy very seriously, there is no doubt that the animal's potential for violence is roughly equivalent to our own. We have seen, indeed, how DeVore's male grassland baboons typically ganged up to confront danger, and also typically threatened (and occasionally attacked) one another as part of their struggle for dominance. Rowell's savanna baboons, on the other hand, could and did escape danger by retreating to nearby trees, with the result that the males showed no taste for violent confrontation with predators—in fact, they usually, thanks to their size, outran the females. And, very significantly, they also showed little interest in playing the dominance game among themselves. Well, if Ardrey's "born criminal" can turn pacifist where the environment recommends this course, perhaps there is hope for man!

Among our primate relatives (and surely among our own ancestors) aggression and violence are (and were) heavily influenced by the amount of stress and tension in the group. A prime source of such stress, as with the baboons, is the presence of enemies in the neighborhood plus the absence of ways to escape them. A second source, it appears, is crowding, whose effects in engendering violence have been observed in both wild and captive primates. Kenji Yoshiba, observing langurs in the Dharwar Forest of southwest India, found aggressive threats between troops far more common than among the langurs described by Phyllis Jay and others. There was virtually no dominance conflict among males of a given troop because most of the troops had only a single adult male, but the area was infested by all-male gangs which on occasion would attack one of the male-female troops, in particular its male leader, sometimes managing to drive him away permanently. There would then ensue a series of fights between the "conquering" males, to the point where all but one of them was driven off. Sometimes, though not always, the new leader would then proceed to kill the troop's infants—those born before his accession to power—which by primate standards is very odd behavior indeed.

The reason for the radical differences between Yoshiba's and Jay's langurs is not altogether clear. Danger from predators is certainly not the answer, since the former were if anything less endangered than the latter. The only significant environmental difference was population density: Yoshiba reports that at Dharwar it was more than thirteen times that reported by Jay. He himself suspects that sexual tension among "unaffiliated" males may also have played a part, but he does not try to guess why so many males were unaffiliated—that is, why most of the mixed troops included only one adult male.

Whatever the precise role of crowding in generating stress and conflict among the Dharwar langurs—and it is hard to believe that it did not play a considerable role—there is no doubt that it can produce serious and sometimes fatal conflicts among captive primates. Again the reasons are not wholly clear, but a very important one is evidently the impossibility of avoiding conflict. In the wild, so long as the population is not too dense, a threatened animal can, and often does, simply remove itself from the situation until the threatener has had a chance to cool off; in captivity, the only "solution" may be to fight it out.

Other factors inducing stress and other abnormal behavior of various types among captive primates are lack of stimulation (in human terms, boredom), sudden changes in environment (in human terms, culture shock), and, possibly, overstimulation of certain kinds. S. D. Singh, comparing urban and rural populations of rhesus monkeys in India, found the former much more aggressive than the latter, both toward one another and toward humans. And a virtually universal source of stress, anger, and often violence among primates—and most or all other mammals—is what is loosely called frustration, in which an animal's normal response to a situation is blocked by some other aspect of the situation. Thus a male chimp attacked by another male may respond by fighting back, but if that response is blocked by fear will often "take out" its anger on a female or smaller male, or may engage in shaking branches and other angry displays until it cools down. Very probably akin to this sort of frustration was the production of "neurosis" in dogs in the famous experiments by Pavlov: the animals, having first been trained to expect food at the sound of a bell, were then given instead an electric shock. Pushed in two contradictory directions by their responses, they rapidly became tense, fearful, and sometimes vicious.

Let us now consider to what extent these stress-and-violence factors may be relevant to violence in man. Specifically, let us examine the environmental, "ecological" situation of the groups in our society that are generally conceded to be a prime focus of violence: the urban, slum poor. These people have committed more than their "share" of violent acts probably for as long as there have been urban slums: in the fifteenth-century Paris of François Villon, in the eighteenth-century London limned by Hogarth, and in twentieth-century New York, Chicago, and Detroit. Neither race nor religion seems to make much difference; in my own city, New York, the "Hell's Kitchen" area of a century ago, populated largely by poor, slum Irish, was quite as dangerous as today's black Harlem or Puerto Rican "El Barrio."

The first thing we can say about these ghetto ecosystems is that their inhabitants feel endangered. The "outside world"—which for them means primarily the (white) landlord and various (usually white) government officials, especially the police—is seen as hostile, and not without reason.* It is seldom possible for the ghetto inhabitant to cope effectively with these threats, since he lacks the power, nor can he escape from them; even could he afford to move to another neighborhood (and he often can't) he is likely to find all sorts of obstacles in the way, from real estate agents who won't sell or rent to him, to neighbors who don't want his kids in school with theirs.

The second thing about the ghetto ecosystem is that it is crowded. Poverty, high rents, and the obstacles to moving out make for the highest population densities in urban America, and some of the highest in the world. Continuing down the list, we find that the ghetto dweller, having been transplanted from the Caribbean or the rural American South, frequently suffers from culture shock and also, since he is often unemployed or underemployed, from boredom. And of course he is frequently frustrated, like the chimp whose urge to fight back is blocked by fear. Nor does frustration stop there: he is also continuously urged, by the press and, especially, television, to buy the beautiful and enticing products of American industry, yet the normal response to this urging—to earn money through a job, or a better job—is blocked by discrimination, by his own lack of skills, or by the simple unavailability of jobs of any kind. *In short, if an expert in primate psychology had set about constructing in his laboratory an environment calculated to produce the maximum stress, tension, and violence among his animals, he would have produced something very like our urban ghettos—dangerous, crowded, frustrating, and boring.*

---

* Many police, of course, perceive the ghetto dwellers as hostile and dangerous, also not without reason.

The result is as predictable as any of Skinner's rat and pigeon experiments: violence. And of course the violence feeds on itself. To the extent it is directed at other ghetto dwellers (as most ghetto violence is) it makes the environment even more dangerous and stressful; to the extent it is directed toward outsiders, such as the police, the ultimate result is the same. For the cops, of course, are primates too, and the more endangered *they* feel, the more aggressive and trigger-happy they become.

Thus far we have considered the ghetto dweller simply as a primate; let us now consider him as a human primate. As we saw in the preceding chapter, man is the most curious and manipulative of the primates, and the only creative one. Evolution has designed him, as it were, to make patterns, and enjoy doing so, from the pattern of a flint hand axe to that of a computer. He is an animal that needs to keep busy, and if he is prevented from doing so in socially approved ways, on the job, he is quite likely to devise less attractive ways of his own. In this sense, Ardrey is perfectly correct in saying that "we" enjoy destruction; we do—so long as we can find no constructive activity to occupy us. The old principle that Satan finds work for idle hands is something that all of us have from time to time seen at work in our own children; it is no less true of other people's children, or of adults.

Man is also the primate most prone to imitate, the most adept at observation learning. And if we look at the flickering images which children, in and out of the ghetto, daily observe, we find them saturated with violence, from John Wayne to Superfly. The man who purveys sexual images to teenagers goes to jail; he who purveys violent ones goes to the bank. What effect these violent images have on the normal, middle-class kid is arguable; their probable effect on the ghetto teenager, predisposed to violence by the tensions and stresses —and, by now, also the traditions—of his environment, is not. In this sense, too, Ardrey is right: violence *is* applauded in our culture, but not much of the applause comes from "us." Rather, it comes from a relatively small group of men who have become rich and powerful by portraying violence as romantic, admirable, and manly.* I am all

* The plot of a recent John Wayne horse opus can be summed up as follows: little boys become men by learning to kill. Also worth noting is that a good deal of Wild West movie and TV violence has only the most tenuous connection with the historical realities of life on the American frontier. Psychiatrist Kent E. Robinson has pointed

in favor of ending this applause—and reinforcement—for violence. If we can legitimately prevent kids from observing copulation on the screen or tube—and I know of no one who disputes this—then I see no reason why we cannot equally restrict their exposure to mayhem and murder. While we are about it, we might also devote some thought to the curious situation whereby military pilots who engaged in wholesale violence are feted at the White House while men who refused to take the violent way are pilloried "without pity" from the same quarter.

But muting our culture's applause for violence, though it may ameliorate the problem, will not solve it. Such positive reinforcement is, in Skinnerian terms, merely the contingency that makes violence more likely to occur; it does not itself generate violence. Much the same can be said of such "negative reinforcements" as tougher courts and cops and longer jail sentences for the violent; they may, just possibly, somewhat diminish violence but they will leave untouched the forces that generate it. To tackle *that* problem means to set about changing the environment which subjects millions of our fellow citizens to the daily fears, tensions, stresses, and frustrations which beget violence in primates as predictably as clouds beget rain.*

I do not propose to specify just how we should set about this; space, and a certain modesty, forbid it. Were I asked for a good place to start, however, I would suggest a governmental guarantee of a job at decent wages for every man and woman able to work. This would, quite rapidly, abolish both the poverty and the idleness that are among the important roots of violence—and would incidentally end the hypocrisy of sermonizing about the work ethic to people for whom no work is available. Economists and sociologists, to be sure, will at this point exclaim "But most of these people have no marketable skills— how can they be given jobs?" I have no patience with this argument. If people don't have the skills, train 'em. I don't mean poverty-program training in the "skills" of *how to get* a job, which in the

out, for example, that Wyatt Earp, an archetype of the rough, tough, shoot-'em-up western sheriff, in fact killed just one man during his three years as marshal. He established law and order not by his readiness for shoot-outs but because he established the first U.S. gun-control law: a system of fines for anyone wearing or discharging firearms in the town. Modern law-and-order advocates, please note.

* Ironically, Ardrey, who dislikes Skinner's theories as much as I do, has in this area unwittingly joined the behaviorists, since his proposals for dealing with violence amount to no more than changing the reinforcements which it entrains.

absence of jobs to be gotten is merely an expensive con game.* Nor do I mean the abstract skills involved in "learning a trade" into which the trainee may then find his way blocked by limited opportunity or trade-union exclusiveness. Rather I mean the concrete skills of a veritable job into which the trainee will literally move immediately on graduation—or, better, before it, working while he is learning.

And if the trainee should prove, because of limited literacy or for other reasons, to be untrainable? Then let us for God's sake find, or invent, some job he can do without training; if a man can only dig sewer ditches, there are surely plenty of sewers that need digging if our rivers and lakes are to be cleaned up. For something like a quarter of a century the federal government has been subsidizing numbers of technologically backward and/or managerially incompetent industries, two prime examples being railroading and shipbuilding; is it too much to suggest that it also subsidize technologically backward individuals?

In proposing that we attack idleness and the other environmental factors that breed violence, I will surely be accused by some biopoliticians of bleeding-heartism, do-goodism, and similar sins: in Ardrey's words, of offering alibis for violence, "presenting greater sympathy for the violator than the violated." As it happens, I have only modest sympathy for the violator—and none at all if he threatens to violate me—but my sympathy is irrelevant to the argument. To cope with the problem of violence, I submit, we do not need sympathy—which, as somebody once observed, is good for a handout at the Salvation Army and not much else—but simple common sense: a willingness to accept the law of cause and effect as it applies to our own species. One does not need sympathy to recognize the fact that if you kick a dog he may bite you, and that if you kick a man he'll kick you back if he can. The study of human evolution, as I have noted earlier, tells us that man, in the specifics of what he does, can be the most unpredictable of animals, but it also tells us that under certain circumstances his nature makes him predictably likely to do certain *kinds* of things. And since we are evidently not going to change his nature, we are foolish indeed if we do not get on with changing the circumstances.

---

* And is seen as such by the trainees, who are by no means as dumb as some psychologists and educationists would like to believe.

Cholera, once a terrifying plague in Europe and America, is an "environmental" disease, in the sense that if the food or drinking water in your environment is contaminated with Vibrio cholerae it is very likely to make you very sick. Nowadays, cholera can be treated quite effectively with antibiotics and quantities of intravenous fluids; at the same time, of course, the sufferer is segregated so that his body wastes cannot infect others. Yet cholera continues to flare up periodically where conditions permit, which is to say in most places where pure water supplies and adequate sewage systems are lacking, sickening tens of thousands and killing at least hundreds. It is the same with violence. We can, and should, segregate the violent; we can and should learn to treat them so that they are no longer violent. But unless we clean up the environmental conditions that stimulate, aggravate, and liberate the potential for violence that evolution has bred into us, it will continue to flare up from time to time—and kill some of us.

13

THE PAST AND THE FUTURE:
Evolution and Freedom

"Human beings have a right to be human in the same sense as cats have a right to be cats."
—A. H. MASLOW

"We have to show the world a society in which all relationships, fundamental principles, and laws flow directly from moral ethics, and from them alone."
—ALEXANDER SOLZHENITSYN

"Man is a long time coming. . . "
—CARL SANDBURG, The People Yes

"I am a human being: do not spindle, fold, or mutilate."
—GRAFFITO, BERKELEY, CALIFORNIA, 1965

People with naïve views on human nature (often they are young people) have sometimes been heard to declare that what is wrong with the world is not man but man's societies and cultures, which have, they allege, warped his true nature into something odious. At times, they even speculate on what sort of creature man might be in a State of Nature, freed from the burden of his cultural and societal baggage.

The answer, of course, is that he would not be man. As we have seen, our ancestors were living in societies—groups—long before they became men; had they not done so, they could not have survived, nor could we, today. Likewise, our ancestors became human as, and to the extent that, they became able to create cultures, the collected tools, tongues, and traditions that men learn from their seniors in society and teach—by precept or simply by example—to their juniors. Robinson Crusoe, the literary prototype of man outside society, survived only by grace of the tools and other products of his society that he salvaged from his wrecked vessel, plus the skills he had acquired growing up in an English village. Depending on the society we inhabit and our place in it, we may be more free or less so, but we are never so free as to be able to dispense with society altogether, even should we wish it, as not one man in ten thousand does. The best we can do is decide, within limits, what kind of society we want, and either seek it out, if it exists, or make a stab at constructing it, if it does not.

In this final chapter I propose to consider how well our society serves our needs, given the kind of animals we are—and given the technology we command. For human freedom, in a very basic sense, is ultimately limited by human technology; the tools and skills whereby man reshapes the natural world to meet his material needs. As we know very well, there is a lot more to freedom than mere technology; a rich society is not necessarily a free one. On the other hand, a poor society is inevitably a relatively unfree one, in the sense that it offers far fewer choices to its members. Man the hunter and gatherer—which until about ten thousand years ago included every human being on earth—was and (in the few places he survives) is free only to be a hunter and gatherer; he cannot, for example, choose to be a poet or a painter except in his spare time. Man the primitive agriculturalist—a category that even today probably includes a majority of the human race—is scarcely better off; born a farmer, he has at the most generous estimate only one chance in ten of being anything else because the productive technology of his society will support no greater proportion of nonfarmers.* In modern industrial societies, disposing of enormous sources of artificial energy, far more choices are open to far more people.** Yet even here the choices are not unlimited; we cannot *all* choose to be poets or painters or professors, doctors, lawyers, or merchants, since if we did we would all starve to death. Yet recognizing the limitations that technology and resources impose on our choices, we can still inquire what choices should be open to us, what freedoms we should be able to exercise— *what our rights are as human beings.*

Now if the term "human rights" means anything, it means the right to be human: to enjoy the pleasures and, so far as circumstances

---

* Even in America and Europe, it is only a hundred and fifty years or less since the proportion of farmers in the employed population first dropped below 90 per cent.

** As long as the energy sources hold out, at least!

permit, avoid the pains for which twenty million years of evolution have equipped us. I take it, then, that the best society is the most human society: that which gives its members maximum scope to exercise and enjoy their humanity.

Put that way, the statement sounds tautologous if not flatulent. Yet I must stress that it is in no sense a scientific statement, as are, to one or another degree, most of the propositions I have hitherto put forward in this book. It is not subject to the rules of logic or evidence; no ethical, evaluative statement is. Scientific methods can tell us, with reasonable certainty, how our species evolved and what kind of creatures we are, but they cannot tell us what is good. To say that a society (or anything else) is "good" immediately raises the question "Good for whom, and by what standards?" And the only answer likely to satisfy any of us, let us face it, is "Good for me, by my standards." Some of us, to be sure, tell ourselves that we are obeying God's commandments, not our own—but it is we, after all, who have chosen the commandments we seek to follow, even leaving aside the question of whether God was in fact their author. Nor, for that matter, is *that* question subject to scientific proof. If God exists, science cannot prove it; if He is dead, science has not signed the certificate. Either you believe in Him, and His commandments, or you don't.

My own statement about the nature of a good society is of precisely the same sort: either you believe it or you don't. Like "all men are created equal," it is a self-evident proposition—which can be defined as one that most people believe but none of them can prove. It is self-evident to me—is, in fact, the fundamental assumption on which I shall base my argument—but those who do not like the assumption will probably not like the argument either.

Accepting that assumption, how good is our society? Putting it another way, just what is involved in "the right to be human"? What needs and drives has evolution implanted in us, and how well does society—can society—satisfy them?

Man, before he becomes man—or woman—is a child, and before that an infant. And it is here that our catalogue of human rights begins.

Every human baby has the right as a bare minimum, to two things: a mother to feed and comfort it and a father to protect and play with it—or, since in human beings parenthood is not so narrowly defined by gender as in our primate relatives and ancestors, vice versa. Obviously this does not necessarily mean the biological mother and/or father. Solomon, in one of his better-known judicial decisions, justly awarded the baby to the woman who showed her love for it; he did not, as the lawyers say nowadays, "reach" the question of whether she was literally the child's mother. Nor am I suggesting that the mother and father, biological or otherwise, must, under all circumstances, inhabit the same house, so long as the child has regular contact with both of them; if broken homes pose emotional problems for kids, as they undoubtedly do, then so, surely, do some unbroken ones.

Some kids, of course, are unlucky enough to be deprived of both a father and mother, by death or desertion. It is then the responsibility of any society that calls itself human to remedy that lack, by arranging for foster or adoptive parents if these can possibly be found, as they can, more often than not. This is, indeed, supposedly routine in our society, but not always quite so routine as we like to think. Even apart from the bureaucratic paperwork which too often encumbers the adoptive process, many adoption agencies are sectarian in the worst sense, meaning that parents are only acceptable if they are of the "right" religion—right, that is, from the agency's standpoint, not the baby's, who knows nothing about doctrinal differences. These agencies, too, are acting inhumanly, putting the interests of their own Catholic, Protestant, or Jewish sect ahead of the child's welfare. From an evolutionary standpoint, parenthood came long before religion, and if the choice is between having religion and no parents or parents and no religion, there can be no doubt which is best for the child. Much the same criticism could be made of certain black social workers who recently have been attacking adoption agencies for placing black children with white parents when black parents are not available. Given the present widespread idiocy about skin color in our society, it is probably better for any child to have parents of its own color—but any color at all is better than none.

The right to a mother and father is obviously a minimum, not a maximum, right. Considering both our primate ancestry and the structure of most human societies, a child is probably better off in an "extended family" than in our predominant "nuclear family"; the more grandparents, aunts, and uncles in the neighborhood, the better. These surrogate parents provide emotional backstops in case of the death, desertion, or simple unkindness of the real parents; they also familiarize the child from an early age with a fundamental and important fact about human beings: they can vary considerably in intelligence, skills, and temperament and yet can love and be loved. It is natural for parents and children to love one another, but nothing like so natural for the parents to be the only (rather than merely the brightest) constellation in the child's emotional firmament.

Given the fragmenting tendencies of modern urban and suburban society, in which a child and its parents are likely to live in one place, its grandparents perhaps in a "retirement community" tens or hundreds of miles away, and its aunts and uncles God knows where, extended families of the good old primate-human pattern are becoming an endangered species. Which is why I view with interest attempts by some communes to re-create it in a social-emotional rather than a biological form. Whether those quasitribal groupings can survive the centrifugal forces of modern individualism and the often hostile attitudes of the larger society is not yet clear, but if they can, the children in them should benefit. Always assuming, of course, that these synthesized extended families can maintain a stability and continuity approximating that of their natural prototype. The "crash pad" type of commune, where numbers of screwed-up youngsters are perpetually drifting in and out, is no place for kids—or anybody else—to grow up.

Children need play and playmates, possibly even more than they need parents; Harlow's experiments with young monkeys showed that they could survive even the catastrophic effects of separation from their mothers if they were allowed regular play with others of their own age.

Fortunately, the playmate problem is something that kids solve by themselves almost automatically; so long as there are other kids available (as there almost invariably are), a child will generally find playmates. The main exception is the child who, because of its parents' geographical mobility, is frequently thrust into new groups of children; these, though they may not be actively hostile toward the newcomer, will like other primates probably be slow to accept him as a full-fledged member of the play group. If this happens repeatedly, the child will come to feel itself a more or less permanent outsider, a distinctly unpleasant condition.*

---

* As it happens, I speak from personal experience here; without going into the reasons, my entire childhood and adolescence involved no more than two successive years in the same neighborhood or school.

I have no figures on how often this sort of thing happens, but thanks to the rise of the modern national and supernational conglomerate corporation it seems to be becoming fairly common among rising young executives. Alvin Toffler cites the case of one such family forced to uproot itself twenty-three times in eighteen years of married life, and while this is doubtless an extreme case, even half that number of moves would have placed severe stresses on the children—and, I dare say, on their parents as well. Primates, as we have seen, need stability as well as variety in their environment, and while human beings, thanks to their high intelligence and curiosity, can assimilate much more variety than other primates, there are limits. People have a right to roots, and roots grow slowly; all the Welcome Wagons in the world cannot change that fact.

I don't know whether any studies have been made of how a tumbleweed existence of this sort affects its victims, but I would expect them to show a higher than average incidence of alcoholism and divorce, plus, among the adolescent children, a rise in drug usage and the kind of depersonalized promiscuity which is for me far more of a "perversion" than anything in the Kama Sutra. During the past half dozen years, I have often thought that the main fault of America's young, middle-class political radicals was not that they were excessively radical (though a few were) but that they were insufficiently political. That is, their activities too often centered not on changing the minds and hearts of their countrymen, and thereby changing their country (which is what politics of any kind is about), but on an existential search for a sort of instant brotherhood *among themselves* —the sort of thing that is a by-product of any intense common experience, but which seldom outlasts the immediate event. Some among them have subsequently pursued the same elusive brand of salvation in hippie communes, the "Jesus movement," and Indian mysticism. It now occurs to me that an intense desire for instant brotherhood is exactly what one would expect to find among the rootless products of corporate suburbia.

Be that as it may, I would say that any corporation which imposes rootlessness on its personnel and their kids as a condition of employment, or even of promotion, is presumptively guilty of un-human activities, which pose a considerably greater threat to our national security, I would say, than un-American ones. Perhaps what we need is a new antitrust law in which companies guilty of such conspiracy in restraint of humanity can be heavily fined. Management, no doubt, would complain that, given their companies' far-flung interests, they could not do business any other way. Much the same thing, however, was said a hundred and fifty years ago by companies employing eight-year-old kids on twelve-hour shifts, yet when child labor was outlawed as inhuman they managed, somehow. If a company is truly so big that it must turn its executives and their children into drifters, this is by itself an excellent reason for breaking it up into more manageable—and more human—fragments.*

Children are not just children; they are boys and girls. And they have a right to grow up *as* boys and girls—that is, to play in ways compatible with their gender.

Unless I and a lot of other people are totally wrong about human evolution and psychology, most little boys if their natural impulses are not systematically and forcibly suppressed—are always going to be more drawn to vigorous, rough physical activities than most little girls, while the latter, with the same reservation, are mostly going to find dolls more interesting than boys generally do. I am all in favor of bringing up kids with as few preconceptions as possible about what is "manly" or "ladylike." At the same time, however, if we operate on the assumption that boys and girls will behave exactly the same if treated the same—*and that if they don't there is something wrong with them (or us)*—we (and they) are in for some unpleasant shocks. If women's rights means anything, it is the right of a woman *to be a woman,* not to be nudged or coerced into becoming a poor imitation of a man.

From my own observation, indeed, most women *like* being women, though more and more of them are coming to resent, quite justly, the artificial disadvantages imposed on them, none of which has anything to do with either physical or psychological gender. Not the least of these disadvantages, I would suggest, is the not uncommon assumption—implicit in the writings even of some feminists—that femininity is somehow inferior to masculinity; for example, that if women are less aggressive than men—as they are to some degree in all species of primate and virtually all human cultures—they are therefore inferior to men, a view which is of course merely another variation on the old male-supremacy tune.

And if little girls should not be pressured into being either mascu-

* As we shall see later, there are also other human reasons for doing so.

line or ultrafeminine, neither should little boys be pressured into being ultramasculine. Left to themselves, young male primates will naturally engage in a certain amount of mutual roughhousing, aggression, and "competition"—as well as in all sorts of other more pacific and cooperative pursuits. Our own culture, unfortunately, too often reinforces boys' aggression and competition as against the other side of their natures. Little Leaguers on the baseball diamond, ten-year-olds helmeted and padded for tackle football, and the thousands of boys (and some girls) subjected to intensive coaching in competitive swimming are all being indoctrinated in the importance, the absolute necessity, of competing and winning—for reasons, one suspects, having more to do with the emotional needs of their fathers and the economic needs of the professionals who oversee these activities than with any benefits accruing to the young participants. (We have already noted the phenomenon of machismo propaganda in TV and the movies.)

There is certainly a lot to be said for boys and their fathers doing things together from time to time. But if we look at the typical primate and primitive human pattern, we see that such activities focus on the boy's learning the adult activities that go with being a man—hunting, fishing, making a bow or a net, paddling a canoe, or what have you. Our overemphasized, overstructured, and overcompetitive juvenile athletics seem to have reversed the pattern: instead of the boys learning how to be men, the men are learning how to be boys again, or trying to.

The macho image of manhood, still a prominent feature of many cultures and especially prominent in (among other places) America, is an obvious source of social violence, as we noted in the last chapter. Less widely appreciated, perhaps, is that it is also a prime source of male frustration, since in almost no culture today can men live up to the image unless they embrace a life of violent crime. Man the Mighty Hunter and Warrior is out of date, and boys imbued with that image of masculinity may well find themselves troubled about whether they are "really" masculine.*

As infants, children, and adults, humans are eternally curious; they

---

* No more desirable, of course, is that other pervasive American masculine image, Man the Blithering Idiot, dominated by his wife and manipulated by his children. Blondie and Dagwood are hardly a satisfactory alternative to Bonnie and Clyde.

enjoy exploring, discovering, and learning, and therefore have a right to these enjoyments.

A great deal of human learning, of course, requires no special assistance from society; it happens automatically. This is the case with such basic physical skills as walking, running, and using the hands to manipulate things; it is also true of the most fundamental human psychological skill, language. Any child that is not grossly abnormal will, by five or six, have effortlessly picked up virtually the entire grammar and a sizable part of the vocabulary of whatever language is spoken in the vicinity—or languages, for that matter.*

As children learn language they also learn to use it as a tool for learning other things. They ask what things are, and later why they are. Often they evolve ingenious theories of their own on the nature of the bewildering world about them, like the city child who, on first seeing a cow, wanted to know which of the four spigots was the one for chocolate milk. They do these things not because anyone has told them to, but because they enjoy learning. Thus when I survey the appalling record of some American schools in teaching children so elementary a skill as reading, my immediate reaction is: who or what has turned these kids off learning? Sometimes the culprits are doubtless the parents; children who are regularly smacked for bothering their parents with questions will soon learn not to ask questions, and eventually, perhaps, not even to think them. A few poorly educated parents actively resent their children learning more than they did, as did Huck Finn's alcoholic father. And if the parents are of a class or ethnic group that has learned, through generations of experience, that learning is unlikely to improve their economic and social status, they may well put a low value on it—and convey that attitude, directly or indirectly, to their children.

But with due allowance for these family and environmental factors,

---

* This fact is for me the most telling argument against the current proposal that black children be taught "black English" in school. By the time most black children get to school, they *know* black English—know it better than almost any white teacher; better, I would wager, than some black teachers. There is perhaps a case to be made for teaching black slum children *in* black English, if they in fact have trouble comprehending standard English, as there is a much stronger case for teaching children who know little or no English—this would include many Hispanic-American kids—in their own tongue for the first few years. But the English that the black—or the Hispanic—child needs to *learn* is standard English. Not because it is "good" English but because it is more widely used and understood than any other dialect of English.

it still seems to me that some schools and educationists have gone to considerable effort to insure that their students *don't* learn, or don't learn too much. They have carefully compiled circumscribed "word lists" supposedly appropriate to each age group, and woe betide any schoolbook, no matter how otherwise attractive and stimulating, that strays beyond the prescribed limits of vocabulary. The result, of course, is textbooks of the "Run, Spot, run!" variety, in which sense and content are sacrificed to educational "method," providing plentiful negative reinforcement—in the shape of boredom—to any child unlucky enough to be assigned them. For the middle-class child the results are seldom catastrophic; having had books read him at home, he is aware that not all of them are about Dick and Jane. But a child for whom these dreary little volumes constitute the first experience of reading is likely to conclude—very sensibly—that if that's all reading is good for, who needs it?

Two other notable examples of systematic diseducation contrived by alleged educational experts are the so-called word-recognition method of learning reading, which seeks to replace our imperfect but serviceable system of alphabetic phonetics with one more appropriate for learning Chinese ideographs, and that scientific chimera, the New Mathematics. Fortunately, both these systems of diseducation seem (at long last) to be on the way out, though not before having provided negative reinforcement to a generation of schoolchildren.

All this, however, does not imply that we should pick educational materials and methods *only* on the basis of how well they hold the child's interest and provoke his natural curiosity; education must obviously take account of the child's future as well as his present needs. In primates and primitive human cultures alike, the young learn the information and skills they will need to survive and function as adults in their particular environment and group with little choice involved on anyone's part; they learn primarily by watching adults who have themselves survived, and who therefore, by definition, possess the knowledge and practice the skills. Things are much more complicated in our own culture, since it embodies many different environments and groups, requiring quite different survival techniques—and teacher and student frequently come from quite different environments, while the bureaucrats who set up curricula and syllabuses inhabit yet another. The result is that what the child is given to study often has only the most tenuous relationship to the realities and demands of the world beyond the schoolhouse door.

For example, unless civics courses have changed a lot more than I think since my own high school days, they say little or nothing about graft, though it is (and has always been) one of the basic factors in shaping the activities of government. Many city kids, and most slum kids, know this as a matter of course, and if their civics and government texts ignore this fundamental fact, they will feel, quite rightly, that they are being handed a crock of nonsense. I doubt if many hygiene or biology texts deal at any length with the problems of rats, roaches, and lead poisoning, which some slum dwellers must cope with every day; classes in business-letter writing seldom involve instruction on how to address the city health department if the landlord won't fix the toilet; physical-education instructors do not go into what you do if somebody pulls a knife on you. Yet all these things are far more relevant to survival in a city slum than, say, how an amoeba consumes its prey, how the electoral college works, or what Shakespeare was getting at when he wrote *Macbeth.*

Don't get me wrong—I do not downgrade these and similar "nonrelevant" subjects; a purely utilitarian curriculum would probably be as bad as a purely nonutilitarian one, stultifying the imagination and deadening the creative impulse. But creativity comes second, survival first. Not, indeed, that I seriously expect any American board of education to adopt the sort of "survival curriculum" implied in the preceding paragraph, if only because it would involve confronting too many unpleasant truths about American society. Nonetheless, it would be educational all around if a group of slum parents, teachers, and kids were to put their heads together, draw up a hard-nosed, realistic curriculum of this sort, and present it to the appropriate authorities—and the press.

One final point about education. We saw much earlier that even kittens learn more quickly from adults with whom they have formed some sort of emotional bond, and there is no reason to doubt that the same is true of young humans—probably, in view of man's greater capacity for forming bonds, more true. And if this is so, it seems that teachers are being selected on largely irrelevant grounds—whether they have taken the right courses and obtained the proper certificates, rather than whether they can win the affection and respect of their charges. A teacher who can do that, I would venture, is almost bound to teach the kids something, whatever the state of her "professional" qualifications; conversely, a teacher who can't will be a poor teacher be she ever so highly certificated.

A teacher's human qualities—her (or his) ability to establish rapport with her charges—are, of course, far less easily measurable than her technical qualifications; even less are they "objectively" measurable. Boards of education therefore find it easy to ignore these qualities, as the behaviorists for so long ignored man's other "subjective" traits; if it isn't objectively measurable, it doesn't exist, or at least isn't important. And since educational systems are run first for the benefit of their administrators, second for the benefit of their teachers, and last of all for the benefit of the pupils, the result is far too large a proportion of teachers who at best are highly "qualified" mediocrities and at worst couldn't teach a cat to lap cream.

The need to explore and learn about the environment does not, of course, vanish with childhood, in man or any other primate; adults too derive satisfactions from acquiring new information and skills. The most potent threat to this human right in our own society comes from various powerful groups, in and out of government, who seek to shield their own dehumanizing activities from public scrutiny, both by blocking public access to information and by disseminating misinformation.* This dehumanizes us not merely by blocking our desire to acquire information but especially by making us less capable of controlling our environment, leading to frustration and, if the process is carried far enough, anger and violence.

As children grow up and reach the age of indiscretion, their desire to explore and learn acquires a new focus: sex. Man—and woman—is a sexual being.

We cannot, however, add to our catalogue of human rights the "right to sexual love," since satisfying this need obviously depends heavily on individual temperament, enterprise, and skill. What we *can* do is to grant every human being the right to pursue sexual love in whatever way he or she deems best—provided, naturally, that this does not involve coercion or violence toward other human beings; what people do in bed, and with which, and to whom, is nobody's

---

* In some societies, though not yet our own, this process extends even to discouraging communication among members of the society of such information as they have managed to acquire about its workings.

business but their own. And it is high time that society—meaning here both the government and the millions of sex-meddlers of all ages and genders—stopped trying to make these things its business.

There is, I am told, not a single human sexual practice, saving only *conventional* copulation between husband and wife, that is not outlawed in at least some American legal jurisdictions; some, such as male homosexuality, are outlawed in all of them, with prostitution almost as universally proscribed. Of course laws haven't stopped these things; they never do and never will. What they have done is create a fertile source of blackmail, police corruption, and individual human misery.

Why Americans—and many other peoples of the Judeo-Christian cultural tradition—should be so troubled about what may or may not be going on in their neighbors' bedrooms is a fascinating question, but too complex for discussion here. No less fascinating and complex is the question of why outcries against sexual "permissiveness" should be especially high-pitched among those conservatives who in other connections inveigh against "government interference" with individual rights. If government, as they tell us, should not interfere with people's right to make money or their right to own guns, what on earth gives it the right to meddle with a far more fundamental human right, one of far greater evolutionary antiquity than either guns or money?

Perhaps the most prominent sexual target in recent years has been pornography, which has drawn the fire not only of long-time religious and political conservatives but of liberals—or whilhom liberals—such as Irving Kristol. For example, he and others have charged more permissive liberals and radicals with inconsistency, in that the latter tolerate explicit sex in books, plays, and films while deploring explicit violence. Well, I for one am willing to accept the analogy: if books and films about killing make some people more likely to kill, as they probably do, then we can reasonably expect that books and films about fucking will make some people more likely to fuck. Given the choice of banning one or the other, I know very well which I would vote for!

The plain fact is that nobody has ever offered any evidence that reading and viewing pornography—or any other variety of noncoercive sexual behavior—is bad for society, or even bad for the individual. The latter, indeed, has been claimed from time to time, but the claim always seems to translate as "pornography (or whatever) is bad for *you,*" never "pornography is bad for *me.*" In the case of such known social evils as alcoholism and drug addiction, we have mountains of firsthand testimony on their destructive effects; any member of Alcoholics Anonymous can tell you in detail how liquor messed up his life. I have yet to hear anyone recount how his life was ruined by smut. And without such testimony, or other convincing evidence that pornography is in fact harmful, there seems to me an overwhelming case for ignoring it. In the area of sex perhaps more than in any other field of human activity, the least government is the best.

The evolutionary view of man's sexual nature and rights, while it suggests that social interference with sex is antihuman, does not provide any recipe for individual sexual happiness. It does, however, suggest certain guidelines that are worth noting briefly, though many readers will doubtless find them wholly unsurprising. Given our hairless condition, with all that it implies for more and stronger stimulation during sex, it seems certain that, other things being equal, sex will be more exciting naked than clothed. Given our sensitivity to visual sexual stimuli—unquestionably highly developed in men, and probably no less marked among women, though the specific stimuli are less understood—it seems hardly less certain that sex in the light will be more exciting than sex in the dark. Perhaps most important of all, given our capacity for empathy, the more we are aware of our partner's excitement, and the more he or she communicates his or her excitement to us, the greater will be our own excitement. It is this fact that provides the most telling argument against casual, dehumanized sex. To the extent we do not know, or do not trust, or do not "mesh" emotionally with our partner, we cannot be fully aware of his or her humanity, or allow him or her to be fully aware of ours. As we saw in Chapter 10, sexual love is an extraordinarily intense and powerful experience precisely because it is so uniquely human. Thus when we engage in sex with partners, or under circumstances, which downgrade its (and our) human qualities, we are necessarily settling for second—or third, or tenth—best.

In protohuman and primitive human societies, sex necessarily implied babies. Nowadays, of course, it doesn't most of the time; no woman—at least in most Western societies—need produce a child that is not wanted. By the same token, however, most of us want to produce one or more of them sooner or later and obviously should be able to do so. If as children human beings have a right to parents, then as adults they have a right to parenthood. This is so generally accepted that it hardly seems worth mentioning, except that parenthood carries with it other rights that are less widely recognized. Being a parent, as we noted much earlier, involves not merely producing a baby but raising it to adulthood—meaning, among other things, that it and its parents must be fed, clothed, and sheltered. As parents—or, for that matter, as nonparents or "post-parents"—human beings have a right to subsistence, which for simplicity I shall call the right to food.

Man's need for "food" is in some respects much more complicated than his need for sex, since it has always been intimately tied up with his need to manipulate his environment—making a spear or a digging stick, organizing a hunt, setting a snare, gathering and preparing berries and roots, and so on. Food was important not simply because it alleviated hunger (who of us would choose food that did no more than that?) but because the quest for it gave occupation to man's active mind and body, and often scope to his burgeoning creative impulses.

It is in this area that modern society has probably moved farthest from our evolutionary past. No primitive human society (or, even less, any prehuman primate band) could guarantee its members enough to eat: that depended on the environment. Where the environment was rich (as, for example, on the northwest coast of North America), people ate well; where it was not rich, they ate not so well. And if, thanks to drought or other natural catastrophe, the environment became really poor, they starved—as they still do in some parts of the world. On the other hand, however, no primitive society, rich or poor, could—or would—have prevented its members from working, from exerting their skills to obtain whatever food (or other desirable things) the environment offered.

Modern industrialized societies have exactly reversed this situation. On the one hand, they can, thanks to their expanded productive powers, provide adequate food, clothing, and shelter to all their members, and almost invariably do so, though in some cases on a pretty niggardly scale. I doubt if anyone has actually starved to death recently in America, but some hundreds of thousands, if not millions, of Americans are known to suffer from severe and chronic malnutrition sufficient to produce sickness and disability if not death. There is, of course, no excuse for this. On the other hand, virtually all modern societies can and, at least on occasion, do prevent some of their members from working; currently, at least five million Americans are condemned to idleness. And there is no excuse for this either. Unemployment, indeed, is not always the product of specific human decisions; it may be rather the by-product of a particular set of antihuman economic institutions. In other cases, however, governments—in recent years including those of both Great Britain and America—have deliberately set about fostering unemployment as a way of "cooling off" their inflationary economies. Either way, the result is quite as humanly destructive as "simple" starvation. Work—engaging in some sort of constructive and gainful occupation—is a basic human need, and therefore a basic human right; societies that ignore this are antihuman.

The socially imposed divorce between work and subsistence applies, of course, not only to the idle poor but also to the idle rich, whose characters are no more improved by parasitic otiosity than are those of their less affluent fellow citizens. The same can be said, in measure, of those rich who work, as of course many of them do. Unlike other people, however, they work when they please, for as long as they please, and—especially—at what they please, while their material life-style bears little if any relationship to the quantity and quality of their work. A life so different from that of most men inevitably isolates them from their fellows, begetting the conviction that they are in fact not as other men, whence the sort of well-bred, if sometimes well-concealed, contempt for the commonality found in such disparate tribes as the Kennedys, Rockefellers, and Buckleys, all of whom would be considerably more human—and easier to take—had they been forced to work for a living like the rest of us.*

Happily, it is possible to solve the human problems of both the poor and the born rich simultaneously: all we need do is confiscate all inherited wealth. Reserving a portion of this money for the support

---

* The self-made millionaire, who is if anything even more obnoxious than the silver-spoon-in-the-mouth variety, becomes dehumanized in another way. To achieve real wealth—not just affluence—nowadays requires either extraordinary luck or an extraordinary willingness to manipulate other human beings, downgrading their humanity and therefore one's own.

of those heirs too old or too young to work, we can apply the remainder, plus the added billions now wasted in welfare payments for the able-bodied unemployed, to a program of public works that would provide jobs for these same unemployed, and for the sometime idle rich. Such a program would humanize the (formerly) poor, humanize most of the (formerly) rich, and humanize the rest of us (as suggested in the previous chapter) by sparing us much of the violence of the former—and much of the arrogance of the latter. As an added bonus, it would do more to purify American politics than all the corrupt-practices acts ever passed. So long as people have large amounts of money to invest in politicians, it is almost impossible to prevent them from doing so; greed, like love, will find a way. But to the extent we abolish the money, we will abolish the corruption if not the greed.

Leaving aside these embellishments, I maintain that it is any society's human obligation, one way or another, to provide work, at reasonable wages, for everyone able to work—and, moreover, to compel every such person to work at the work provided, whether his distaste for it stems from inherited wealth or acquired inertia. Recently, a few social workers and other self-appointed spokesmen for the poor have gone further: it is not enough for society to provide work, they say; it must be "meaningful" work. Just what "meaningful" is supposed to mean is anyone's guess, but if it refers to stimulating, interesting work, somebody is kidding himself or trying to kid the rest of us; there are simply not that many stimulating jobs.

From the evolutionary human standpoint there is no doubt that there ought to be. I don't profess to know whether the life of a Paleolithic hunter or his wife was "meaningful," but I'll wager it was far more interesting than that of a modern typist, key-punch operator, miner, or assembly-line worker, though the latter enjoy a far higher standard of living than their Stone Age forebears. It is hardly a secret that a high proportion of the jobs in our society are boring, sometimes excruciatingly so. It is also becoming apparent that the people holding these jobs aren't going to put up with them indefinitely; some of them are already beginning to demand that their work be restructured so as to give more scope to their human needs, making it less fragmented, less repetitive, less deadly dull. And in a few places, management is finding that restructuring of this sort actually "pays dividends" in the shape of less absenteeism and reduced turnover among their workers.

This is, of course, a welcome development; any steps by management to make work more human, for whatever reasons, can hardly be faulted. But in a basic sense it does not and will not solve the problem of dehumanization at work, because its basic assumption remains antihuman: changes in the conditions and organization of work are tolerable *only* if they pay dividends, or at least don't reduce them; the important thing is still what is produced, and how cheaply, not who produces it and under what conditions. A truly human society must, by definition, give the producer equal weight with the product, but to do so will involve far more fundamental changes in the productive processes than any management is likely to accept voluntarily.

For example, consider the automobile industry. It is in some respects one of the most mechanized in the world, yet its assembly lines are equally among the world's most dehumanizing productive institutions. It has long been recognized that many repetitive assembly-line (and other) jobs could in principle be performed by machines; indeed, the more repetitive the job, the more it lends itself to mechanization. But the complex machines required for this type of mechanization are expensive—probably too expensive to be scrapped or rebuilt at the end of a single year, when the industry changes models. Thus really comprehensive mechanization might well imply a model change once in three years, or in five. And a serious proposal to this effect would surely evoke screams of rage and pain from the plushier offices of Detroit and points adjacent, whose inhabitants have apparently convinced themselves that Americans will stop buying cars if the models don't change annually.

I may be underestimating Detroit's technological ingenuity. It is possible that the automotive moguls could solve the problem in ways requiring a far less drastic shift in their business habits. But of one thing I am absolutely certain: they won't do it unless and until somebody twists their arms—hard. At one time I had a very high opinion of what used to be called American know-how; today it has taken a back seat to un-American know-how. It was the Japanese, not the Americans, who made the rotary gasoline engine, so much simpler and lighter than its conventional prototype, a going concern. It was the Japanese who devised the "stratified charge" technique of reducing automotive pollution, while Detroit was busy explaining why pollution couldn't be reduced. And when Amtrak needed a turbine-driven train that would not constantly break down, they found—after unhappy experiences with several American manufacturers—that they had to go to France. Yet I doubt that all this happened because the Japanese and French has suddenly become technological wizards while American engineers had succumbed to epidemic feeble-mindedness; what was lacking in America was not ingenuity but will.

Given the will, the problem of humanizing work in America's factories could very possibly be solved in ways far simpler than anyone now suspects. But the will is unlikely to come from management; it will have to be supplied by the organized producers themselves, who as the victims of dehumanization have the most powerful motive for insisting that it be ended.

Nor does the impact of dehumanization at work fall only on the corporate rank and file, though they certainly bear the main brunt of it; the men of middle management, especially the engineers, are also frequent if often unwitting victims. An enormous amount of their work is devoted to paper shuffling and other activities not worth a grown man's time—in the auto industry, such vital questions as exactly where to place a strip of chrome, how to restyle the hood for the nth time, and so on. Perhaps some engineers in this situation don't give a damn, but I'll wager many of them do, finding their human desire to experiment, to tinker, to innovate, deeply frustrated by top management's disinterest in these matters. The American automobile today is in all essential respects the same machine it was twenty years ago, a fact which can hardly be the source of much satisfaction for its designers.

What ails the auto industry, along with many, many other branches of American industry, is not, I think, any lack of creativity down below but bureaucratization at the top: an organizational structure which divorces technological creativity from power and which assigns decisions to people who are ultimately selected for their *lack* of imagination, their willingness not to rock the boat, and who can impose their dead hand on the rest of the organization.

If this sort of thing is increasingly true of industry, in general, as I am convinced it is, it is doubly true of those economic monstrosities known as conglomerates, in which not one or two but three or four levels of top management are in a position to paralyze imagination and generally foul up the works. The conglomerate, as more and more people are coming to realize, has little or nothing to do with the satisfaction of any evolutionary human need, whether it be the need of its personnel to innovate or that of its customers for the goods it produces. It is the creature of lawyers and accountants whose creativity, such as it is, expresses itself in beating the tax laws and shuffling assets from one balance sheet to another. There may somewhere be a conglomerate that is more, not less, efficient at producing goods or services than were its constituent parts before takeover, that is a more, not a less, satisfying place for lower and middle management to work. I wish somebody would tell me about it.

Yet having said all this, having insisted that American industry, given the will, can do far, far more than it has done toward making its mills, factories, and offices human places for human beings to work, I must still warn against expecting too much. We can greatly reduce the number of repetitive dehumanizing jobs in our society, but short of returning to a handicraft, village economy, with the low standard of living which that implies, we cannot abolish such jobs. Ten or twenty or fifty years from now, somebody will still have to collect the garbage from our streets, change the oil in our cars, sweep the floors and wash the windows in our great skyscrapers, and perform all the other dull jobs on which any complex civilization depends today and will depend in the foreseeable future. The "post-industrial society" in which every job that is repetitive and dehumanizing will be handled by machines, may arrive eventually, but it is by no means breathing down our necks as some naïve writers appear to think. Indeed, if we do not turn loose some of our really superior innovators to devise new energy sources to power the machines, it will not arrive at all.

There is one final point about man's enjoyment of work and (to the extent his talent and circumstances permit) of creativity: it applies equally to woman. Though evolution, as I have indicated, has given women and men somewhat different temperaments, there is not a shred of evidence that the differences involve any greater tolerance of idleness or any less enjoyment of experiment and innovation on the part of the female.

In modern industrial societies, woman's right to work is distorted in two ways. On the one hand, she is told by traditionalists that she "ought" to find fulfillment as a housewife and mother, and if she chooses to work outside the home she generally finds that she is paid less than men, and less likely than they to be promoted. On the other hand, she is being increasingly told by some radicals that she "ought" to work outside the home, since housekeeping and motherhood are "degrading."

In primitive human societies, the questions of whether women should work, and at what, didn't arise. Simply as a matter of survival, they *did* work, usually as hard as the men if not harder. Primarily, though not exclusively, they worked at child care, food preparation, and other close-to-home activities. This focus on the home did not come about through any man's contriving; somebody had to look after the baby, and that somebody was woman—in part, probably because of temperamental differences, but certainly because only she could feed it. Thus any other tasks she took on could not take her too far from the infant; either she remained near home or carried the baby along with her.

In economically advanced societies today, a woman's life seldom need be anything like so restricted. She can usually limit her babies to a few or none, nor is there any physical reason she need personally feed them. Much housework is mechanized, as are sizable areas in food preparation (how many American women bake their own bread, except as a hobby?). I have heard it said that the "average American housewife" spends over eighty hours a week—nearly twelve hours a day—on housework, but neither I nor my wife believes this for a minute; we have calculated that the two of us together spend only about a quarter of this time on keeping our five-room apartment clean and ourselves (and any visitors) fed. The eighty-hour figure (a feminist writer recently raised it to ninety-nine!) may apply to a minority of women with many small kids and few household appliances, who do their own ironing, but they are hardly average; millions of women, after all, have only grown children, or none at all.*

Thus even if the woman of the family does most or all the housework—and there is, of course, no evolutionary reason why she should—she is still likely to have a good deal of time left over for which she has a right to find occupation, whether in an actual job, in volunteer work, or in personal creative activities such as gardening, gourmet cooking, home canning, or designing and/or making her own clothes. In citing activities of this sort as possible outlets for woman's

---

* As Betty Friedan long ago observed, however, housework follows Parkinson's law, expanding to fill the time available for it. Particularly when the housewife is daily deluged with the advertising industry's whiter-than-white, cleaner-than-clean propaganda.

creativity I will doubtless be accused of wanting to "keep women in the home," which is nonsense. It is not a question of whether women "ought" to find these activities satisfying, but rather of the fact that many of them—some of them friends of mine—demonstrably do, certainly more satisfying than working in an office all day. A woman who doesn't, obviously has the right to seek her satisfactions in "outside" work, and to be paid and promoted on the same basis as men.

I have absolutely no sympathy with the argument that housework, or home-based work generally, is intrinsically degrading—certainly not until somebody explains to me why it is degrading for a woman to sweep the floor but not degrading for a man to sweep the streets.* A good deal of housework is unquestionably *dull* (and I've done enough of it myself to know), but so, as we have already noted, are plenty of jobs outside the home (and I've done enough of *them* to know, too). Moreover, there can be no doubt whatever that a disproportionate amount of America's dull work, in and out of the home, is done by women, and this is clearly unfair. At the same time, let us bear in mind that simply shifting the dull jobs from one sex to the other is not going to solve the basic problem of satisfying both man's and woman's human need for stimulating, creative activity. Unless all of us, men and women, begin to concern ourselves with making work in general less dehumanizing, we will merely be robbing Peter to pay Paula. And while Paula unquestionably has a human right to more than she's getting, so, in measure, does Peter. Thus if Peter and Paula focus their attention merely on who's getting the biggest slice of pie, they can easily lose sight of the fact that the entire pie, as currently baked by American corporate management, is not very tasty.

There is an exact parallel here with the problem of unemployment among different ethnic groups. While it is obviously unjust that blacks should be unemployed at two or three times the rate of whites, simply transferring a portion of the available jobs from whites to blacks will not solve the basic human problem, which is the destructive effect of idleness on human beings regardless of color. To solve *that* problem will require not just equal-opportunity employment but *more* employment. And unless both blacks and whites recognize this fact and act

---

* For that matter, even if we choose to define street sweeping as "degrading," the streets have still got to be swept. Also the floors.

on it, the likely result is increasingly heated confrontation between whites and blacks over who gets how many of the available jobs. Blacks quite justifiably resent limitations on their job opportunities; to suppose that whites will not resent future limitations on *their* opportunities, for the benefit of blacks, is to demand more of man's altruistic impulses than they can possibly fulfill.

The conflict between black and white, and the developing conflict between men and women, over who is to have jobs, or better jobs, points up one of the more depressing facts about our society: in terms of giving scope to man's altruistic, helping impulses, it is one of the most antihuman in the world. Our national motto, *E pluribus unum,* has somehow become transmuted into "I'm all right, Jack!" Children are encouraged and at times almost compelled to compete with one another, not only in sports but in school; among middle-class children, competition for marks easily passes into competition to get into a "good" college. As workers, men and women, blacks and whites compete for jobs and promotions; as consumers, they compete for the status conferred by material possessions, being continually encouraged to do so by the competitive misrepresentations of corporate advertising. Corporations compete for bigger shares of the consumer's dollar and also for bigger profit margins—which is to say, for smaller value returned to the consumer on the dollars spent. Corporations, through their bought or rented politicians, compete for bigger shares of government expenditures; management and labor compete for bigger shares of corporate expenditures. Self-interest is the goal, not the public interest.

Now there is obviously nothing evolutionarily unnatural about pursuing one's self-interest; men have always done so and always will. But during most of man's evolution—particularly the "human" phase of his evolution surveyed in Chapter 8—self-interest was intimately and irrevocably bound up with the public interest, which is to say the interest of the group. It was this basic ecological fact which, as we saw in Chapter 9, encouraged the evolution of man's altruistic impulses; men and women who persistently pursued their own interests at the expense of the group's interests either destroyed the group —and themselves—or were destroyed by it.

In our own society, the shoe is on the other foot: we are encouraged and at times virtually compelled to pursue our own interests at the expense of other people's. A carpenter or plumber who encourages new workers to enter his trade is likely to find his own chances of employment diminished—and therefore discourages them; the fact that some of them are blacks, whom he has been taught to dislike anyway, supplies a convenient excuse for following his own self-interest, but even if they weren't he would probably do much the same thing. A man who encourages and publicly recognizes the work of a clever woman in his department may find her getting the promotion he covets—and therefore finds it easy to convince himself that women really are less competent than men. A corporation that seeks to reduce the pollution its operations are vomiting into the environment will probably find itself at a competitive disadvantage as against its more self-interested competitors; a politician who too resolutely pursues the public interest at the expense of the private concerns of his campaign contributors stands a good chance of being removed at the next election.

And all of us, of course, are continually exposed to the drumming propaganda of the advertising industry, which with the rarest of exceptions can be summed up as "Consume!" I have never been among those who credited advertising with some occult power to make people do whatever it chose; the black arts of the motivational researchers and other hidden persuaders seem to me to have achieved their chief success in persuading advertisers and ad agencies, not their consumer targets.* It is rather that advertising as a whole promulgates a philosophy of pure selfishness, of "Ask not what you can do for your fellows but what you can do for yourself." Given man's natural propensity to pursue his own interests, there is no human reason for reinforcing it to the tune of some billions of dollars a year, and plenty of reasons not to.

Though our society is far more complex and infinitely richer than that of the hapless Ik, it engenders many of the same behavior patterns in us that Colin Turnbull found so repellent in them; as their natural environment of drought and famine compelled them to follow a policy of every man—and woman and child—for himself as the price of survival, so our social environment encourages us to pursue a similar strategy as the price, if not of physical survival, then of success and

---

* Some years ago I read an advertisement for a sports car which, in accordance with the scientific precepts of motivational research, portrayed the car as a "mistress," its text leaving the reader in some doubt as to whether the machine was to be driven or screwed. The car is no longer manufactured.

affluence. Not because we are intrinsically evil or antihuman, any more than the Ik were, but because the pattern of rewards and punishments built into our environment systematically reinforces antihuman activities.

Reinforcement theory, as we noted in Chapter 3, tells us very little about how we learn the things we learn, but it tells us an enormous amount about why we learn certain things rather than others, and especially why, of the many things we learn, we do some more often than others. A society, like an individual, gets what it pays for, and if its payoffs—in money, creative satisfaction, or praise—reward selfish, even predatory behavior, then that is the behavior it will get.

All of us know the truth of this basic principle from personal experience and observation; what is extraordinary is how often it is ignored in constructing human institutions. A classic case was described some years ago by the sociologist H. Cohen, in a work appropriately titled *The Diabolics of Bureaucracy.* His study concerned an employment bureau which, though unnamed, could without difficulty be identified as a branch of the New York State Employment Service. The ostensible purpose of this organization was of course to find jobs for the unemployed, which involved—in theory—interviewing job seekers, seeking out jobs from employers, referring the job seeker to the job, and following up to determine if he or she had gotten a job, and if not, why not. In actual practice, however, personnel were rated, promoted, and reprimanded by their superiors simply on the basis of how many interviews and referrals they carried out; time spent in ascertaining the exact requirements of jobs, in matching the job to the job seeker, or in follow-up with either employers or job seekers, was treated as time wasted. The result was of course utterly predictable: lots of interviews and referrals, but very few jobs—and a flagrant waste of public money.

The institutionalization of selfishness in our society—the system by which it is richly rewarded while altruism is seldom rewarded and sometimes punished—goes back to the beginnings of the industrial revolution and some varieties of the doctrine known as utilitarianism. Man, according to these utilitarians (notably David Ricardo), is basically governed by self-interest, by the motives of the marketplace. Society, therefore, should be so constituted as to give maximum scope to the pursuit of self-interest, from which will automatically flow the good of all.

Like the much later behaviorists, the self-interest utilitarians constructed a self-proving theory. The behaviorists, having dogmatically declared that learning was a fragmented, atomisitic process, set up their Skinner boxes in which animals were systematically reinforced for learning atomized bits of behavior; when the animals learned, this proved that the behaviorists were right. So the utilitarians, having dogmatically declared that man was fundamentally selfish, helped construct a societal Skinner box in which men were systematically rewarded for being selfish; the results, of course, proved that the utilitarians were right.

When the late Richard Titmuss began examining the contrasts between the altruistic, voluntary British blood donors and the self-interested, commercialized blood banks of the United States and other countries, he soon found himself forced to examine "the extent to which specific instruments of public policy encourage or discourage, foster or destroy the individual expression of altruism and regard for the needs of others." His conclusion was that "modern . . . technical, professional, large-scale, organized society" allows few opportunities for ordinary people to behave altruistically toward others "outside their own network of family and personal relationships." He found the explanation in "the explicit or implicit institutionalization of separateness, whether categorized in terms of income, class, race, color, or religion, rather than the recognition of the similarities between people and their needs . . . and the atomistic private market systems [which] free men from any sense of obligation to or for other men." Human beings, he declared, have the right to give, and to the extent a marketplace society coerces or constrains them from giving, it is antihuman. I couldn't agree more.

Chiefly for reasons of space, I have restricted the foregoing discussion to the ways in which our society dehumanizes *us*. That America (along with various other societies, both industrialized and underdeveloped) also dehumanizes other peoples is by now an all-too-well-known fact. The methods include economic domination, assistance to repressive, antihuman native governments, and (as recently in Southeast Asia) the violent disruption of entire societies and destruction of their inhabitants by the hundreds of thousands. And the process works both ways: those of us who, willingly or under compulsion, participate in or even condone these activities do so at the price of injuring our own humanity; the soldiers at Mylai, though they were not destroyed as were their victims, did not emerge unscathed. We cannot deny the humanity of others without to some degree denying our own.

I believe we can do better.

If our society, as I have argued, dehumanizes too many of us in too many ways—diseducating our children, frustrating our adult desire to learn about our world, meddling with our sex lives, deadening our minds with repetitive and trivial tasks, frustrating our creative and altruistic impulses, condemning some of us to the environments of stress, frustration, and idleness that breed violence, and compelling others to be agents or accomplices in the dehumanization of their fellows—we do not have to put up with it; we can choose to arrange things differently. In productive capacity, we are still the richest country on earth; though the choices open to us are—and always will be—limited by our technology, these limits constrain us less than any people in history. Nor are we constrained by any lack of imaginative, innovative talent; we are as richly endowed with these traits as any country on earth, and perhaps a bit more than some.* All that is needed is the will, the determination, to apply those talents to human ends, to the construction of a society in which man will truly be the measure of all things.

This is not the place nor yet the time to try to depict what such a society would be like; my own guess would be something like a cross between Czechoslovakia under Dubček, before the Russians marched in, and Sweden. But that is one man's view, and visions of a new world, if they are to mean anything, must embody the dreams, aspirations, and hopes of thousands and millions. The important thing is *to begin to dream, hope, and aspire,* to rediscover in ourselves and in our fellows those human qualities—imagination, creativity, and concern for one another—that the institutions of our present world express imperfectly at best and suppress at worst, if they do not destroy them outright. We are the descendants and heirs of the ape-men who first learned to shape tools to a pattern, and with those tools began reshaping their environment; of the near-men who first evolved the capacity to deal in symbols and to reshuffle those symbols into new meanings; of the artists who first carved reindeer bone and mammoth

---

* Thanks to a certain empirical, experimental bias in our culture, some of the reasons for which are recounted in Chapter 38 of *Climate, Man, and History.*

tusk into images of what they knew and what they imagined; of the men who guarded the tribal cave, of the women who guarded the tribal fire; of all those nameless bands of primitives who over five million years survived by grace of their concern and love for one another. And all these human qualities and capacities, however suppressed, distorted, or violated, are still alive within us, bearing an inexhaustible potential for joy in our awareness of our own and our fellows' humanity.

To rediscover the humanity which is too often spindled, folded, and mutilated by the impersonal institutions of a mass, marketplace society will be a long and sometimes painful process; even longer, and perhaps more painful, will be the process of reshaping those institutions so that they serve man- and womankind, not "the people in the black limousines." Yet I am convinced we can do it; we have done harder things. Men and women have prevailed against the twilight pounce of the leopard, the onslaught of the hyena or wolf pack, the parching drought of the tropical grassland, the frost and blizzard of the glacier-edge tundra, the miasmas and fevers of swamp and rain forest. We may, as Thornton Wilder has written, have survived only by the skin of our teeth, but we have survived—and will keep on surviving.

Some twenty years ago, the conservative philosopher Daniel Bell proclaimed "the end of ideology," a state of affairs in which social and political conflict in the Western world was being submerged by the rising tide of material prosperity. Some ten years ago, the radical philosopher Herbert Marcuse, arguing from different premises, reached much the same conclusion, seeing Western man as "one dimensional," so tranquilized by affluence that he had lost all interest in social change. A few years later, mass ideological protest movements forced the virtual resignation of an American president and almost brought down a French government. Man, that complex, restless, and unpredictable animal, perversely refuses to conform to the philosophers' scenarios; give him what you think he wants, or even what *he* thinks he wants, and he—or his children—will discover that they want something else.

Evolution has designed us to solve problems, and to enjoy doing it, so that we no sooner find the answer to one problem than we begin searching for a new one with which to busy ourselves. Full fed after hunt or harvest, we scratch the mammoth's image on the wall of our cave, mold the river bank's soft clay into a new shape of pot, compose a sonorous tale of a great hero's anger and recite it to the twanged strings of a lyre, brew herbs and berries gathered along the roadside into a potion that will cool a sick child's fever, found a religion, write a book—or brood over the world's ills and how they can be healed.

Man is neither god nor beast; he is both, and neither. The complex of impulses bequeathed him by evolution, plus the traditions and myths he has evolved out of his own fancy, can combine to make him more destructive than any beast that ever walked the earth—or more benevolent than most gods who ever reigned in heaven; few of us could bring ourselves to do to our fellows what the Almighty did to Job. For nearly all man's time on earth, he confronted the problems of being a beast: how to get enough to eat, to avoid being eaten, and to feed and tend his children. He coped with those problems, first as a beast among beasts, later as a man among men, well enough to spread from the African grassland to the uttermost ends of the earth.

In some places he still confronts those same problems, unable to take his daily bread for granted, threatened daily, if not by the dwindling ranks of wolf and lion, then by the swarming microbes and parasites that can consume him quite as surely if less bloodily. But other societies, including our own, are more fortunate; for all practical purposes we have solved the problems of being beasts: unless we grossly mismanage our affairs, or permit others to so mismanage them, neither starvation nor plague need vex us. Yet we cannot stop there—and will not. The same restless curiosity and capacity to learn new ways of surviving that took us from the safe treetops of the forest to the open and dangerous grassland, from campsite to cave, from cave to village, and from village to city, still drive us on to the moon and stars—and to the nearer yet dimmer goals of comprehending our own natures and needs and of reordering our societies to more perfectly satisfy them. We have learned how to be beasts, and so effectively that we have unwittingly become almost as gods, masters under natural law of the earth and all that is in it. Now it is time to learn how to be truly human.

Notes

To make life simpler for the reader—and myself—I have tried to eliminate all but the most essential source notes. I have not, for example, attempted to give sources for facts that are generally accepted by prehistorians or primatologists. Where the text gives *both the author and the title* of a work listed in the bibliography, the reader should look there, not here; the same goes for *named authors with only one listed work*. References below are, of course, to items in the bibliography, where the reader will find the complete title, publisher, and so forth.

Chapter 1: TO BEGIN WITH

pp. 8–9: "testimony from a whole menagerie." Notable offenders are Lorenz and Ardrey.

p. 9: On the ecology of baboons and of primitive man, see DeVore's and Hall's paper in DeVore, ed.

p. 10: On observations of captive primates and the resulting misconceptions of their nature, see Eimerl and DeVore.

Chapter 2: INSTINCT, LEARNING, AND INCENTIVES

Nearly all the material in this chapter is fairly elementary zoology and psychology. Whether the particular built-in human likes and dislikes I have cited evolved in precisely the way I have suggested can be argued. What is certain, however, is that these likes and dislikes exist, that they are the product of evolution, and that they almost certainly did not evolve by chance—i.e., they conferred some advantage on those animals in which they did evolve, enabling them to survive more successfully than those of their relatives who evolved different likes and dislikes. On the problematic role of "instinct" in man, see Eisenberg.

Chapter 3: HOW ANIMALS LEARN

p. 22: The material on Watson and the early history of behaviorism is mostly from Heidbreder.

p. 24: The quotation from Harlow is from his paper in Riopelle, ed.

p. 25: The material on Hull is from Hilgard.

p. 26: On drive-reduction theory, see Hilgard.

p. 27: The material on Skinner is from Hilgard, and Skinner (1966); quotations from Skinner are from the latter. See also Skinner (1953).

p. 29: The "best seller" is, of course, *Beyond Freedom and Dignity*, which I have not included in the bibliography because it is irrelevant to this book.

p. 30: The "standard textbook" in question is Hilgard.

p. 31: Harlow's experiments with infant monkeys are described in Pfeiffer, Harlow (1959), and Harlow and Harlow (1967).

p. 33: On rats' preference for "earned" versus free food, see Carder and Berkowitz. For similar findings with children, see Devendra Singh. The Institute for Research on Poverty study was reported in the *New York Times* and elsewhere.

p. 34: Miller's attempt to salvage drive-reduction is described in Hilgard.

p. 35: Harlow's experiments on learning sets are described in his paper in Riopelle, ed.

p. 37: Watson's "refutation" of imitation learning is described by Chance, in Riopelle, ed.

p. 38: Darby and Riopelle's account of their work on imitation learning is in Riopelle, ed.

p. 41: The American Psychological Association's eulogy of Skinner was reported in the press—and also was included in the promotional material for Skinner's *Beyond Freedom and Dignity*.

Chapter 4: THE FAMILY OF MAN

Most of the material in this chapter is from Halstead, LeGros Clark, and Napier; see also Eimerl and Devore, and Howell.

p. 48: On Aegyptopithecus, see Simons, December 1967.

p. 51 *n*: For a good discussion of the complexities of hominoid classification, see Simons, November 1967.

p. 53: Coon on tree-shrews is quoted in Eimerl and DeVore. For a contrasting view of these animals, see Sorenson's paper in Rosenblum, ed. (1970).

p. 56: On group learning among Japanese macaques, see Frisch's paper in Jay, ed.

p. 57: On group learning in baboons, see Eimerl and DeVore. On play, see especially the special supplement to *Natural History* magazine listed under "Play" in the bibliography.

p. 59: The description of tree-shrews is from Sorenson, op. cit.

Chapter 5: MOTHER AND CHILD

p. 60f.: Virtually all the material on langurs, and all the quotations on them, are from Jay's classic paper in DeVore, ed. See also Poirier in Rosenblum, ed. (1970) and Yoshiba in Jay, ed.

p. 64: The material on mother-child relationships in other primate species is mostly from papers in DeVore, ed. See also Eimerl and DeVore.

p. 65: Goodall on adult primate tolerance of infants: from Goodall (1971); see also other citations for this chapter.

p. 66: On male interest in infants among baboons and chimps, see Goodall, op. cit., and Eimerl and DeVore, from which the quotation is taken.

p. 68: Harlow's experiments on the importance of playmates are described in Pfeiffer and in Solomon.

p. 70: The quotation on mutual attraction in infants is from Harlow and Harlow.

p. 72: On experimental studies of curiosity, see Butler, and Berlyne.

p. 74: The description of a young chimp playing at nest-building is from Goodall (1971).

Chapter 6: THE PRIMATE MYSTIQUE

p. 78: On behavioral differences between the sexes in various species see, e.g., Schaller (1972). On long-term bonds between mother and child in chimps, see Goodall (1971)

p. 79: The quotation on sex differences in young monkeys is from Harlow and Harlow.

pp. 80–81: On "presenting," see, e.g., Eimerl and DeVore, and DeVore, ed.

pp. 84–85: On hormones and sex differences, see Levine, Hamburg, and Hamburg and Lunde in Maccoby, ed., also Money and Ehrhardt.

p. 88: On the male role in baboon and rhesus groups, see, e.g., Eimerl and DeVore, and Southwick, et al. in DeVore, ed. For a contrasting view of the male baboon in a quite different environment, see Rowell, and Pilbeam.

p. 89: On hunting as a male activity in chimps, see, e.g., Teleki (1973a); for the same phenomenon in humans, see Lee and DeVore, eds.

p. 91: On the female chimp's defense of her young, see Goodall (1971).

p. 92: The falsity of Tiger's and Fox's account of meat-eating is clearly shown in Goodall (1968), and further in Telecki (1973a and b) and Goodall (1971). The latter actually includes a picture of a dominant male "begging" for meat from one of his "subordinates," which is reproduced in this volume.

Chapter 7: EVOLUTION AND EVIL

Some good general sources on this topic are Montagu, and Russell and Russell.

p. 95: The Stanley Kubrick quotation appeared in the *New York Times;* unfortunately I have mislaid the clipping.

p. 98: The figures on the incidence of killing in the U.S. are rough estimates based on homicide statistics in the FBI's *Uniform Crime Reports;* halving or doubling the figure would obviously not invalidate my basic point, which is that in virtually every human culture homicide is an uncommon activity. The account of Elsa is taken from Ardrey (1961).

p. 99: For more on the Evasive We and similar rhetorical devices, see Claiborne (1971). The quotation from Reynolds and Reynolds is from their paper in DeVore, ed.

p. 100: The Goodall quotation is from Goodall (1971).

p. 101: Wingfield and Hall's observations are described in Hall and DeVore, in DeVore, ed.

p. 102: The DeVore quotation is from Eimerl and DeVore, as is the account of male baboons changing groups. On the latter, see also Lindberg.

p. 103: The Walter Reed–Yerkes Center studies of aggression, dominance, and testosterone are described in Rose, et al. (1971 and 1972). See also Hamburg.

p. 105: The extraordinary account of sex-reversal in fish is in Robertson.

p. 107: The Goodall quotation is from Goodall (1971).

p. 109: The feeble role of dominance in several primitive peoples is described in Coon; the Tasaday were reported extensively in the mass media.

p. 111: On contrasts in the behavior of male baboons in different situations and environments, compare, e.g., Eimerl and DeVore with Rowell.

Chapter 8: THE LAST MILLION YEARS

The factual material in this chapter—very little of it is controversial—is culled from a variety of sources, especially Pfeiffer and Howell. See also Constable.

p. 119: For more on the early use of fire, see Claiborne (1970).

p. 120: The Goodall quotation is from Goodall (1971).

p. 122: On Washoe's accomplishments with sign language, see Gardner and Gardner. On Sarah's use of symbols, see Premack, and Premack and Premack.

p. 124: The Levallois technique is depicted step by step in Howell.

p. 130f.: The material on insight learning is taken mostly from various papers in Riopelle, especially Chance and Birch.

p. 131: Mike's use of kerosene tins is described in detail in Goodall (1971).

pp. 134–35: On territoriality in chimps, see Goodall (1971) and Reynolds and Reynolds in DeVore, ed.; in gorillas, see Schaller (1965); in baboons, see Eimerl and DeVore, and Hall's fifth paper (pp. 149ff.) in Jay, ed.

p. 137: On the relative importance of hunting and gathering among contemporary primitives, see Lee's paper in Lee and DeVore, eds.

Chapter 9: THE GIFT RELATIONSHIP

p. 140: The quotation from Jay is from her paper in DeVore, ed.

p. 141: On reassurance gestures among chimps, see Goodall (1971).

p. 142: Darby and Riopelle on empathetic learning: in Riopelle, ed.

pp. 143–44: "lack of consideration" in chimps: quoted from Goodall (1971).

p. 144: The quotations are from Teleki (1973a); the subject is treated more extensively in Teleki (1973b).

p. 147: The experiments in altruism are described in Weiss, et al.; see also Macaulay and Berkowitz.

p. 155: The quotation from Brecht is in the Marc Blitzstein translation of *Dreigroschen Oper.*

Chapter 10: THE SEX RELATIONSHIP

p. 157: Hall's twenty-one copulations in the baboon group are reported by Hall and DeVore in DeVore, ed., as are DeVore's observations of the less frenzied sexual activities in Kenya.

pp. 158–59: On non-competitive sex among chimps, see Goodall (1971). On the relationship between hunting and female availability, see Eimerl and DeVore. The quotations are from this book, and from Hall and DeVore, op. cit.

p. 161: Gebhard's survey of sexual positions around the world is in Marshall and Suggs, eds.

p. 166: The source of the Paul Goodman interview is given in the bibliography under "Goodman."

p. 167: The studies of female sexual secretions in rhesus monkeys are reported in Michael, et al. On "pink ladies" see Goodall (1971).

p. 168n: The quotation is from Marshall's paper in Marshall and Suggs, eds.

p. 169: Some relevant cave drawings are reproduced in Ucko and Rosenfeld.

p. 171: On rank and sexual attraction in langurs, see Jay, op cit.; in baboons see Hall and DeVore, op. cit.

p. 172: On women of the Turu tribe, see Schneider's paper in Marshall and Suggs, eds.

p. 173: Gebhard on premarital and extramarital sex: in ibid. On the effect of the male presence on menstruation, see McClintock.

p. 174: The "generalized" primate family is discussed at length in Rowell.

p. 177: On primate "incest taboos," see ibid.

p. 178: Marshall on sex in Mangaia—see Marshall and Suggs, eds. On the *kitesha,* see Merriam in ibid.

p. 181: The Cro-Magnon drawing is described (and reproduced, though not very clearly) in Ucko and Rosenfeld.

Chapter 11: THE CREATIVE IMPULSE

p. 183: The more-or-less orthodox view of the relationship between Neanderthal and modern man is set forth in Constable. I see the problem somewhat differently, for reasons which the balance of the chapter should make clear. I have, however, drawn fairly heavily on his *factual* account of the Neanderthals. See also Howell.

p. 188: On the dating of the Krapina finds see Oakley, and Oakley, et al., eds.

p. 190f.: On innovations among the Cro-Magnons and subsequent modern men, see, e.g., Prideaux. Even the most resolute partisans of the Neanderthals as a subspecies of modern man are constrained to admit that as innovators they were at a pretty low level.

Chapter 12: A MIRROR TO MAN

p. 202: On female orgasm in Mangaia, see Marshall in Marshall and Suggs, eds.

p. 204: For a more detailed discussion of Schlock Sociology, see Claiborne (1971).

p. 208: On violence among the Vikings, see, e.g., Claiborne (1970); among the Navaho and Apache, see, e.g., Driver.

p. 209: Yoshiba's account of aggression in langurs is in Jay, ed.

p. 211f.: One of the best descriptions on ghetto life and its mingled tension and boredom is Liebow. On sources of abnormal behavior in primates, see Mitchell in Rosenblum (1970).

p. 212*n*: Robinson's dissection of the Wyatt Earp myth is quoted in Atkins.

Chapter 13: THE PAST AND THE FUTURE

p. 221: Toffler's account of enforced mobility in an American executive family is in his *Future Shock.* I should emphasize in citing Toffler that while I consider him a useful source of facts, his interpretations seem to me generally worthless—for reasons given in Claiborne (1971).

p. 226: On the importance of the emotional bond in learning among kittens, see Chesler.

p. 232: Protests against dehumanization on the job have been especially vocal at the General Motors plant in Lordstown, Ohio, widely reported in the press.

p. 233: On managerial rigidity in the auto industry, see Rothschild.

Bibliography

While all the sources listed below have been used in preparing this book, some are obviously more important than others—especially for readers interested in delving further into the subject.

On the overall course of human evolution, the best single short source is still Howell, though it is unavoidably a bit dated. Pfeiffer is full of valuable information but is somewhat disorganized; Edey and Constable are good on specific periods. On the environmental background, Claiborne (1970) is the best concise source—if only because there is no other single work on the subject.

On primate behavior, Rowell, Goodall (1971), Eimerl and DeVore, and DeVore, ed., are absolutely invaluable, with Jay, ed., hardly less so; Riopelle, ed., is excellent in its own limited area (learning). References on specific subjects will be found in the notes to the appropriate chapters.

Starred* titles are available in paperback.

*ARDREY, ROBERT. *African Genesis.* New York: Dell, 1961.
*————. *The Territorial Imperative.* New York: Dell, 1971.
*————. *The Social Contract.* New York: Dell, 1971.
ATKINS, HARRY. "The Freudulent West." *The Sciences,* August–September 1971.
BERLYNE, D. E. "Curiosity and Exploration." *Science,* July 1, 1966.
BITTERMAN, M. E. "The Evolution of Intelligence." *Scientific American,* January 1965.
*BOURNE, GEOFFREY H. *The Ape People.* New York: New American Library, 1972.
BUTLER, ROBERT A. "Curiosity in Monkeys." *Scientific American,* February 1954.
BUTZER, KARL W. *Environment and Archeology.* Chicago: Aldine, 1964.
CARDER, BROOKS, and BERKOWITZ, KENNETH. "Rats' Preference for Earned in Comparison with Free Food." *Science,* February 1970.
CHESLER, PHYLLIS. "Maternal Influence in Learning by Observation in Kittens." *Science,* November 14, 1969.

CLAIBORNE, ROBERT. *Climate, Man, and History.* New York: Norton, 1970.
———. "Future Schlock." *The Nation,* January 25, 1971.
———. *The First Americans.* New York: Time-Life, 1973.
*CLARK, GRAHAME. *The Stone Age Hunters.* New York: McGraw-Hill, 1967.
*CLARK, J. DESMOND. *The Prehistory of Africa.* New York: Praeger, 1970.
CONSTABLE, GEORGE. *The Neanderthals.* New York: Time-Life, 1973.
COON, CARLETON S. *The Hunting Peoples.* Boston: Little, Brown, 1971.
DEVORE, IRVEN, ed. *Primate Behavior.* New York: Holt, Rinehart, & Winston, 1965.
*DRIVER, HAROLD E. *Indians of North America.* Chicago: University of Chicago, 1969.
EDEY, MAITLAND A. *The Missing Link.* New York: Time-Life, 1972.
Editors of Time-Life Books. *The First Men.* New York: Time-Life, 1973.
EIMERL, SAREL, and DEVORE, IRVEN. *The Primates.* New York: Time, Inc., 1965.
EISENBERG, J. F., *et al.* "The Relation between Ecology and Social Structure in Primates." *Science,* May 26, 1972.
EISENBERG, LEON. "The *Human* Nature of Human Nature." *Science,* April 14, 1972.
GARDNER, R. ALLEN, and GARDNER, BEATRICE T. "Teaching Sign Language to a Chimpanzee." *Science,* August 15, 1969.
GILMAN, RICHARD. "The FemLib Case Against Sigmund Freud." *The New York Times Magazine,* January 31, 1971.
GOODALL, BARONESS JANE VAN LAWICK. *My Friends the Wild Chimpanzees.* Washington, D.C.: National Geographic Society, 1967.
———. *In the Shadow of Man.* Boston: Houghton Mifflin, 1971.
"An Interview with Paul Goodman." *Psychology Today,* November 1971.
HALSTEAD, L. B. *The Pattern of Vertebrate Evolution.* San Francisco: W. H. Freeman, 1968.
HAMBURG, DAVID A. "Psychobiological Studies of Aggressive Behaviour." *Nature,* March 5, 1971.
HARLOW, HARRY F. "Love in Infant Monkeys." *Scientific American,* June 1959.
HARLOW, HARRY F., and HARLOW, MARGARET. "The Young Monkeys." *Psychology Today,* September 1967.
HEIDBREDER, EDNA. *Seven Psychologies.* New York: D. Appleton-Century, 1933.
HILGARD, ERNEST R. *Theories of Learning.* New York: Appleton-Century-Crofts, 1948.
HOWELL, F. CLARK. *Early Man.* New York: Time, Inc., 1965.
HOWELL, F. CLARK, and BOURLIÉRE, FRANÇOIS, eds. *African Ecology and Human Evolution.* Chicago: Aldine, 1963.
JAY, PHYLLIS C., ed. *Primates: Studies in Adaptation and Variability.* New York: Holt, Rinehart, & Winston, 1968.

JOHN, E. ROY, *et al.* "Observation Learning in Cats." *Science,* March 29, 1968.

KELLOGG, WINTHROP N. "Communication and Language in Home-Raised Chimpanzees." *Science,* October 25, 1968.

LEE, RICHARD B., and DEVORE, IRVEN, eds. *Man the Hunter.* Chicago: Aldine, 1968.

LEVINE, SEYMOUR. "Sex Differences in the Brain." *Scientific American,* April 1966.

LIEBERMAN, PHILIP, and CRELIN, EDMUND S. "On the Speech of Neanderthal Man." *Linguistic Inquiry,* March 1971.

LIEBOW, ELLIOT. *Talley's Corner.* Boston: Little, Brown, 1967.

LINDBERG, D. G. "Rhesus Monkeys: Mating Season Mobility of Adult Males." *Science,* November 28, 1969.

LORENZ, KONRAD. *On Aggression.* New York: Bantam, 1970.

MACAULAY, J., and BERKOWITZ, L., eds. *Altruism and Helping Behavior.* New York: Academic Press, 1970.

MCCLINTOCK, MARTHA K. "Menstrual Synchrony and Suppression." *Nature,* January 22, 1971.

MACCOBY, E. E., ed. *The Development of Sex Differences.* Palo Alto, Calif.: Stanford University Press, 1966.

MARSHALL, DONALD S., and SUGGS, ROBERT C., eds. *Human Sexual Behavior.* New York: Basic Books, 1971.

MICHAEL, RICHARD P., *et al.* "Pheromones: Isolation of Male Sex Attractants from a Female Primate." *Science,* May 28, 1971.

MONEY, JOHN, and EHRHARDT, ANKE A. *Man & Woman, Boy & Girl.* Baltimore: Johns Hopkins University Press, 1972.

*MONTAGU, M. F. ASHLEY. *Man and Aggression.* New York: Oxford University Press, 1973.

MORGAN, ELAINE. *The Descent of Woman.* New York: Stein and Day, 1972.

*MORRIS, DESMOND. *The Naked Ape.* New York: Dell, 1967.

NAPIER, JOHN. *The Roots of Mankind.* Washington, D.C.: Smithsonian Institution Press, 1970.

NISHUDA, T. "The Social Group of Wild Chimpanzees in the Mahali Mountains." *Primates* 9 (1968).

OAKLEY, KENNETH. *Frameworks for Dating Fossil Man.* Chicago: Aldine, 1964.

OAKLEY, KENNETH, *et al.,* eds. *Catalogue of Fossil Hominids.* London: British Museum, 1971.

*PFEIFFER, JOHN E. *The Emergence of Man.* New York: Harper & Row, 1972.

PILBEAM, DAVID. "The fashionable view of man as a naked ape is . . ." *The New York Times Magazine,* September 3, 1972.

Play (supplement to *Natural History* magazine), December 1971.

PREMACK, ANN JAMES, and PREMACK, DAVID. "Teaching Language to an Ape." *Scientific American,* October 1972.

PREMACK, DAVID. "Language in Chimpanzee?" *Science,* May 21, 1971.

PRIDEAUX, TOM. *The Cro-Magnons.* New York: Time-Life, 1973.

*RIOPELLE, J. A., ed. *Animal Problem Solving.* Baltimore: Penguin, 1967.

ROBERTSON, D. R. "Social Control of Sex Reversal in a Coral-Reef Fish." *Science,* September 15, 1972.

ROSE, ROBERT M., *et al.* "Plasma Testosterone, Dominance Rank and Aggressive Behaviour in Male Rhesus Monkeys." *Nature,* June 11, 1971.

ROSE, ROBERT M., *et al.* "Plasma Testosterone Levels in the Male Rhesus: Influences of Sexual and Social Stimuli." *Science,* November 10, 1972.

ROSENBLUM, LEONARD A., ed. *Primate Behavior.* Vol. 1. New York: Academic Press, 1970.

————. *Primate Behavior.* Vol. 2. New York: Academic Press, 1971.

ROTHSCHILD, EMMA. *Paradise Lost: The Doctrine of the Auto-Industrial Age.* New York: Random House, 1973.

*ROWELL, THELMA. *Social Behaviour of Monkeys.* Baltimore: Penguin, 1972.

RUSSELL, CLAIRE, and RUSSELL, W. M. S. *Violence in Monkeys and Man.* London: Macmillan, 1968.

*SCHALLER, GEORGE B. *The Year of the Gorilla.* New York: Ballantine, 1964.

————. *The Serengeti Lion.* Chicago: University of Chicago Press, 1972.

SCHALLER, GEORGE B., and LOWTHER, GORDON R. "The Relevance of Carnivore Behavior to the Study of Early Hominids." *Southwestern Journal of Anthropology* 25, no. 4 (1969).

SHERFEY, MARY JANE. "Ancient Man Knew His Place." *The New York Times,* November 14, 1972.

SIMONS, ELWYN. "The Significance of Primate Paleontology for Anthropologic Studies." *Am. J. Phys. Anthropology,* November 1967.

————. "The Earliest Apes." *Scientific American,* December 1967.

SINGH, DEVENDRA. "The Pied Piper vs the Protestant Ethic." *Psychology Today,* January 1972.

SINGH, SHEO DAN. "Urban Monkeys." *Scientific American,* July 1969.

SKINNER, B. F. *Science and Human Behavior.* New York: Macmillan, 1953.

————. "The Phylogeny and Ontogeny of Behavior." *Science,* September 9, 1966.

SOLOMON, JOAN. "With a Little Help from a Friend . . ." *The Sciences,* October 1971.

TELEKI, GEZA. "The Omnivorous Chimpanzee." *Scientific American,* January 1973a.

————. *The Predatory Behavior of Wild Chimpanzees.* Lewisburg, Pa.: Bucknell University Press, 1973b.

THOMAS, ALEXANDER, *et al.* "The Origin of Personality." *Scientific American,* August 1970.

*TIGER, LIONEL. *Men in Groups.* New York: Vintage Books, 1970.

*TIGER, LIONEL, and FOX, ROBIN. *The Imperial Animal.* New York: Holt, Rinehart, & Winston, 1971.

*TITMUS, RICHARD M. *The Gift Relationship.* New York: Random House, 1972.

TURNBULL, COLIN M. *The Mountain People.* New York: Simon and Schuster, 1972.

UCKO, PETER J., and ROSENFELD, ANDREE. *Paleolithic Cave Art.* New York: McGraw-Hill, 1967.

WASHBURN, S. L. "Behavior and the Origin of Man." *The Rockefeller University Review,* January–February 1968.

WASHBURN, S. L., and DEVORE, IRVEN. "The Social Life of Baboons." *Scientific American,* June 1961.

WEISS, ROBERT FRANK, *et al.* "Altruism Is Rewarding." *Science,* March 26, 1971.

WEISSTEIN, NAOMI. "Woman as Nigger." *Psychology Today,* October 1969.

Index